THE DEMOCRATIC PARTY
Jefferson to Jackson

Thomas Jefferson

THE DEMOCRATIC PARTY

Jefferson to Jackson

by

HERBERT J. CLANCY, S. J.

Foreword by
JOHN W. McCORMACK,
Speaker of the
House of Representatives

FORDHAM UNIVERSITY PRESS : NEW YORK

For My Mother
with
Deep Gratitude

Acknowledgments

Few portrayers of the past would disagree with Leopold von Ranke that "the historian must record a thing as it really occurred." Indeed the correct attitude of the historian in face of his subject finds classic expression in the words of Othello: "Paint me as I am. Nothing extenuate nor aught set down in malice." I have tried to use the philosophy contained in this quotation as my guiding star in the writing of this book. I trust I have succeeded.

Some thirteen years ago I had the good fortune to meet Mr. Herman Kahn. Currently a special assistant to the Archivist of the United States, he was at that time director of the Franklin D. Roosevelt library. I asked him what he thought about the feasibility of my undertaking the task of writing a documentary history of the Democratic party. We were both aware that no such history had as yet been attempted. His advice was so sound that it proved to be vital in initiating this work. He has probably forgotten all about the incident, but nevertheless I want to record my gratitude to him.

My next step was to immerse myself in the rich personal correspondence of the founders and leaders of the Democratic party. The papers of such distinguished Democrats as Jefferson, Madison, and Monroe were graciously put at my disposal in the manuscript division of the Library of Congress. The competent staff of this important division then proceeded to make available to me the letters and diaries of hundreds of other statesmen who had important roles in shaping the destiny of our political parties.

As a result of my researches I have tried to portray both the origins of the Democratic party as well as its history from Thomas Jefferson to Andrew Jackson. In subsequent volumes I hope to bring my study up to date.

As this book emerged from the research to the writing stage, I became deeply conscious of a large personal debt to a group of friends and advisors. Mr. Charles C. Tansill, distinguished author and scholar, has placed his large fund of historical knowledge at my disposal. His friendship has meant very much to me. The Reverend Harry J. Sievers, S.J., of Bellarmine College, Plattsburgh, New York, took time out from his teaching and writing to give me the benefit of his wise counsel. When I came to my chapter on the Monroe Doctrine I realized what the distinguished majority leader Senator Mike Mansfield meant when he referred to the Reverend Joseph F. Thorning as "the padre of the Americas." Fr. Thorning, author and professor of Latin American history at Marymount College, Virginia, has made me more than ever aware of the real meaning of friendship.

This book was written within the friendly walls of the Library of Congress. I am greatly indebted to Mr. L. Quincy Mumford, Librarian of Congress, and to his staff. Particular thanks are due to Mr. John M. Hunt, director of the Microfilm Reading Room, and to Mr. John S. de Porry of the Division of Manuscripts, whose aid has been invaluable. The Reverend Edwin A. Quain, S.J., director of the Fordham University Press, and his assistant editor Miss Donna A. Thomas have made the tedious process of book-making a real joy. Miss Mary Helen Woods and Miss Mariemmi Wanek, both of Washington, D.C., not only typed my manuscript but provided sage editorial suggestions.

I would never have been able to finish this book but for Jane and James Matthews of Arlington, Virginia, and Catherine and Frank Heller of Scarsdale, New York. In the National Archives of the United States, Mrs. Kieran J. Carroll and Mrs. William A. Dowling provided me with the dispatches and instructions of our Ambassadors and Secretaries of State for the years 1800 to 1828. They made working in the Foreign Affairs Section of the Archives a real pleasure.

CONTENTS

ILLUSTRATIONS

Foreword

As Speaker of the House of Representatives I have, as would be expected, a deep interest in the Democratic party. Therefore, I am pleased to find this book a report which admirably portrays the party's origins and development.

I first met the author in the summer of 1958 on the occasion of his leading the House in prayer. I thought his prayer that day made sense, and I am firmly convinced that it still does. I was especially impressed with his concluding petition which seems to me to go to the heart of our crisis in international affairs. I have never forgotten it, and could almost repeat it from memory. It goes like this:

May this House by its words and deeds make clear to our enemies that America will never be intimidated by the threat of violence. In our Judaic-Christian concept, dignity and freedom take precedence over mere biological survival.

Father Clancy's book, like his prayer, goes to the heart of the matter. His is a well-documented study. He has made excellent use of the rich treasure house of archival material both in the manuscript division of the Library of Congress and the National Archives. This is an important and indeed an indispensable book for students of American political history.

With Western civilization facing the greatest crisis in its history, Democrats and Republicans alike will do well to peruse this volume. The philosopher George Santayana once wrote that "those who cannot remember the past, are condemned to repeat it." My dear friend, the Reverend Dr. Herbert J. Clancy, S.J., by his painstaking research, has recalled the magnificent history of the first twenty-eight years of the Democratic party. May his work serve us as a sure guide for the future.

JOHN W. McCORMACK
Speaker
U.S. House of Representatives

THE DEMOCRATIC PARTY
Jefferson to Jackson

1

Beginnings

PROFESSOR SAMUEL E. MORISON once wrote that he was confident that the "well-springs of political action can be traced mainly through the personal correspondence of the actors."[1] And eighty-seven years before Dr. Morison penned the above words, Thomas Jefferson, the founder of the Democratic party, insisted that the true history of the "conflict of parties will never be in possession of the public, until by the death of the actors in it the hoards of their letters shall be broken up and given to the world."[2] Convinced that the Morison-Jefferson approach is essential, the present writer has undertaken the task of writing a history of the Democratic party based upon the personal correspondence of its leaders.

With some few exceptions the letters and diaries of the builders of the Democratic party are on deposit in the manuscript division of the Library of Congress. I have tried by the use of these sources to get at the heart of my subject. I have not neglected presidential messages, formal state papers, and the comparatively few edited editions of the letters of our statesmen. However, I felt that if I relied on these alone, I would be in danger of presenting a somewhat partisan view. I felt I had to get behind the scenes, as it were. Therefore, my main effort has been to meticulously scrutinize the private correspondence of the major and minor actors involved in my story.

For foreign affairs, I have relied primarily on the dispatches and instructions on file in the National Archives. In seeking background material and color, I attempted to consult as many contemporary newspapers as possible.

I am in great debt to the host of scholars who have preceded me in the field of American political history. I would have been lost

---

[1]Samuel Eliot Morison, *The Life and Letters of Harrison Gray Otis* (Boston: Houghton Mifflin Co., 1913), Vol. I, p. X.
[2]Jefferson to Short, January 8, 1825, *Jefferson MSS.*

in an ocean of manuscripts had it not been for the guidance of their monographs, biographies, articles, and special studies. My footnotes will indicate the names of these distinguished men and women.

NO PARTIES

The notion of political parties was so alien to the Founding Fathers that Vice-President John Adams merely gave expression to a prevailing opinion when he declared that there "is nothing I dread so much as the division of the Republic into two great parties, each under its leader. . . . This, in my humble opinion, is to be feared as the greatest political evil under our Constitution."[3] Jefferson himself was initially content with this theory, and as our first Secretary of State wrote President George Washington that "my chief comfort will be to work under your eye, my only shelter the authority of your name, and the wisdom of measures to be dictated by you."[4] Washington joined the chorus and wrote Jefferson that he was "no party man," and it was his "first wish," that "if parties did exist to reconcile them."[5]

Alexander Hamilton, our first Secretary of the Treasury, did not set out to found a political party. In fact, the Federalists denied the very legitimacy of a political party. Hamilton's purpose was to save a paper Constitution that he himself had little faith in. As he saw it, it was his task in 1788 to interest the merchant ship-owners, the public creditors and financiers in underwriting the new government. These forces were at that time the most dynamic in America; they had been most potent in making the Constitution. If he could involve them in such a way that the collapse of the new government would threaten them with economic ruin, then the Constitution might function. By his mighty measures of funding, assumption, and banking, he accomplished this task. These merchants, creditors and financial wizards soon came to be known as the Federalists, and it was not long before they succeeded to their own satisfaction in making the terms "Federalists" and "patriot" synonymous.[6]

---

[3]Wilfred E. Binkley, *American Political Parties: Their Natural History* (New York: Alfred A. Knopf, 1943), p. 19.
[4]Jefferson to Washington, December 15, 1789, *Jefferson MSS.*
[5]Washington to Jefferson, July 6, 1796, *Jefferson MSS.*
[6]Wilfred E. Binkley, *American Political Parties: Their Natural History, op. cit.,* pp. 29-52. Excellent for the origins of Federalism.

The first mention of the name by which the Democratic party was to be known for about twenty-eight years, occurs in a letter from Jefferson to Washington dated May 13, 1792. Jefferson wrote Washington that the "Republican party, who wish to preserve the government in its present form, are fewer in number than the monarchical Federalists."[7] The phrase "monarchical Federalists" used by Jefferson is based, in part at least, on Hamilton's freely expressed admiration for monarchy and the British Constitution, and his contempt for "the people."[8] Continuing, Jefferson wrote that the Republicans were "fewer even when joined by the two or three or half-dozen anti-Federalists, who though they dare not avow it, are still opposed to any general government."[9] Thus Jefferson not only named his party in 1792, but he also renounced the anti-Federalist tag which the Hamiltonians delighted in using. In his repudiation of this taint, the founder of the new party was careful to admit to Washington that the anti-Federalists were less opposed to Republicans than to upholders of monarchy, and that they "naturally join those whom they think pursuing the lesser evil."[10] It seems quite unfair to assert that the Democratic party was built on the anti-Federalist party. In the Constitutional Convention, the anti-Federalists opposed any general government. Neither Jefferson nor Madison had any sympathy with this movement. In fact the compromises by which the Constitution had been made acceptable to the planters of the South saw Madison and his followers ride roughshod over the anti-Federalists in the successful fight for ratification.[11]

DEMOCRACY IS BORN

While it is true that the Jefferson letter of 1792 fixes the birth date of the Democratic party, yet its origins go back at least to the Constitutional Convention of 1787. It was here in Philadelphia that the future followers of Jefferson fought for a limited federal government with all the powers possible left close to the people in their state governments. On the other hand, Hamilton and his fol-

[7] Jefferson to Washington, May 13, 1792, cited in Frank R. Kent, *The Democratic Party: A History* (New York: The Century Co., 1928), p. 14.
[8] Hamilton made these statements behind the closed doors of the Constitutional Convention. Binkley, *op. cit.,* p. 31.
[9] Jefferson to Washington, May 13, 1792, *Jefferson MSS.*
[10] Jefferson to Washington, May 13, 1792, *Jefferson MSS.*
[11] Jefferson was in Paris during the Constitutional Convention.

lowers wanted a strong, centralized government. Hamilton wished to abolish the states. "They are not necessary," he said, "for any of the great purposes of commerce, revenue, or agriculture."[12] Jefferson stood squarely for states' rights, and he reminded Washington that Hamilton "wished the general government should have power to make laws binding the states in all cases whatever. Our country has thought otherwise."[13] Frederick Jackson Turner goes back over a hundred years before the Constitutional Convention in his quest for the origins of Jeffersonian democracy. He finds that from "Bacon's rebellion to the La Follette revolt there are almost continuous manifestations of sectional contests of East and West, of the frontier and older areas."[14] Turner argues that the genesis of the Democratic party is to be found in what our early historians called the "Old West." On the eve of our Revolutionary War, about a million people lived in this long strip of back country extending from Maine to Georgia. Common problems along this western frontier soon produced a homogeneous society. Composed of transient mechanics, and the impecunious whites of the Eastern settlements, as well as immigrants from Europe, especially the Scotch-Irish, these settlers had either bought or squatted upon the lands of speculators. By and large, these people were debtors to the towns and nursed a feeling of deep resentment against the older settlements. It was these multitudes that Albert J. Beveridge had in mind when he said that the Constitution "was to the masses something new, vague, and awful; something to oppress the poor, the weak, the debtor, the settler; something to strengthen and enrich the already strong and opulent, the merchant, the creditor, the financial interests."[15]

About a month after Jefferson had christened his party Republican, he wrote Madison that Hamilton still had the audacity "to call the Republican party a faction."[16] In 1810, ten years after the Republicans had captured the White House, the word Democrat was generally accepted as meaning the same thing as Republican.

[12]Henry A. Minor, *The Story of the Democratic Party* (New York: Macmillan Co., 1928), p. 1.
[13]Jefferson to Washington, September 9, 1792, *Jefferson MSS.*
[14]Frederick J. Turner, *The Significance of Sections in American History* (New York: Henry Holt & Co., 1932), p. 196.
[15]Albert J. Beveridge, *John Marshall* (Boston: Houghton Mifflin Co., 1919), Vol. I, p. 37.
[16]Jefferson to Madison, June 29, 1792, *Jefferson MSS.*

Finally, in Andrew Jackson's time, the designation of the Jefferson party became definitely Democratic. Whether one uses the name "anti-Federalist," "Republican," "Democratic," or "Jacobin" in describing the thousands of Jeffersonians, they were, by 1792, composed of the agrarian masses led by an aristocracy of slave-owning planters. It was their intent, on the retirement of George Washington, to capture the seat of government by means of the ballot, and at least in theory, they repudiated the right to use the government for the benefit of any capitalistic groups: fiscal, banking, or manufacturing.

As far as the documents show, Jefferson was in no great rush to assume the helm of the ship-of-state. We find him writing to Washington in 1792, pleading with him to stay on for another four years. In the same letter he cautioned the Chief Executive about forcing the citizens to pay excise, and of building up a huge national debt.[17] There is little doubt that the leaders of the Republican party looked on Washington as a brake on the extremist tendencies of the Federalists. A little less than two months after Jefferson's plea to Washington, Monroe wrote the Sage of Monticello that the "partisans for monarchy are numerous and powerful."[18] Fearful of a geographical division of the country along party lines, the President wrote Jefferson, now Secretary of State, that it was his "earnest wish, and my fondest hope . . . that there may be . . . mutual forbearances and . . . yieldings on *all sides* . . . attacks have been made upon almost all the measures of government."[19] As long as Washington remained on the scene and agreed with the Federalists, the Republicans realized they had little chance of taking over the control of government. Jefferson understood the futility of arguing with the President, and "finding him really approving the Treasury system . . . avoided entering into argument with him on these points."[20] Early in his political career, the founder of the Democratic party concluded that such was "the popularity of the President that the people will support him in whatever he will do or will not do with-

---

[17]Jefferson to Washington, May 23, 1792, *Jefferson MSS*. In our first two presidential elections, 1788 and 1792, Washington was unanimously chosen President, receiving all the electoral votes.
[18]Monroe to Jefferson, July 17, 1792, *Jefferson MSS*.
[19]Washington to Jefferson, August 23, 1792, *Jefferson MSS*.
[20]Jefferson's notes on talk with President, July 10, 1792, *Jefferson MSS*.

out appealing to their own reason."[21] Never one to allow political theory to interfere with good political practice, Jefferson wrote that since Washington's mind "has been so long used to unlimited applause . . . I have long thought . . . it was best for the Republican interests to soothe him by flattery."[22] If anything further was needed, Hamilton's use of the militia in 1794 to compel the farmers of western Pennsylvania to pay the excise on whiskey, convinced the Republicans that the only way they could redress the grievances of the agricultural man was to win the next election. Jefferson, whose political philosophy was shot through with such expressions as "those who labor in the earth are the chosen people of God," and the farmers "are the true representatives of the great American interest,"[23] assured his agrarian followers that the moment Washington "retires," the Republicans would replace the Federalists in the White House.[24]

PRELUDE TO THE ELECTION OF 1796

Besides the domestic issues of funding, banking, and manufacturing, foreign policy played a major role as a divisive element in our early political history. While quietly organizing his party, Jefferson, as Secretary of State, wrote in cipher that "Adams, Jay, Hamilton, Knox . . . pant after union with England," and "are most determined Antigallicans." The pro-French author of the Declaration of Independence concluded with the observation that "it is prognosticated that our government is to end with the President's life, but I believe they will find themselves all head and no body."[25] As the election of 1796 came on apace, Jefferson, having retired as Secretary of State, lamented from his Monticello home that "against us are the Executive, the Judiciary, two out of three branches of the legislature, all the officers of the government." Continuing in this

[21]Jefferson to Archibald Stuart, January 4, 1797, *Jefferson MSS.* Stuart was a leader of Jeffersonian Democrats in Virginia.

[22]Jefferson to Archibald Stuart, January 4, 1797, *Jefferson MSS.*

[23]Richard Hofstadter, *The American Political Tradition and the Men Who Made It* (New York: A. A. Knopf, 1948), p. 27.

[24]Jefferson to Monroe, July 10, 1796, *Jefferson MSS.*

[25]Jefferson to William Short, July 28, 1791, *Jefferson MSS.* As late as the summer of 1796, the Jeffersonians felt that Washington would stand for a third term. Jefferson was the choice of the Republicans as early as 1794. Stephen G. Kurtz, *The Presidency of John Adams: The Collapse of Federalism, 1795-1800* (Philadelphia: University of Pennsylvania Press, 1957), pp. 86-90.

vein, the future President informed the Italian philosopher, Philip Mazzei, that the

. . . aspect of our politics has wonderfully changed since you left us. In place of that noble love of liberty and republican government which carried us triumphantly through the war, an Anglican, monarchical and aristocratical party has sprung up, whose avowed purpose is to draw over us the substance, as they already have done the forms, of the British government. The main body of our citizens, however, remain true to their republican principles.[26]

Later on, in the campaign of 1800, the Mazzei letter would be used by the Federalists in an attempt to prove that Jefferson disapproved of the great George Washington. But Jefferson would never publicly take issue with Washington, and when campaigning, he always disassociated the great Washington from the Federalists. The Jay Treaty was such an important issue in the election of 1796 that some consider that contest to have been a referendum on the treaty. Signed in the midst of a bitter war between England and France, the Jay Treaty was tantamount to an Anglo-American alliance. The Federalists rejoiced over the treaty, but the Francophile Democrats blasted it all the way from Maine to Georgia.

It is not surprising that thousands of Americans who had recently won their freedom from England by a long and successful war should resent this American-British *rapprochement*. France, whose aid was so essential in winning our independence, underwent a revolution in 1789. This was followed by a French declaration of war on Great Britain, February 1, 1793. News of this conflict reached Philadelphia by April. George III, the recent enemy, whose government still refused to make a treaty of amity with the United States, was now at war with France, the old ally of American independence. Despite the economic reasons which had inclined Hamilton and the Federalists to a pro-British policy, the majority of Americans undoubtedly favored France. By the Franco-American Alliance of 1778, the United States was still the ally of France, pledged to defend the French West Indies in case of war. What should its attitude now be toward the strictly European war?

The answer was not long in coming. President George Washington issued a proclamation of neutrality. The new French Minis-

---

[26]Jefferson to Philip Mazzei, April 24, 1796, *Jefferson MSS.*

ter, Citizen Edmond Genet, was received without qualification. France did not choose to demand military aid in defending the West Indies according to the terms of the alliance. Although Genet was instructed not to invoke the alliance, he was under orders to use neutral American soil as a base for organizing attacks on British colonies and commerce. He proceeded to do this so well that he soon irritated President Washington and his entire cabinet. When he appealed to the American people over the head of the President, he became *persona non grata* and was recalled by his government.

No sooner had George Washington settled the delicate Genet case when he found himself confronted with a possible war with England. The orders-in-council of June 8, 1793, and November 6, 1793, ordered British naval commanders to capture any ship engaged in trade with France or any of her colonies. Under these orders 300 American ships were suddenly captured while trading with French islands in the Caribbean.

News of the Caribbean captures reached the President in March, 1794, simultaneously with a report that the Governor-General of Canada had made a speech to a delegation of hostile Indian tribes from the Western Territory of the United States which General Wayne's army was preparing to pacify. The naval attacks were thus joined with the perennial problem of frontier relations. A war crisis flared up. The public at large, still sympathetic to France, was seething with indignation. Congress had become convinced that Great Britain had no intention of making a treaty of commerce or of negotiating a settlement of any of the outstanding disputes.

Hamilton, as expected, saw in any break with England the ruin of American credit and the collapse of America. In this crisis he and other Federalist leaders convinced Washington that he should send Chief Justice John Jay on a special mission to London to see if some sort of a *modus vivendi* could be arranged. Jay succeeded in doing this in a treaty signed on November 19, 1794. Pitt was just as eager for peace as Jay. England's main anxiety was her European war. At the moment she abhorred any American distraction. Besides, the United States was her most profitable foreign customer.

By the terms of the Jay Treaty the United States guaranteed the payment to Great Britain of bona fide private debts contracted before the peace. Great Britain agreed to evacuate the seven fortified posts of Dutchman's Point and Pointe-au-Fer at the boundary end of Lake Champlain, Oswegatchie, on the New York shore of the St. Lawrence, Oswego, on the southern shore of Lake Ontario, Niagara, in New York, Detroit and Michilimackinac, dominating the passages where Lakes Superior, Michigan and Huron join their waters. She also agreed to pay compensation for spoliations on American shipping. A mixed boundary commission was to determine the identity of the true St. Croix River which had been made a part of the northeastern boundary by the Treaty of 1783. The navigation of the Mississippi was again declared free to the citizens of both countries. The treaty also established commercial relations between the two parties on a non-discriminatory basis.

Downhearted, but still confident, Jefferson wrote from his Monticello retreat to Monroe in Paris that "tho' the Anglomen have in the end got their treaty through, and so far have triumphed over the cause of republicanism . . . the moment he retires [Washington] his successor if a monocrat will be overborne . . ."[27]

The pro-French Republicans were forced to admit that the Genet episode of 1793 had strengthened the Federalists. For Genet had incurred the wrath of an aroused American people by his intrigues to violate American neutrality. The sympathies of the American common man in the struggle between France and England were with our former ally, for French help was essential in winning our independence. But even though France was now engaged in a fight to overthrow monarchy, neither Hamiltonians nor Jeffersonians would brook the French Minister Genet's insulting diplomatic practice of appealing to the people of the United States over the head of President Washington. Citizen Edmond Charles Genet did just this, and in so doing did harm to France, and to the Republican party of America. It is clear that foreign policy was an important

---

[27]Jefferson to Monroe, July 10, 1796, *Jefferson MSS*. In the Jay Treaty signed in 1794, the British promised to evacuate the chain of forts on United States soil. They also agreed to pay damages for their recent seizures of American ships, but Jay failed to win any concessions on future maritime seizures, impressments, or Indian butcheries. See Samuel F. Bemis, *Jay's Treaty* (New York: Macmillan Co., 1923), pp. 252-271.

factor as sixteen states prepared to choose a president in 1796.[28] In the summer of that year, the Federalist members of Congress held a conference wherein it was agreed that John Adams should be the candidate for President, and Thomas Pinckney of South Carolina, vice-president. About the same time, Jefferson and Burr were agreed upon by a conference of Republican members of Congress. Jefferson, the organizer of the party, was to stand as the candidate for president, and Burr, who by his political adroitness had recently replaced George Clinton as the New York leader of the Republican party, was to run as the candidate for vice-president. Tennessee, having been admitted to the Union on June 1, 1796, was the sixteenth state. Only fifteen states had participated in the election of 1792. The electors in Tennessee were chosen by the legislature as they were in Vermont, Rhode Island, Connecticut, New York, New Jersey, Delaware, South Carolina, Georgia, and Kentucky. The people, voting by districts, chose the electors in Pennsylvania, Maryland, Virginia, and North Carolina. In Massachusetts and New Hampshire, the people and the legislature divided the duty. In other words, there were certain districts where the people selected the electors, and others where the legislature appointed them.[29]

By the year 1796, the Fourth Estate was a potent factor in American politics. At that time, the United States proudly boasted of seventy weeklies, ten semi-weeklies, three tri-weeklies, and eight daily newspapers. The leader of the Hamiltonian press was John

---

[28]Genet, in December 1793, appealed directly to our two Houses of Congress. He was severely rebuked by Secretary of State Jefferson for this action. Finally, on demand of our government, he was recalled, but wisely chose the altar instead of a possible guillotine in France. He married Governor Clinton's daughter, and lived happily ever after in America. Fauchet, who succeeded Genet, was accused of attempting to bribe Secretary of State Randolph in 1795. Randolph resigned as a result of the investigation. See John Alexander Carroll and Mary Wells Ashworth, *George Washington: First In Peace* (New York: Charles Scribner's Sons, 1957), pp. 265-344 for a scholarly discussion of Randolph's guilt. Washington tended to believe that Randolph was guilty but the evidence is not conclusive. This book by Carroll and Ashworth is the seventh and final volume of Douglas S. Freeman's monumental study of George Washington. The Jay Treaty was important in shaping the two parties which until this time were somewhat nebulous. *Joseph Charles, The Origins of the American Party System* (Williamsburg: Institute of Early American History and Culture, 1956), pp. 91-118.

[29]See Edward Stanwood, *A History of the Presidency* (Boston: Houghton Mifflin Co., 1912), pp. 38-48. Hamilton wanted a Southerner for vice-president in order to garner Southern votes. His first choice was Patrick Henry. When Henry, now a Federalist, declined, then Hamilton turned to Pinckney. Manning J. Dauer, *The Adams Federalists* (Baltimore: The Johns Hopkins Press, 1953), p. 95.

Fenno, editor of the *United States Gazette*.[30] The key figure among the Jeffersonian journalists was Benjamin Franklin Bache, grandson of the great Franklin, and editor of the Philadelphia *Aurora*.[31] During the campaign of 1796, both party presses teemed with bitter, personal attacks. The Federalist Adams became a defender of the red-coated assassins of the Boston massacre, an enemy of the masses, a monarchist, a panter after titles, an aristocrat. The Republican Jefferson was an atheist, a Gallophile, a friend of anarchy, an enemy of the Constitution, an inciter of the Whiskey Insurrection, a foe to public credit.[32] In addition to the slander in the press, Pierre Adet, the French Minister, was distributing money liberally to elect Jefferson, and had sent agents into the Western country in his behalf.[33] In a desperate effort to distract the people from the Jay Treaty, the Federalists focused on the celebrated Adet letter to Secretary of State Timothy Pickering. The letter, issued on the eve of the election, reviewed the complaints of France against the American government, and mentioned Jefferson favorably. Handed to the press, as well as given to Secretary of State Pickering by Adet, the note was a bombshell. The Federalists roared that France was secretly campaigning to make Jefferson president, and that her minister was electioneering. The Adet letter soon became a paramount issue. Bache accepted it but countered in the pages of the *Aurora* by urging Fenno to spare some of his indignation for the "scourging of an American at a British gangway" and the shooting of a brother of a member of Congress trying to escape from a British press gang.[34]

---

[30]John Fenno, with Alexander Hamilton's encouragement, established the Federalist paper, the *Gazette of the United States,* in New York, April 11, 1789. A year later he moved the paper to Philadelphia. During most of its life, the paper was embroiled in bitter controversies with the Jeffersonian journals, Philip Freneau's *National Gazette,* and Benjamin Franklin Bache's *Aurora.* It was continued until 1800 by the founder's son, John Ward Fenno.

[31]Philip Freneau was Jefferson's original choice. Freneau was succeeded by Bache, who in turn was succeeded by William Duane. Freneau was employed by Jefferson in the Department of State. When Freneau edited the *Aurora,* it was known as the *Gazette of the United States.*

[32]Donald H. Steward, *Jeffersonian Journalism, 1789-1801,* p. 511 sq., for press coverage of election of 1796. This is an unpublished thesis on microfilm in the Library of Congress.

[33]*Memoirs of the Administrations of George Washington and John Adams,* ed. by George Gibbs (New York: W. Van Norden, 1846), Vol. I., p. 332, 350-352.

[34]*Aurora,* December 27, 1796. Madison regretted the Adet letter and felt that it hurt Jefferson very much. Madison to Jefferson, December 5, 1796, *Madison MSS.*

While editors vied with each other in vituperation, strange things were happening in certain Federalist circles. Hamilton, convinced that Adams was a man who would not be dictated to, was busy with a plan to substitute Pinckney for Adams. The plan was simple: he arranged for certain Federalist electors to vote to a man for Pinckney, while at the same time casting a few Adams votes for other men. As the high man was elected president, and the second, vice-president, the scheme appeared to be foolproof.

Apparently, however, not all of Hamilton's followers were enthusiastic about the plan. His devoted friend, Oliver Wolcott, feared that the maneuvering might result in the election of Jefferson to the presidency, or at least to the vice-presidency. If Jefferson attained the presidency, Wolcott hoped that "the Northern states would separate from the Southern."[35] Adams' friends, suspecting treason within the ranks, decided to offset any possible Adams losses by dropping a few Pinckney votes to a third party. As a result, of the thirty-nine New England votes, Pinckney received but twenty-two, while all thirty-nine went to Adams. Deeply chagrined, Hamilton read the final result: Adams, 71; Jefferson, 68; Pinckney, 59. The hated leader of the Democrats was now Vice-President of the United States. It may well be that Hamilton, by his underhand methods, elected Jefferson as Vice-President.

JEFFERSON DOES NOT WANT TO WIN?

Thus it was that in 1796, the Federalists elected their last President, John Adams, by the narrow margin of three votes. The distribution of the electoral votes presents all the appearance of a referendum on the Jay Treaty. South of the Potomac, Adams received one vote in Virginia and one in North Carolina; while north of the Potomac, Jefferson received fourteen votes in Pennsylvania and four in Maryland. Practically speaking, the Democrats controlled everything south of the Potomac, and the Federalists everything north of it.

Jefferson appears to have been aware of Hamilton's chicanery, for he wrote Madison that "I have no expectation that the Eastern states will suffer themselves to be so much outwitted as to be made

---

[35]Gibbs, *op. cit.,* Vol. I, pp. 408-409. Wolcott was from Connecticut and succeeded Hamilton as Secretary of the Treasury.

the tools for bringing in P. instead of A." He was convinced that Hamilton's strategy would considerably help the "Republican vote," and in the event of a tie between himself and Adams "I pray you and authorize you fully to solicit in my behalf that Mr. Adams may be preferred."[36]

When the final result was known, the Hamiltonians realized their mistake. Wolcott sighed that Jefferson in the vice-presidency "would be more dangerous than as President."[37] Chauncey Goodrich agreed with Wolcott and said that we "must expect him to be the nucleus of a faction."[38] Fisher Ames joined the wailing, and looked on Jefferson's election as "a formidable evil."[39] Hamilton buried his embarrassment in cynicism:

Our Jacobins say they are pleased that the Lion and the Lamb are to lie down together. Mr. Adams' personal friends talk a little the same way . . . Skeptics like me quietly look forward to the event, willing to hope but not prepared to believe. If Mr. Adams has vanity, 'tis plain a plot has been laid to take hold of it.[40]

Jefferson declared that he would have served as President if elected, for "on principles of public respect, I should not have refused." But he wrote, "I protest before my God that I shall from the bottom of my heart rejoice at escaping. I know well that no man will ever bring out of that office the reputation which carries him into it."[41]

As soon as Jefferson was certain that Adams had won, he wrote him that although the newspapers had placed them "in a point of opposition to each other, I confidently trust we have felt less of it in ourselves." He went on to say that with him, the "issue was never doubted. I knew the impossibility of your losing a single vote north of the Delaware, and even if you should lose that of Pennsylvania . . . you would get enough south of that to make your election sure." Jefferson assured Adams that he had "no ambition to govern men" and reminded him of the "trick worthy of the subtlety of your arch-

---

[36]Jefferson to Madison, December 17, 1796, *Jefferson MSS.*

[37]Gibbs, *op. cit.,* Vol. I, pp. 400-403.

[38]*Ibid.,* Vol. I, pp. 411-413.

[39]*Ibid.,* Vol. I, p. 208.

[40]Charles R. King, *Life and Correspondence of Rufus King* (New York: G. P. Putnam's Sons, 1898), Vol. II, p. 148.

[41]Jefferson to Rutledge, December 27, 1796, *Jefferson MSS.*

friend of New York who has been able to make of your real friends tools to defeat their and your just wishes."[42]

As Jefferson prepared to take over the vice-presidency, he entertained the thought of supporting John Adams in future elections if he "could be induced to administer the government on its true principles, quitting his bias for an English Constitution." For after all "he is the only sure barrier against Hamilton's getting in."[43] About a month and a half before the inaugural, having lost none of his love of France, Jefferson wrote his son-in-law, Thomas Mann Randolph, that " . . . in spite of the most copious profusion of English lies . . . it appears that the French are eminently successful . . . I really believe him [Adams] disposed to . . . arrest English violences."[44] As the inaugural drew closer, Jefferson's confidence in Adams increased, and he depicted him as "my most ancient and respected friend," whose "principles founded on the immutable basis of equal right and reason have continued pure and unchanged."[45]

Now that peace with England had been purchased by the hated Jay Treaty, something had to be done about our relations with France. For if French spoliations against American ships continued, Adams would have no other recourse but to follow the Federalists into war. Adams, like Washington, had no desire for war, but the situation that faced him on March 4, 1797, was most complex. In the summer of 1796, Washington replaced the Republican Monroe as Minister to France with the Hamiltonian Federalist Charles Cotesworth Pinckney. The Directory, now in power in France, refused to have anything to do with him, and gave point to its refusal by a demonstrative and affectionate farewell for Monroe. Adams met the situation with characteristic practicality. He wanted to send Jefferson,[46] but the project was opposed by Pickering, and was

---

[42]Jefferson to John Adams, December 28, 1796, *Jefferson MSS.*

[43]Jefferson to Madison, January 1, 1797, *Jefferson MSS.*

[44]Jefferson to Thomas Mann Randolph, January 22, 1797, *Jefferson MSS.* Jefferson did not take an active part in the election of 1796. Noble E. Cunningham, Jr., *The Jeffersonian Republicans: The Formation of Party Organization, 1789-1801* (Chapel Hill: University of North Carolina Press, 1957), p. 107.

[45]Jefferson to James Sullivan, February 9, 1797, *Jefferson MSS.* James Sullivan, a Jeffersonian Republican, was Governor of Massachusetts.

[46]Adams to Gerry, April 6, 1797. Charles F. Adams, *The Works of John Adams* (Boston: Charles C. Little and James Brown, 1851), Vol. VIII, p. 538. Elbridge Gerry was an old friend and supporter of John Adams.

vetoed by Jefferson himself. It was finally determined to send a commission to Paris to be composed of three members, one of them being Charles C. Pinckney. John Marshall of Virginia and Elbridge Gerry of Connecticut were chosen as the other two members. They met Pinckney in Paris, and on October 5, 1797, announced their arrival to the Directory. Day after day the Americans waited for a communication from the French government. None came. Instead two bankers, Hottinguer and Bellamy, and two other persons, M. Hauteral and Madame de Villette, visited them. These agents suggested that the United States should lend money to the French government, and also make a gift of a large sum of money to the Directors. Confronted with this attempted blackmail, Pinckney spoke for the United States, and his phrase, "No. No, not a sixpence," has become famous in American history. Negotiations ended abruptly in March, 1798. Marshall and Pinckney departed, and Gerry alone remained at Paris, for Talleyrand had told him that France would declare war if he, too, abandoned the mission.

When Adams read the dispatches from his envoys, he was greatly stirred. In successive communications to Congress, he explained the duplicity of France, advocated preparations for war, and declared that he would "never send another minister to France without assurances that he will be received, respected and honored as the representative of a great, free, powerful, and independent nation."[47] The Jeffersonians felt that Adams was acting intemperately and unconstitutionally, and demanded the publication of all the Paris dispatches. Adams obliged them by sending all the papers to Congress —the names of the French agents being replaced by the letters X, Y, and Z. The publication of the papers produced intense excitement both in Congress and all over the country. "Millions for defense, but not one cent for tribute," became the dominant mood. The Republican majority in Congress rapidly dwindled, the members either going home or voting with the Federalists.[48] The President recalled

[47]Edward Channing, *A History of the United States* (New York: Macmillian Co., 1929), Vol. VII, p. 189. See Albert J. Beveridge, *The Life of John Marshall*, Vol. VI, pp. 257-290, for the best detailed account of XYZ affair. Beveridge makes excellent use of Marshall's journal.

[48]The Boston *Independent Chronicle*, April 16, 1798, claimed that the XYZ revelations were "unpleasant but not alarming." The Republican press insisted on the above attitude and even praised Adams for his eventual peace negotiations. See Donald H. Steward, *Jeffersonian Journalism 1789-1801*, pp. 546 sq.

Gerry. Defense preparations were immediately undertaken. Plans were made to protect American shipping in the West Indies. Washington and Hamilton were nominated by Adams to take charge of raising and training the new army. Washington was to be commander-in-chief, and Hamilton his inspector-general. A naval force was also to be fitted out, and for greater efficiency the Navy Department was separated from the War Department, and placed under the direction of our first Secretary of the Navy, Benjamin Stoddert.

Just when the Hamiltonian junto in Congress was beginning to look with friendly eyes on Adams, he infuriated them by sending a special minister, William Vans Murray, to Paris. This surprise move, which the Federalists tried desperately to block, resulted in the Convention of 1800, and peace with France. Professor Bemis, in dealing with this action, writes that "Without loss to American honor, President Adams had prevented the Federalists from rushing the country into war with France."[49] Even though it meant his own political death, and the wrecking of the Federalist party, Adams consoled himself with the thought that "my missions to France . . . were the most disinterested and meritorious actions of my life." In fact he desired no other inscription over his gravestone than "Here lies John Adams, who took upon himself the responsibility of the peace with France in the year 1800."[50] A good many Federalists never forgave Adams, for they felt that war with France would have perpetuated their party in power.

FREEDOM VS. SECURITY

Foreign policy always has its repercussions on the domestic scene, and this was never more true than during the administration of John Adams. The Federalist-inspired Alien and Sedition Acts of 1798 not only gave rise to the Virginia and Kentucky resolutions of the same year, but also presented the Republicans with a very live issue for the presidential campaign of 1800. Hamiltonian hostility to foreigners was due in no small measure to French propaganda of recent years, and to the persistent effort of the French to

---

[49]Samuel F. Bemis, *A Diplomatic History of the United States* (New York: Henry Holt & Co., 1936), p. 125.
[50]Adams to James Lloyd, January, 1815. *Works of John Adams,* Vol. X, p. 113. Lloyd was a Senator from Massachusetts.

separate the American people from their government. America, in 1798, seemed filled with exiles from France, Santo Domingo, England, and Ireland. These newcomers, save those from England, proved obnoxious to the Federalists. The extreme radicalism of their views, so venomously expressed in the press and on the public platform, brought a strong reaction from the party in power. Furthermore, the majority of them became Jeffersonian Democrats. Thus it was that four laws were passed by the Federalists during June and July of 1798. The Naturalization Act extended from five to fourteen years the period required for citizenship. This would disenfranchise the recent immigrants for some years to come. The two Alien Acts gave the President the power to order any alien out of the country or license him to reside in the United States at some designated place. Finally, the Sedition Act dealt with all persons, native or foreign, who conspired against the government, or who, through printing or writing, did anything to bring it or any one of its officials into disrepute. The federal courts were given jurisdiction over these laws and the punishment was limited to five years' imprisonment and $5,000 fine.

The Sedition Act struck hard at the powerful Jeffersonian press. Callender, Cooper, Duane, Holt, Greenleaf, all prominent Democratic editors, were hauled into court under the Sedition act.[51] The overbearing manner of Judge Samuel Chase who presided at most of these trials added to the indignation felt throughout the country. The fact that there was no national law controlling the picking of jurors led to the cry of "packed" juries, and caused a good deal of scandal. The Republican press warned that America was being depopulated of some of her most competent people, and asserted that four hundred families in the summer of 1800 crossed into Canada because of the Alien Acts. The Jeffersonians coupled their statistics with a vigorous plea for the votes of anyone who had any

---

[51]Cooper, of Sunbury and Northumberland *Gazette,* got 6 months and $400 fine. See *Aurora,* November 5, 1800 in Donald H. Steward, *Jeffersonian Journalism, 1789-1801,* p. 899. Callender of Richmond *Examiner* got 9 months and $200 fine. See Richmond *Examiner,* October 10, 1800 in Steward, *op. cit.,* p. 902. Duane, held for contempt, was actually let off. See *Aurora,* May 13, 1800, as cited by Steward, p. 901. Greenleaf, of theNew York *Argus,* died, and a journeyman of the same paper, Frothingham, was fined $100 and given 4 months in prison. See New London *Bee,* January 1, and February 12, 1800, in Steward p. 876. Holt of the *Bee* got 3 months and $200 fine, see Steward, *op. cit.,* p. 897.

ties to any foreign country—and that, of course, meant all Americans.[52]

Besides influencing public opinion through Democratic newspapers, Jefferson drew up a series of resolutions condemnatory of the Alien and Sedition laws. He gave them to his friend, William C. Nicholas, expecting that the North Carolina Assembly would adopt them. In October 1798, Nicholas gave John Breckenridge, a member of the Kentucky Assembly, a copy of the resolutions. Nicholas then informed Jefferson that Breckenridge was confident that the "legislature of Kentucky will adopt them."[53] The resolutions were adopted by the Kentucky legislature in November, 1798. In substance, they set forth the theory that the general government exists by compact; that there were certain definite powers delegated to it, but the "residuary mass of right" was reserved to each state; and that whenever the general government assumes undelegated powers "its acts are unauthoritative, void, and of no force." Finally, the resolutions declared that the Alien and Sedition laws were void and called for their repeal by Congress. Kentucky then called upon its co-states to say whether or not the acts were authorized by the federal compact. The Virginia resolutions, adopted in December, 1798, came to pretty much the same thing as those of Kentucky. Somewhat briefer, they declared the Alien and Sedition legislation unconstitutional, and called on their sister states to take the necessary action to preserve "unimpaired, the authorities, rights, and liberties, reserved to the states respectively or to the people."[54] The response from the other states was nil, which must have been somewhat disappointing to Jefferson and his party. However, by January of 1800, Virginia, reacting to Northern condemnation, voted money for arms, military supplies, and an armory. Washington was deeply worried and pleaded with Patrick Henry to return to public life. Responding to Washington's entreaty, Henry made his last memorable speech from a tavern in Charlotte, Virginia, in March, 1799. Admitting the right of revolution if a people were

[52]New London *Bee,* October 1, 1800, in Donald H. Steward, *Jeffersonian Journalism, 1789-1801,* p. 903.

[53]William C. Nicholas to Jefferson, October 4, 1798, cited in Edward Channing, *A History of the United States,* Vol. VIII, p. 225. Nicholas was one of the foremost Jeffersonians of Virginia.

[54]The Virginia Resolutions were written by James Madison after consultation with Jefferson.

intolerably oppressed, he begged his fellow-Americans to wait until some infringement was made on their rights which could not otherwise be redressed. He asked them not to split into factions but to preserve their strength for the English, the French, or the Germans, or anyone else who might dare invade our territory. In a grand finale, he asserted that if the Virginians opposed the general government, Washington would have to lead the army against them. Where, he declared, is the American "who will dare to lift his hand against the father of his country? . . . No, you dare not do it; in such a patricidal attempt the steel would drop from your nerveless arms."[55] And that was that. The danger from Virginia evaporated. As long as George Washington lived and backed the Federalists, they could be fairly sure of success. If Washington would consent to run for president in 1800, the Federalists would be sure to stay in power.

---

[55]William W. Henry, *Patrick Henry: Life, Correspondence and Speeches* (New York: Charles Scribners Sons, 1891), Vol. II, pp. 608-610.

2

The Revolution of 1800

THE PRESIDENTIAL ELECTION OF 1800, which saw Adams and Charles Cotesworth Pinckney pitted against Jefferson and Burr, has been called the Second American Revolution. Essential for an understanding of how this revolution was accomplished, which was to give the Democratic party almost uninterrupted power for sixty years, is a knowledge of the election machinery of that period.[1] In the first place, there was no direct voting by the people for the candidates. There was no general election day. The electors in eleven of the sixteen participating states were chosen by the legislatures meeting in joint session. Only in the remaining five was there any semblance of a direct, popular vote. The electors cast their votes for two men, without any distinction between them as to office. The candidate receiving the highest number of all the ballots cast became president, the candidate with the second highest number, vice-president.

It therefore followed that the national campaign was fought in the local elections for members of the state legislatures. A Federalist majority in the combined houses of any legislature would mean the choosing of Federalist presidential electors; or vice-versa, if a majority of Republicans were elected, the result would be Republican presidential electors.

Another factor of importance in 1800 was that rigid property qualifications made eligible voters of only one-fifteenth of the adult male white population of the entire country. Even this fraction was still further reduced owing to the difficulty of reaching the polls on the appointed day, and because of the non-secrecy of the voting. The picture of the wealthy merchant, Mr. John Murray, sacrificing

---

[1]The Taylor-Fillmore Whig regime of 1848-1852 was the one real exception. The Whig Harrison died in 1840 a month after his inaugural address and was succeeded by Tyler who was in reality a Democrat.

an entire day in order to observe how his employees voted, gives an idea of the courage it took in 1800 to vote according to one's convictions.[2]

Generally speaking, 1800 was expected to be a repetition of 1796 in that the Southern states could safely be counted in the Republican column and the New England section in the Federalist. This was, in the main, the division that Madison described when, on July 14, 1787, he remarked in the Constitutional Convention: "It seems now to be pretty well understood that the real difference of interests lay, not between the large and small, but between the Northern and Southern states. The institution of slavery and its consequences formed the line of discrimination."[3]

Politicians knew only too well that the contest of 1800 would turn in large measure on the electoral votes of New York, Pennsylvania, and South Carolina. Of these, New York was most important. Unless that state could be won, victory would almost be impossible. As early as March, 1800, Jefferson informed Madison that the Republicans were in, if New York City could be carried.[4] In this case, Burr was Jefferson's informant, and it was Burr who by his political brilliance was to win New York. The Federalist Gouverneur Morris agreed with Jefferson's interpretation, and he wrote in his diary that the "New York election has been carried by the Democrats, and it is from thence concluded that Jefferson will be President."[5]

Five days after the election of the new legislature in New York, Hamilton wrote to Governor John Jay proposing the calling of the old legislature for the purpose of providing for the choice of presidential electors in districts by popular vote. This would, he argued, save New York and the country for the Federalists. Jay was warned by Hamilton that "it is easy to sacrifice the substantial interests of society by a strict adherence to ordinary rules." Hamilton argued that the scruples of delicacy and propriety ought not "to hinder the taking of a legal and constitutional step to prevent an atheist in

---

[2]George M. Troup to King, June 5, 1799, *Rufus King MSS.* Troup was a Georgian and a Democrat.
[3]*The Records of the Federal Convention of 1787*, ed. by Max Farrand (New Haven, Yale University Press, 1937), Vol. II, p. 10.
[4]*The Writings of Thomas Jefferson*, ed. by Paul L. Ford (New York: G. P. Putnam's Sons, 1899), Vol. X, pp. 134-136, 154-159.
[5]*Diary of Gouverneur Morris*, May 3, 1800, *Gouverneur Morris MSS.*

religion, and a fanatic in politics from getting possession of the helm of state." Jay, ardent Federalist though he was, would not stoop to conquer, and he commented on this remarkable letter with the words: "Proposing a measure for party purpose which it would not become me to adopt."[6]

Deeply embarrassed at the political defeat administered to him by Burr in New York, Hamilton was further chagrined when Burr somehow got possession of the above letter, and it appeared in a Republican newspaper the very day after Hamilton had dispatched it. Burr's Revolutionary War intelligence service experience was a great help to him in political life. It would help him more than once in the campaign of 1800.

Rumblings of civil war were to be heard now and again during the campaign. William Duane, Jefferson's chief newspaper editor, writing of Hamilton's plan "to prevent the effects of the recent change in the people's mind from taking effect" asserted that some held the opinion that "a civil war would be preferable to having Jefferson for President."[7]

There were three important reasons why Burr was able to defeat the Federalists in New York: Hamilton's duplicity, Burr's careful choosing of a slate of candidates, and Burr's enfranchising hundreds of Democrats. As in 1796, so in 1800, Hamilton tried to undermine Adams. Again his conniving was to prove his undoing, for instead of nominating a group of outstanding Federalists, Hamilton picked a group of mediocrities—men who would be his willing tools in deserting Adams and supporting Charles Cotesworth Pinckney. Federalists of high caliber would not have lent themselves readily to such a work. Fifteen years later, John Adams could relate with considerable complacency, even though it cost him the election, how Hamilton called a secret caucus

To prepare a list of representatives for the City of New York, in their State legislature, who were to choose electors of President and Vice-President. He fixed upon a list of his own friends, people of little weight or consideration in the city or in the country. Burr, who had friends in all circles, had a copy of this list brought to him immediately. He read it over, with great gravity

---

[6]*The Works of Alexander Hamilton*, ed. by Henry Cabot Lodge (New York: G. P. Putnam's Sons, 1904), Vol. VII, p. 549.
[7]Philadelphia *Aurora*, May 7, 1800.

folded it up, put it in his pocket, and without uttering another word said, "Now I have him all hollow."[8]

Burr's first move had been a tactical one: he had refused to publish a ticket until the Federalists completed theirs. Now that Burr knew his opposition, he "immediately went to Governor Clinton, General Gates, Chancellor Livingston, etc., etc., stirred them all up, and persuaded the Governor and the General to stand candidates, with a list of the most respectable citizens to represent the city in the legislature."[9] John Adams added that "Burr's list was chosen, as common sense must have foreseen, by a great majority, who went to Albany, and chose electors who voted unanimously for Mr. Jefferson, though New York at all antecedent elections voted unanimously for Adams."[10]

But Burr did not depend solely on the merits of his ticket. For many years he had been forging a compact, strong, political machine. Based upon a group of young men of ability and zeal, bound together by a fanatical devotion to Burr, the organization acted with formidable unanimity. The Federalists, and even later the Republicans, sneered at this "little band," the "Myrmidons," but Theodosia, Burr's daughter, proudly called them the "tenth legion."

There was also a much larger group, the Society of St. Tammany, founded in 1789 by William Mooney, an ex-soldier. It was the logical successor to certain societies of the Revolutionary years: the Sons of St. Tammany and the Sons of Liberty. Composed of groups of laborers, mechanics, and the dispossessed, they insisted on fighting until independence was attained. They opposed and made fun of Tory organizations possessing the high-sounding titles of St. David, St. Andrew, St. George, etc. These predecessors of Tammany disbanded at the end of the war, only to rise again during the fight over the Constitution. Followers of George Clinton, in his first battles against the ratification of the Constitution, they had dissolved again under the penetrating acid of Hamilton's triumphs.

When a new order of aristocrats, the Society of the Cincinnati, composed of officers only, emerged, William Mooney was stirred to action. These Cincinnati, with hereditary membership for their

---

[8]John Adams to James Lloyd, February 17, 1815, *John Adams MSS.*
[9]John Adams to James Lloyd, February 17, 1815, *ibid.*
[10]John Adams to James Lloyd, February 17, 1815, *ibid.*

families and resplendent insignia, completely overlooked the common soldiers who had fought the Revolutionary War. Hamilton became the president of the New York chapter, and Burr was also a member.

As a protest, William Mooney, a private during the Revolution, formed the Society of St. Tammany. Originally a social and not a political force, it was equipped with an elaborate ritual and an array of Indian titles such as Sachems, Grand Sachems, Sagamores, Scribes, and Wiskinies. Their meeting place was called the Wigwam, and Barden's Tavern at Broad and Beekman in downtown Manhattan served as the first Wigwam.

For some years, Burr had his eye on the political possibilities of Tammany. He never joined the Order, but he gradually achieved control, becoming, in fact, its real leader. Many of Burr's "little band," John and Robert Swartwout, Matthew Davis, John and William P. Van Ness, Isaac Pierson, John P. Hall, Jacob Barker, and others joined Tammany, and became in time its Sachems and Grand Sachems. Davis acknowledged that "Burr was our chief."[11]

By 1798, the society had entered its political phase. Through his lieutenants, Burr now controlled Tammany policies, formed its members into an effective organization, and led them to the polls on election day where they voted according to his wishes. The fact that most of the Tammanyites were disenfranchised by the existing property qualifications presented a problem to Burr. He met it squarely by having groups of propertyless and landless Republicans purchase sufficient land as joint tenants. Funds for the purpose were furnished by wealthy Republicans. Each tenant, according to the law, was now owner of the entire piece of property, and thus had a vote. Burr had found a loophole in the restrictions which men of property had placed in the Constitution against the rabble. Burr's enfranchisement of these hitherto voteless citizens was to prove a considerable help in winning New York and the White House in 1800.[12]

John Adams, aware of Hamilton's machinations, struck back by firing James McHenry, Secretary of War, and Timothy Pickering, Secretary of State. These men were Hamilton partisans, and Adams

---

[11]New York *American Citizen*, July 18, 1809, cited by Nathan Schachner, *Aaron Burr: A Biography* (New York: Frederick A. Stokes Co., 1937), p. 175.
[12]Burr made a card index of every voter in New York City.

would have fared much better had he discharged them much sooner.[13]

Furious, Hamilton determined to fight Adams to a finish. He composed a pamphlet in which he attacked the Administration and John Adams in intemperate language. His first instinct was to publish it anonymously to the world. He only changed his mind after the repeated pleadings of his friends. It was now agreed that he would sign it and circulate it privately among the leading Federalists. Hamilton now thought this to be the most effective way to replace Adams with Pinckney. He again reckoned without Burr. The pamphlet had been sent to the editor of the New York *Gazette* to be secretly printed. Again Burr's sleuthing experience stood him in good stead, for somehow or other he got hold of a copy of the printed pamphlet even before Hamilton received his own. Burr promptly saw to it that it was printed with appropriate comments in the Philadelphia *Aurora* and the New London *Bee*. The Adams Federalists were shocked. The party was split wide open.[14]

After the dust of the great battle of 1800 had settled, it was agreed by both Federalists and Republicans that the newspapers had won for Jefferson.[15] When Jefferson, as Secretary of State, wrote Madison that he should have given Freneau "the perusal of all my letters of foreign intelligence," he was following normal political practice.[16] Both parties fed their respective presses. There is hardly anything worth mentioning in the private correspondence of the politicians that did not make the newspapers. Duane, in 1800, editor of Jefferson's most important newspaper, wrote that there were really three parties in the field: the Republicans, the friends of the President, and the followers of Hamilton. The Democratic press pounced on Hamilton. Dictator of the aristocratical party, and fa-

---

[13]McHenry was asked to resign, and did so on May 6, 1800. Pickering, refusing to resign, was dismissed on May 10, 1800. The commonly accepted thesis that Burr organized his voters through Tammany in 1800 is challenged by Noble E. Cunningham, Jr., in *The Jeffersonian Republicans*, p. 181-182. Among other things, Cunningham does not feel that Tammany was potent enough in 1800.

[14]Nathan Schachner, *Aaron Burr: A Biography, op. cit.*, p. 183. In the summer of 1800, Hamilton stated: "The only way to prevent a fatal error in the Federal party, is to support General Pinckney." Hamilton to Theodore Sedgwick, May 10, 1800. *Hamilton MSS.* Sedgwick was a Federalist Congressman from Massachusetts.

[15]Donald H. Steward, *Jeffersonian Journalism, 1789-1801*, p. 1.

[16]Jefferson to Madison, July 21, 1791, *Jefferson MSS.* At the time Freneau was Jefferson's leading editor.

ther of the funding system, Hamilton was pictured flying around the country rallying his partisans to Pinckney.[17]

In the main, Jeffersonian newspapers made their appeal to small farmers, mechanics, former soldiers, small merchants, Germans, and Irish. Duane, Callendar, Cooper, Holt, and other Jeffersonian editors constantly reminded their readers of the high cost of the army and navy and the frequent outrages of idle soldiers. The excise law, the eight percent loan, the increasing national debt, Wolcott's admission that another eight percent loan would be necessary, all these made good reading for prospective Republicans. Duane hammered the Federalists over the Dayton scandal and boldly asked

Jonathan Dayton . . . do you or do you not hold in your possession thirty thousand dollars, the property of the good people of the United States—which was advanced to you for public uses, but which you never returned to the proper owners thereof for more than two years?[18]

Dayton, Federalist leader of New Jersey, while Speaker of the House, made written application at the end of the 1798 session for thirty-three thousand dollars. The money was requested for the current expenses of Congress. It was proved that the amount was not needed. When the Secretary of the Treasury, Wolcott, attempted to defend himself by saying he did not know he had given Dayton more than necessary, the Jefferonian press greeted him with salvos of sarcasm. It was not until the winter of 1799 that it was discovered that Dayton had retained more than eighteen thousand dollars since July, 1798. Wolcott, being apprised of the scandal, demanded and received the money from Dayton, but not the interest. Wolcott, who at this time was secretly working with Hamilton to seat Pinckney instead of Adams, was accused by the Republicans of saying that Adams "did not deserve a vote for President." In addition, the Jeffersonians asserted that the Secretary of the Treasury's "monstrous suppression of the true state of the financial affairs of the country" was part and parcel of the "whole system of Anglo-federal party."[19]

---

[17]*American Mercury,* September 11, 1800, as cited by Claude Bowers, *Jefferson and Hamilton,* p. 465.

[18]*Aurora,* May 23, 1800. Also Newark *Sentinel of Freedom,* May 27, 1800. Both cited by Donald H. Steward, *Jeffersonian Journalism, 1789-1801, op. cit.,* p. 190.

[19]Richmond, Virginia *Argus,* September 2, 1800, in Donald H. Steward, *ibid.,* p. 202. Also see Wolcott to Hamilton, July 7, 1800, *Hamilton MSS.*

Bloody but unbowed, the Federalists rushed into print with an issue that was to recur again and again in American political campaigns. Religion always makes good copy, and no one was more aware of this than the supporters of Adams and Hamilton. They were quick to stress the religious theme, especially in New England. After a speech by Abraham Bishop, the fighting leader of the Jeffersonians in Connecticut, the Hartford *Courant* declared that the audience contained "every open reviler of religion," and that all of them were "highly gratified."[20] All over New England, and in New York and Philadelphia, ministers were preaching politics. Federalist strategy was to picture Jefferson as an atheist, a scoffer at religion who laughed at the Bible. This part of the campaign was entrusted to the ministerial corps. It was a form of calumny that pursued Jefferson from the moment he obtained religious toleration and liberty for Virginia. The only time Jefferson answered any campaign canard was when the Reverend Cotton Smith accused him of obtaining his property by robbing a widow and her fatherless children of their estate. "If Mr. Smith thinks that the precepts of the Gospel are intended for those who preach them as well as for others," Jefferson answered, "he will some day feel the duties of repentance and acknowledgment in such forms as to correct the wrong he has done. All this is left to his own conscience."[21] When the Reverend Dr. Abercrombie of Philadelphia warned his congregation against voting for an atheist, the *Aurora* replied that he "is the man who opposed reading the Declaration of Independence of 4th of July last . . . need we wonder at his hatred of Mr. Jefferson?"[22] In answer to a Federalist pamphlet which declared that Jefferson was not even a Christian, the *American Mercury* dwelt on Jefferson's contributions to the church and to needy clergymen. The *Mercury* insisted that while Mr. Jefferson is "practicing the blessed religion of Jesus Christ by acts of charity and benevolence . . . these political parsons are abusing that holy religion . . . by fulminating lies and slander against Mr. Jefferson."[23] When Federalists urged Catholics to vote against Jefferson, Duane dryly commented: "We presume the . . . reason to be that it was owing to Mr. Jefferson that the Catholic priest was saved

[20]*Courant,* September 15, 1800.
[21]Jefferson to Uriah McGregory, August 13, 1800, *Jefferson MSS.*
[22]*Aurora,* September 1, 1800.
[23]*American Mercury,* October 2, 1800.

from being hanged for going into . . . Virginia . . . and that to his toleration law it was owing that the Catholic can now build churches and adore God without incurring penalties of fine and imprisonment."[24] And so that battle of the press rolled on, and by the summer of 1800 Uriah Tracy had to admit that at least in Pennsylvania the Republicans were "establishing presses and newspapers in almost every town and county in the country and the Federalist presses are failing for want of support."[25] The press was vital in promoting the revolution of 1800. At least, that was the opinion of Federalist and Republican leaders of 1800. John Adams swore that "a group of foreign liars," Duane, Freneau, Callendar, Cooper, and Lyon, had upset the virtue and property of the country.[26]

1796 VS. 1800

The election of 1800 invites comparison with that of 1796. In 1796 Adams had received all of New York's twelve electoral votes. If he had received half of them in 1800, he would have been President. For in 1800, Jefferson received seven fewer electoral votes from states outside of New York than he had in 1796. A change of two hundred and fourteen votes in New York City would have spelled victory for Adams. In 1800 as well as 1796, Adams received the whole thirty-nine votes of New England. Not counting New York, Adams received in 1796 twenty electoral votes from New Jersey and the states to the southward. In 1800 Adams did better, he received twenty-six votes from those states. Laurels for Burr seem mandatory when one considers that, omitting New York, Adams had more electoral votes in 1800 than he had in 1796.

There is no doubt that the Democratic victory of 1800 was due in no small measure to the effective work of Aaron Burr, but, in spite of the victory, the country was confronted with an unprecedented situation. For the final election results showed that Jefferson and Burr were tied: 73 to 73. Adams had 65 and Pinckney 64. As the Constitution required in 1800, the electors had cast their ballots for two men, without differentiating between them as to

---

[24]*Aurora,* October 14, 1800.

[25]Uriah Tracy to Oliver Wolcott, August 7, 1800, cited in *Memoirs of the Administrations of George Washington and John Adams,* ed. by George Gibbs, Vol. II, p. 399. Tracy was an important Federalist from Connecticut.

[26]John Adams to Benjamin Stoddert, March 31, 1801, *John Adams MSS.*

which was to be designated president and which vice-president. The Constitution also required that, in case of a tie, the choice of a President was to be determined by a majority of the House of Representatives, voting as states for the two highest candidates. Since there were sixteen states in the Union in 1800, nine was a majority, but the Federalists controlled the House, and almost in despair Jefferson wrote Governor Monroe that

after the most energetic efforts, crowned with success, we remain in the hands of our enemies by the want of foresight in the original arrangement. I will thank you for any information you can give me on the subject of the conspiracy.[27]

More than three months before the election, Hamilton thought there was "too much probability that Jefferson or Burr will be President."[28] The Jeffersonians had tried certain precautions to prevent a tie but they had failed. On December 2, Philip Freneau[29] wrote Jefferson that one elector from South Carolina was expected to vote for Clinton instead of Burr to insure the presidency for Jefferson, but that he had failed to do so.[30] Again, on December 12, Jefferson wrote that "it is believed Georgia will withhold from him one or two. The votes will stand probably T. J. 73, Burr about 70, Mr. Adams 65."[31] Three days later he wrote a carefully worded congratulatory note to his running mate:

It was badly managed not to have arranged with certainty what seems to have been left to hazard. It was the more material because I understood several of the high-flying federalists have expressed their hope that the two republican tickets may be equal, and their determination in that case to prevent a choice by the House of Representatives (which they are strong enough to do), and let the government devolve on a president of the senate . . .

---

[27]Jefferson to James Monroe, December 20, 1800, *Jefferson MSS.* At this time Monroe was Governor of Virginia.

[28]Hamilton to James A. Bayard, August 6, 1800, *Hamilton MSS.*

[29]Philip M. Freneau has been called "the poet of the American Revolution." In 1791, with Madison's help, he started the *National Gazette* in Philadelphia. He waged a bitter campaign against the Federalists. Washington referred to him as "that rascal." Jefferson said he "saved the Constitution."

[30]Peter Freneau to Jefferson, December 2, 1800, *Jefferson MSS.*

[31]Jefferson to Thomas Mann Randolph, December 12, 1800, *Jefferson MSS.* Burr had not been supported by the South in 1796, running 38 votes behind Jefferson. When the Democratic delegation approached Burr to stand as Jefferson's running mate in 1800, they gave him assurances on this question. Nicholson to Gallatin, May 7, 1800, *Gallatin MSS.* Nicholson is Joseph Nicholson, a Democrat from Maryland.

Assuming that he was to be President, with Burr as his Vice-President, Jefferson was quick to congratulate Burr

on the issue of this contest; because it is more honorable and doubtless more grateful to you than any station within the competence of the chief magistrate, yet, for myself, and for the substantial service of the public, I feel most sensibly the loss we sustain of your aid in our new administration whose talents, integrity, names and dispositions should at once inspire unbounded confidence in the public mind, and insure a perfect harmony in the conduct of the public business. I lose you from the list, and I am not sure of all the others.[32]

The day after Jefferson penned the above letter, Burr, anticipating the possibility of a tie, wrote to General Samuel Smith of Baltimore, a Republican Congressman and close friend of Jefferson. Burr stated that

It is highly improbable that I shall have an equal number of votes with Mr. Jefferson; but, if such should be the result, every man who knows me ought to know that I shall utterly disdain all competition. Be assured that the federal party can entertain no wish for such an exchange. As to my friends, they would dishonour my views and insult my feelings by a suspicion that I would submit to be instrumental in counteracting the wishes and expectations of the United States. And I now constitute you my proxy to declare these sentiments if the occasion should require.[33]

This letter seemed clear enough, but on the other hand, suppose the representatives of the people in the House decided to elect Burr president in spite of his wishes? This was a distinct possibility.

Two days before Christmas, Burr answered Jefferson's letter of December 15:

Gov. Fenner is principally responsible for the unfortunate result of the election in R.I. So late as September he told me personally that you would have every vote in that state and that Adams would certainly have one and probably two; this he confirmed by a verbal message to me through a confidential friend in October. He has lately given some plausible reasons for withdrawing his name from the Republican ticket. I do not, however, apprehend any embarrassment even in case the votes should come out alike for us. My personal friends are perfectly informed of my wishes on the subject and can never think of diverting a single vote from you. On the contrary, they will be found among your most zealous adherents. I see no reason to doubt of your

[32]Jefferson to Burr, December 15, 1800, *Jefferson MSS.*
[33]Burr to Smith, December 16, 1800, *Memoirs of Aaron Burr*, ed. by Matthew L. Davis (New York: Harpers & Brothers, 1855), Vol. II, p. 75.

having at least nine States if the business shall come before the House of Representatives.[34]

In other words, Burr, while trusting that the South would not betray him, had felt that Rhode Island's vote would insure the primary office for Jefferson. However, Governor Fenner had at the last moment decided not to run as an elector, and his substitute had voted for Jefferson and Burr. Actually, if Jefferson's lieutenants had been successful in withdrawing votes from Burr in South Carolina and Georgia and Tennessee, and Rhode Island had followed suit—Burr would very probably have lost the vice-presidency to Adams.[35]

Burr did not think Jefferson would have any trouble forming a cabinet and he remarked that

as far as my knowledge extends, it is the unanimous determination of the Republicans of every grade to support your administration with unremitted zeal; indeed, I should distrust the loyalty of anyone professing to be a Republican who should refuse his services. There is, in fact, no such dearth of talents or of patriotism as ought to inspire a doubt of your being able to fill every office in a manner that will command public confidence and public approbation. As to myself, I will cheerfully abandon the office of V.P. if it shall be thought that I can be more useful in any active station. In fact, my whole time and attention shall be unceasingly employed to render your administration grateful and honorable to our Country and to yourself. To this I am impelled by the highest sense of duty as by the most devoted personal attachment.[36]

Jefferson, aware of the futility of being a vice-president, had marked Burr for a cabinet post. When the news of the tie reached the Federalists, they were jubilant. Ever since Burr's New York victory in May, many of them had acknowledged defeat, but now John Randolph of Roanoke reported "our Tories begin to give themselves airs . . . I fear that . . . they will give us some trouble."[37] Jefferson, writing to his friend Breckenridge, was sure that

the Federalists in Congress mean to take advantage of this, and either to prevent an election altogether, or reverse what has been understood to have been the wishes of the people as to their President and Vice-President, wishes which

[34]Burr to Jefferson, December 23, 1800, *Jefferson MSS.*

[35]The Madison correspondence and the Nicholson to Gallatin letter cited in footnote 31 indicate that the original arrangement had been one of absolute Southern loyalty to Burr. See *Letters and Other Writings of James Madison* (Philadelphia: J. B. Lippincott & Co., 1865), Vol. II, p. 160.

[36]Burr to Jefferson, December 23, 1800, *Jefferson MSS.*

[37]John Randolph to Nicholson, December 16, 1800. *Jefferson MSS.*

the Constitution did not permit them specially to designate. The latter alternative still gives us a Republican administration, the former a suspension of the federal government for want of a head.[38]

Democrats, generally, accepted Burr's disclaimer, especially since he had designated Samuel Smith, one of Jefferson's closest friends, to act as his proxy in refusing to oppose Jefferson. Stevens T. Mason, writing to Monroe, stated that "I have no doubt [Burr] will cordially cooperate with us."[39] Caesar A. Rodney informed his Maryland friend Nicholson that "I think Col. Burr deserves immortal honor, for the noble part he has acted on this occasion."[40] However, the Federalists considered Burr's letter to Smith to be mere window dressing. Writing to James McHenry, Uriah Tracy was convinced that "Burr is a cunning man. If he cannot outwit all the Jeffersonians I do not know the man."[41] McHenry, in turn, wrote to Rufus King that the Federalists did not consider Burr bound by his letter to Smith "not to accept the office of President, if elected by the House of Representatives."[42] On Christmas Eve, Robert Goodloe Harper confided to Burr that the

votes of Tennessee are come in and decide the the tie. The language of the Democrats is that you will yield your pretensions to their favorite; and it is whispered that overtures to this end are to be, or are made to you. I advise you to take no step whatever by which the choice of the House of Representatives can be impeded or embarrassed. Keep the game perfectly in your hands, but do not answer this letter, or any other that may be written to you by a Federal man, nor write to any of that party.[43]

By this time, it was obvious that the Federalists intended to support Burr in spite of his letters renouncing all competition. On January 5, 1801, Benjamin Hichborn, a Democrat from Philadelphia, wrote Jefferson that "Col. Burr is in the house with me and Gen. Smith from Baltimore has been here. I am convinced that some of our

---

[38]Jefferson to John Breckenridge, December 18, 1800, *Jefferson MSS*. Breckenridge was a Kentucky Democrat and became a United States Senator in 1801.

[39]Mason to Monroe, January 2, 1801, *Monroe MSS*. Mason was United States Senator from Virginia and a Democrat.

[40]Caesar A. Rodney to Nicholson, January 3, 1801, *Nicholson MSS*. Rodney was a Democrat from Delaware.

[41]Tracy to James McHenry, December 30, 1800, *McHenry MSS*.

[42]McHenry to Rufus King, January 2, 1801, *King MSS*.

[43]Harper to Burr, December 24, 1800. In 1823 Harper said that he never heard from Burr on this letter. *Aurora*, July 12, 1808.

friends . . . are willing to join the other party, in case they should unite in favor of Col. Burr."[44]

This meeting in Philadelphia was anything but secret. Even the newspapers carried rumors of it.[45] Smith, acting under orders of his Republican superiors, wanted a second and stronger disclaimer from Burr. In effect, he wanted Burr to state publicly that he would not serve if elected. Burr preferred a decision between himself and Jefferson rather than "a suspension of the federal government for want of a head."[46] When Burr stated at this meeting that if the Democrats "could not get Mr. Jefferson they could take him," Smith was adamant and replied that "that could not be done, for the republicans would not give up on any terms."[47]

The evidence is perfectly clear that if Burr wanted to betray his party he could have had the presidency. On February 12, 1801, with the House in a deadlock, James Bayard, the Federalist leader, approached various Democrats in the name of Burr.[48] A few days later a disappointed Bayard wrote that Burr had the "election . . . in his power, but he was determined to come in as a Democrat."[49] A week after this, Bayard repeated that "Burr had refused the offers of the Federalists."[50] Writing to Alexander Hamilton, Bayard insisted that Burr was determined not to shackle himself with federal principles."[51] Six years after the election, Bayard testified under oath that the Federalist plan to seat Burr was "determined by the party, without consulting Mr. Burr."[52] As the documents indicate, Aaron Burr could have had the presidency if he had cooperated with Bayard.

But what about Jefferson? Is there anything to the charge that he accepted Federalist terms in order to achieve the presidency? On

---

[44]Hichborn to Jefferson, January 5, 1801, *Jefferson MSS.*

[45]Philadelphia *Aurora,* January 6, 1801.

[46]These are Jefferson's words. He claimed this was part of the Federalist plan. Jefferson to Breckenridge, December 18, 1800, *Jefferson MSS.*

[47]Gabriel Christie to Samuel Smith, December 19, 1802, *Samuel Smith MSS.* Smith was a Democratic Congressman from Maryland. Christie was a prominent Democrat from Maryland.

[48]Jefferson, *Anas,* February 12, 1801, *The Writings of Thomas Jefferson,* Vol. I, p. 291.

[49]Bayard to Richard Bassett, February 16, 1801, *James A. Bayard MSS.* Bayard was from Delaware and was the leader of the House.

[50]*Diary of Thomas Rodney,* February 21, 1801, *Thomas Rodney MSS.*

[51]Bayard to Hamilton, March 8, 1801, *Hamilton MSS.*

[52]*Memoirs of Aaron Burr, op. cit.,* Vol. II, pp. 123-125.

February 17, 1801, Bayard wrote to his friend, Colonel Allen Mc-
Lane, Collector of the Port of Wilmington:

> Mr. Jefferson is our President. Our opposition was continued until it was
> demonstrated that Burr could not be brought in, and even if he could he
> meant to come in as a Democrat. In such case to evidence his sincerity he
> must have swept every officer in the United States. I have direct information
> that Mr. Jefferson will not pursue this plan . . .I have taken good care of you,
> and think, if prudent, you are safe.[53]

This letter contains allegations which, if proven to be true, would
certainly mar the reputation of Thomas Jefferson. Let us patiently
look at the evidence. When news of the tie reached Alexander
Hamilton, he immediately approached all important Federalists in
the House. His advice was: Vote for Jefferson. He threatened to
leave the Federalist party unless his wishes were complied with. To
Bayard he wrote that he admitted that Jefferson's "politics are tinctured with fanaticism . . . that he is crafty . . . not scrupulous about
the means of success . . . a contemptible hypocrite."[54] But Hamilton
considered Burr to be twice as bad. Hamilton called him "extreme,
irregular, selfish, profligate, artful . . . a complete Catiline."[55]

Bayard was faced with a torturing dilemma. He temporarily
resolved it by voting for Burr on the first ballot. There were now
eight states for Jefferson, six for Burr, and two tied. The votes of
nine states were needed for the presidency. John Vaughn wrote
Jefferson that "our political destiny is suspended by a slender thread,
while dependent on the integrity of Mr. Bayard."[56] Jefferson himself was well aware that there were "three states, Maryland, Delaware, and Vermont, from either of which if a single individual comes
over, it settles the matter."[57] But these all-important congressmen,
the four members from Maryland (Thomas, Craik, Dennis, and
Baer), and Morris of Vermont, had agreed to act in concert with
Bayard. As Bayard himself explained it: "By the arrangements I
had made, I . . . made myself responsible for the issue."[58]

---

[53]Bayard to McLane, February 17, 1801, *Jefferson MSS.* McLane never was removed by Jefferson.
[54]Hamilton to Bayard, January 16, 1801, Lodge, *Hamilton MSS.*
[55]Hamilton to Bayard, December 27, 1800, *Hamilton MSS.*
[56]John Vaughn to Jefferson, January 10, 1801, *Jefferson MSS.*
[57]Jefferson to Randolph, January 9, 1801, *Jefferson MSS.*
[58]Bayard to Samuel Bayard, February 22, 1801, *James A. Bayard MSS.*

After five days and nights of tiring and fruitless balloting, Bayard let it be known that he was prepared to vote for Jefferson provided Jefferson would agree to certain points. John Nicholas of Virginia, a close friend of Jefferson, asked Bayard what these points were. Bayard replied:

First, Sir, the subject of the public credit; secondly, the maintenance of the naval system; and lastly, that subordinate public officers . . . shall not be removed from office on the ground of their political character, nor without complaint against their conduct.[59]

Nicholas, according to Bayard, thought that these points were reasonable. However, he refused to approach Jefferson. Bayard then approached Samuel Smith and repeated his offer, adding the names of certain officeholders he would like protected: "George Latimer, collector of the port of Philadelphia, and Allen McLane, collector of Wilmington."[60] Smith promised to consult Jefferson and the

next day, upon our meeting, General Smith informed me that he had seen Mr. Jefferson, and stated to him the points mentioned, and was authorized by him to say that they corresponded with his views and intentions, and that we might confide in him accordingly. The opposition of Vermont, Maryland, and Delaware was immediately withdrawn.[61]

In 1806, Jefferson, aware of Bayard's allegations, stated that "no proposition of any kind was ever made to me on that occasion by General Smith."[62] Twenty-nine years later, Smith attempted to clear up the mystery by writing that the all-important conversation was held with Jefferson without Jefferson

having the remotest idea of my object. Satisfied with his opinion on the third point, I communicated to your father the next day—that from the conversation that I had had with Mr. Jefferson, I was satisfied in my own mind that his conduct on that point would be so and so.[63]

As one might expect on the basis of the above evidence, some condemn and some exonerate Mr. Jefferson.

---

[59]Deposition of Bayard in case of *Gillespie v. Smith*, given April 3, 1806, cf., *Memoirs of Aaron Burr*, Vol. II, pp. 130-133.

[60]*Memoirs of Aaron Burr, ibid.*, pp. 130-133.

[61]*Ibid.*, pp. 130-133.

[62]Jefferson, *Anas*, April 15, 1806, *The Writings of Thomas Jefferson*, Vol. I, pp. 311-314.

[63]Samuel Smith to James A. Bayard, II, April 3, 1830, *Burr*, II, pp. 107-109.

There is some evidence, although by no means conclusive, that the Republicans would have resorted to war unless Jefferson was chosen. Four days after Jefferson took the presidential oath, one of his adherents wrote Mrs. Samuel Smith that there was

> . . . One thing that appears to me to be very much against the Republicans . . . they had determined if Mr. Jefferson were not President to involve the country in all the calamities of a civil war (for this assertion I have undoubted authority) and nothing but the yielding of the Federalists saved us from this dreadful scourge . . .[64]

At least two important Federalists corroborate the above thesis. James Bayard asserted that the Federalists finally chose Jefferson when it was clear that unless they did "we must risk the Constitution and a civil war."[65] Robert G. Harper echoes Bayard, and states that "supporters of Mr. Jefferson had come to a determination which was known to have been solemnly made and publicly avowed to risk the Constitution and the Union rather than give him up."[66] While the House was still balloting, John Tyler assured James Monroe that Pennsylvania had twenty-two thousand men ready to take up arms in the event of extremities.[67] Two days before this, Jefferson informed Monroe that "we thought it best to declare openly . . . that the day such an act passed the middle states would arm."[68] Jefferson was referring to one of the Federalists' plans whereby they would continue the deadlock in the House until after March 4, 1801. It was then feared that the Federalists would pass a law which would in some way enable them to have a Federalist president.[69] Whatever the motives, after thirty-five trials and five days consumed in balloting, the House of Representatives finally did choose Thomas Jefferson of Virginia as the third President of the United States.

---

[64]Maria Templeton to Mrs. S. H. Smith, March 8, 1801, *Mrs. S. H. Smith MSS.* Mrs. Smith was the wife of Samuel H. Smith, editor of the *National Intelligencer.*

[65]James A. Bayard to Richard Bassett, February 17, 1801, *James A. Bayard MSS.*

[66]Diary of Robert G. Harper, February 24, 1801, *Robert G. Harper MSS.* Harper was a Federalist member of the House from South Carolina.

[67]John Tyler to Monroe, February 11, 1801, *Monroe MSS.*

[68]Jefferson to Monroe, February 15, 1801, *Monroe MSS.*

[69]Marshall, soon to be Chief Justice, had been consulted as to the legitimacy of the House appointing someone other than Jefferson or Burr in case no selection had been reached by March 4. Marshall stated it would be entirely legitimate. John Adams felt the same way. See Monroe to Jefferson, January 18, 1801, *Monroe MSS.* Also John Adams to Elbridge Gerry, February 10, 1801, *John Adams MSS.*

3

Jefferson and the Court

WHEN THOMAS JEFFERSON ascended the steps of the Capitol on March 4, 1801, he looked out on a continent of some five million souls. Nearly one-fifth of these were Negro slaves. This left about four and a half million free whites. In practice this meant that there were less than one million able-bodied males on whose shoulders the future of America rested.[1] The man they had chosen to lead them was awkward in bearing, shy in manner, sandy-complexioned, and six feet two and a half inches in height.[2] The British minister reported that Mr. Jefferson

came from his own lodgings to the House where the Congress convenes, and which goes by the name of the Capitol, on foot, in his ordinary dress, escorted by a body of militia artillery from the neighboring State, and accompanied by the Secretaries of the Navy and the Treasury, and a number of his political friends in the House of Representatives. He was received by Mr. Burr, the Vice-President of the United States . . .[3]

Mrs. Samuel Harrison Smith, the wife of the editor of the *National Intelligencer,* one of Jefferson's most powerful newspapers, observed that the "Senate chamber was so crowded that I believe not another creature could enter." There were "near a thousand persons within the walls. The speech was delivered in so low a tone that few heard it." However, coming out of the House, "the paper was distributed immediately."[4]

Would the first Democratic president heed the warnings of the Federalists, and "see both his honor and interest connected with

[1] *United States Census,* 1800.

[2] Henry Adams, *History of the United States During the First Administration of Thomas Jefferson* (New York: Charles Scribners Sons, 1921), Vol. I, p. 185.

[3] Thornton to Grenville, March 4, 1801, *British Archives, Henry Adams Transcripts.*

[4] Mrs. Samuel H. Smith to Miss Susan Smith, March 4, 1801, *Mrs. Samuel H. Smith MSS.*

the desirable event of party coalition . . . and receive the blessings of all good men"?[5] Or would he adhere to the temper of Duane who exulted that the "Revolution of 1776 is now and for the first time arrived at its completion"?[6] In answering, the Sage of Monticello appealed to philosophy. He quickly assured the Federalists that

every difference of opinion is not a difference of principle. We have called by different names brethren of the same principle. We are all Republicans; we are all Federalists.

To extreme states' righters, and to admirers of monarchy, the President had a mild but effective answer: "If there be any among us who would wish to dissolve this union or to change its republican form let them stand undisturbed as monuments of the safety with which error of opinion may be tolerated." As for foreign affairs, he pledged, "honest friendship with all nations, entangling alliances with none."[7]

Two powerful Federalist newspapers rushed to accept Jefferson's olive branch. In Boston the comment was that his "propositions are fair and candid . . . we have hitherto opposed Mr. Jefferson from principle, it will give us pleasure in like manner to support him."[8] At the nation's new capital, William L. Rind exclaimed that the "inauguration speech of Mr. Jefferson is replete with wisdom and moderation."[9]

Privately the Chief Executive rejoiced, and confided to the three hundred pound former Secretary of War, Henry Knox, that "my inaugural address is considered as holding out a ground for conciliation and union. I am the more pleased with this . . . I was always satisfied that the great body of those called federalists were real republicans as well as federalists."[10] Aware that his remarks on foreign policy might be ill received at the Court of St. James, he did not delay entrusting His Majesty's Minister with the information

---

[5]Washington *Federalist,* February 17, 1801, January 2, 1801.

[6]*Aurora,* February 20, 1801. The *Aurora* was published in Philadelphia.

[7]*National Intelligencer,* March 4, 1801. The *National Intelligencer* was published in Washington, D.C., and was a Republican paper.

[8]*New England Palladium,* March 20, 1801.

[9]*Washington Federalist,* March 7, 1801. Rind, editor of this paper, was in close contact with John Marshall.

[10]Jefferson to Henry Knox, March 27, 1801, *Jefferson MSS.* Knox was Washington's Secretary of War.

that he "was aware . . . that he had been represented as hostile to Great Britain; but this had been done only for electioneering purposes."[11]

When James A. Bayard read Jefferson's inaugural speech, he must have recalled Hamilton's prophetic words concerning Jefferson:

He is as likely as any man I know to temporize—to calculate which will be likely to promote his own reputation and advantage; and the probable result of such a temper is the preservation of systems, though originally opposed, which being once established, could not be overturned without danger to the person who did it. To my mind a true estimate of Mr. Jefferson's character warrants the expectation of a temporizing rather than a violent system.[12]

Bayard had replied to this letter by voting for Jefferson. Four days after Jefferson's inaugural, Bayard agreed with Hamilton that Burr was "an unprincipled man," and one who would "never have another chance of being President; for by deceiving one man a great blockhead and tempting two (not incorruptible) he might have secured a majority of the States." Bayard was not unhappy that the Federalists had decided on a "legal election," rather than a "breakup of government."[13] Jefferson's inaugural effort had succeeded in bringing peace to the Potomac front. His next move was to form a cabinet.

In 1801 the cabinet consisted of the Secretaries of State, Treasury, Army, Navy; the fifth member was the Attorney General, who because the law business of government was light, was not required to reside permanently in Washington. The President, assisted by the Secretaries of State and Treasury, actually ran the business of government.

Thomas Jefferson immediately chose his fellow Virginian, James Madison, as Secretary of State. Albert Gallatin from Pennsylvania was named Secretary of the Treasury. In an effort to conciliate the Federalists, the new President selected Levi Lincoln of Massachusetts for Attorney General, and Henry Dearborn of the same state for Secretary of War. Robert Smith of Baltimore was

---

[11]Edward Thornton to Lord Grenville, March 7, 1801. Grenville was Foreign Secretary under Pitt. *British Archives, Henry Adams Transcripts.*
[12]Hamilton to Bayard, January 16, 1801, *Hamilton MSS.*
[13]Bayard to Hamilton, March 8, 1801, *Hamilton MSS.*

chosen as Secretary of the Navy. With an eye still bent on converting Federalist New England, Jefferson selected Gideon Granger of Connecticut, Postmaster-General. Although this position was not considered worthy of cabinet ranking at the time, considerable patronage went along with it.

PATRONAGE

On March 4, 1801, when Jefferson was sworn in by John Marshall, he found not a single Democrat in office. He was well aware of the principle that George Washington had laid down, viz., that no one should be appointed to office whose political tenets were adverse to the measures of the government. The new President was in a quandary. He did not want to "revolt our new converts" by depriving them of office "on the ground of political principles alone."[14] He felt like Washington that "the greatest good we can do our country is to heal its party divisions."[15] However, he was conscious of the fact that "the will of the nation calls for an administration of government in accordance with the principles of those elected"; and any practical politician would agree that for "the fulfillment of that will, displacements are necessary."[16] Jefferson realized how absurd it would be to "strengthen the effect of their opposition by the weight of office."[17] He gave lucid expression to his problem when he wrote that "my position is painful enough between federalists who cry out on the first touch of their monopoly and republicans who clamor for universal removal."[18] For the moment at least, the Chief Executive, in keeping with his inaugural address, considered "the pure federalist as a republican who would prefer a somewhat stronger executive."[19] Towards the end of his second administration, Jefferson echoed the political philosophy of Washington on the point of patronage when he proudly proclaimed that "I have never removed a man merely because he was a federalist . . . I have removed . . . those . . . who

---

[14]Jefferson to Monroe, March 7, 1801, *Jefferson MSS.*
[15]Jefferson to John Dickinson, July 23, 1801, *Jefferson MSS.* John Dickinson participated in the Constitutional Convention of 1787 as a delegate from Delaware.
[16]Jefferson to Elias Shipman, July 12, 1801, *Jefferson MSS.*
[17]Jefferson to Governor Williams, July 6, 1805, *Jefferson MSS.*
[18]Jefferson to John Dickinson, July 23, 1801, *Jefferson MSS.*
[19]*Ibid., Jefferson MSS.*

maintained an active and zealous opposition to the government."[20]

Our third President started slowly. In the first fourteen months he removed only sixteen men.[21] By the summer of 1803, he revealed that "of 316 offices in all the U.S. subject to appointment and removal by me, 130 only are held by federalists."[22] By the end of his first administration, he was convinced that "those called federalists, even the honest among them, are so imbued with party prejudice, so habituated to condemn every measure of the public functionaries that they are incapable of weighing candidly the pro and con of any proposition coming from them and only seek in it the grounds of opposition."[23]

The tenderness that Jefferson insisted upon using in New England in order to undermine a Federalist majority was not needed in the other states of the Union. No sooner had the Democrats wrested New York and Pennsylvania from Federalist hands, than they rooted out all vestiges of Federalist influence. In the Empire State, Aaron Burr and George Clinton headed the two rival factions of the Democratic party. When in the spring of 1801, George Clinton was elected Governor of New York, Burr's only chance for influence rested with Jefferson. Jefferson distrusted Burr because of his action in the election of 1800. The Chief Executive in a letter to Governor Clinton surrendered his Vice-President into the hands of his enemies.[24] Unaware of Jefferson's decision, Burr continued to pepper him with letters during the fall of 1801. Finally Jefferson wrote Burr that he had adopted a policy of "not answering letters on office specifically but leaving the answer to be found in what is done or not done on them."[25]

The answer was not long in coming. DeWitt Clinton and Ambrose Spencer, acting in unison with Jefferson, succeeded in alienating the Livingstons from Burr. Chancellor Livingston received the

---

[20]Jefferson to John Page, July 17, 1807, *Jefferson MSS.*

[21]Henry Minor, *The Story of the Democratic Party, op. cit.,* p. 41.

[22]Jefferson to Duane, July 24, 1803, *Jefferson MSS.* Duane was editor of the Philadelphia *Aurora,* which paper had contributed much toward the election of Jefferson.

[23]Jefferson to John Page, July 17, 1807, *Jefferson MSS.*

[24]Jefferson to George Clinton, May 17, 1801, *Jefferson MSS.* In this letter, Jefferson indicates his dislike of two of Burr's requests; viz., Theodorus Bailey for Naval Officer, and Matthew L. Davis for supervisor. Neither received appointments.

[25]Jefferson to Burr, November 18, 1801, *Jefferson MSS.*

mission to France, and Edward Livingston was made mayor of New York. In meetings of the Council of Appointment during the summer and autumn of 1801, the state and city offices were taken from the Federalists and divided between the Clintons and the Livingstons.[26] Burr's influence was practically nil. And Gouverneur Morris was to write Livingston in Paris that the "Clinton party have exclusively the ear of the President for what regards this state."[27]

By this time both the Federalists and their newspapers were screaming about the "displacement of able and virtuous men (many of whom were eminent in the Revolution) in a scandalous abuse of power."[28] It was at this time that the Federalists, meeting at Middletown, Connecticut, offered a toast to Thomas Jefferson: "May he receive from his fellow citizens the reward of his merit— a halter."[29]

JEFFERSON VS. SUPREME COURT

The Democrats had possession of the Executive branch of the government. They also controlled the Congress by sixty-nine to thirty-five. The Federalists, so Jefferson claimed, had "retired into the Judiciary as a stronghold." In the Supreme Court, warned the Sage of Monticello, "the remains of federalism are to be preserved and fed from the Treasury; and from that battery all the works of republicanism are to be beaten down and erased."[30]

Federalist entrenchment in the court had taken place in the waning weeks of John Adams' administration. The Federalist-dominated Congress passed the Judiciary Act of 1801. This measure meant an increased annual expenditure of some thirty thousand dollars. In addition, the circuit duties of the Supreme Court were

---

[26]The Council of Appointment, controlled by young DeWitt Clinton and his friend Ambrose Spencer, had charge of the state patronage. See Henry Adams, *History of the United States During the First Administration of Thomas Jefferson,* Vol. I, p. 228 sq.

[27]Gouverneur Morris to R. R. Livingston, November 28, 1893, *Gouverneur Morris MSS.* See Howard L. McBain, *DeWitt Clinton and the Origin of the Spoils System in New York* (New York: Columbia University Press, 1907), pp. 136-137, for Clinton's triumph over Burr.

[28]John Rutledge, Jr. to James A. Bayard, November 21, 1801, *John Rutledge MSS.* Rutledge was a Federalist Representative from South Carolina.

[29]Edward Channing, *The Jeffersonian System* (New York: Harper & Brothers, 1906), p. 13. See Claude G. Bowers, *Jefferson in Power* (Boston: Houghton Mifflin & Co., 1936), Ch. III for a vivid account of the Federalist attack on Jefferson.

[30]Jefferson to John Dickinson, December 10, 1801, *Jefferson MSS.*

transferred to a new class of circuit judges, eighteen in number. To top all, the Federalist Secretary of State, John Marshall, was made Chief Justice of the Supreme Court. Jefferson understood the challenge, and promptly accepted it. The issue was between Jefferson's concept of the Constitution, and Marshall's. Jefferson felt that "to consider the judges as the ultimate arbiters of all constitutional questions would place us under the despotism of an oligarchy."[31] Marshall's viewpoint was that it was "emphatically the province and duty of the judicial department to say what the law is."[32]

The signal for the commencement of hostilities came in an almost casual reference in the President's first message. The "Judiciary system," said the Chief Executive, "and especially that portion of it recently enacted, will, of course, present itself to the contemplation of Congress."[33] A month later, Senator John Breckenridge, Democrat from Kentucky, moved the repeal of the Federalist National Judiciary Act of 1801. The fight was on. Senator Gouverneur Morris, Federalist from New York, in reply to Breckenridge's motion declared that to repeal the Federal Judicial Law would be "a declaration to the remaining judges that they hold their offices subject to your will and pleasure." Thus, he continued, "the check established by the Constitution is destroyed."[34] Senator Stevens Thomson Mason, Democrat from Virginia, in response to Morris, agreed that the Judiciary should be independent, but not "independent of the nation itself."[35] After many vehement speeches from both sides of the aisle, the Senate, on February 3, 1802, by a strictly party vote of 16 to 15, passed the bill to repeal the Federalist Judiciary Act of 1801.

The debate now moved to the House, where it was opened by

---

[31]Albert J. Beveridge, *The Life of John Marshall*, Vol. III, p. 101. Jefferson felt that as Chief Executive, he had the power to declare Acts of Congress unconstitutional. He compared the Sedition Act with the Constitution and found that Act to be in contradiction to the Constitution. He then considered the Sedition Act as a nullity. See original draft of his first message to Congress, December 8, 1801, *Jefferson MSS.* He deleted this passage at the last minute for fear the Federalists might twist it to their advantage.

[32]*Ibid.*, p. 101.

[33]Jefferson to Congress, December 8, 1801, Richardson, *Messages and Papers of the Presidents*, Vol. I, p. 331.

[34]*Annals of the Congress of the United States* (Washington: Gales & Seaton, 1851), 7th Congress, 1st Session, p. 38.

[35]*Ibid.*, p. 61.

Archibald Henderson, Federalist from North Carolina. The "monstrous and unheard-of doctrine . . . lately advanced, that the judges have not the right of declaring unconstitutional laws void" was, he declared, "the very definition of tyranny, and wherein you find it, the people are slaves, whether they call their government a monarchy, republic, or democracy." If Jefferson's theory of the Constitution should prevail "better at once to bury it with all our hopes."[36] In rebuttal, Philip R. Thompson, Democrat from Virginia, warned that to "give the Judiciary this check upon the Legislature" would mean they, the judges, would have "the power to declare your laws null and void"; permit the Court this prerogative and "in vain have the people placed you upon this floor to legislate."[37] About thirty days after the debate had started in the House, a vote was taken. It was midnight, March 3, 1802, and the final count was 59 Democrats for repeal, and 32 Federalists against. The Washington *Federalist* gloomily announced: "The fatal bill has passed; our Constitution is no more." Defiantly, however, this same paper went on to predict that the judges would declare the repeal "null and void." This Federalist organ concluded by charging the Democrats with a plan to force "a dissolution of the Union," and the newspaper felt that this was likely to happen.[38] Twelve days after these dire forebodings the Democratic *Independent Chronicle* congratulated the public on the final triumph of Republicanism in the repeal of the obnoxious judiciary law.[39]

Senator Breckenridge, who led the fight for repeal in the Senate, wrote that the Federal Judiciary Act of 1801 was a "useless and burdensome extension of the federal courts." It was a "measure . . . increasing executive patronage and power and as having for one of its objects a permanent provision at the expense of the Republic for the friends of an expiring party."[40] Caesar A. Rodney,

---

[36]*Ibid.*, pp. 529-530.
[37]*Ibid.*, pp. 552-553. The threat of secession was made in both Senate and House. See *Ibid.*, pp. 26-183 and 510-986.
[38]Washington *Federalist*, March 3, 1802.
[39]*Independent Chronicle*, March 15, 1802. On March 18, a Democratic Senate Committee was appointed to investigate the Supreme Court. The Committee reported a bill abolishing the June session of the Court, and decreeing that the Court should meet but once each year, and then on the second Monday of February. This bill was passed, and thus a year went by before Marshall could act.
[40]John Breckenridge to 23 People, February 12, 1802, *Breckenridge MSS.*

Democratic Congressman from Delaware, cautioned the Federalists to "remember . . . there is a boundary which they cannot pass with impunity . . . judicial supremacy may be made to bow before the strong arm of legislative authority."[41] William Plumer, Federalist Senator from New Hampshire, bemoaned the fact that "the Judiciary, that bulwark of our rights . . . is to depend upon the whim and caprice of a theoretical President and his servile minions."[42] James A. Bayard, Federalist Congressman from Delaware, asserted that "a judge instead of holding his office for life will hold it during the good pleasure of the dominant party. The judges will of course become partisans."[43]

So far so good for the Democrats, but they were well aware that, if their revolution of 1800 was to endure, they must control the Supreme Court. Now that they had successfully repealed the Judiciary Act of 1801, what about the Judiciary Act of 1789, that triumph of Federalist centralization? This Act had conferred on the Supreme Court jurisdiction over the final judgment of state courts in cases where the powers of the federal government had been drawn in question and the decision was unfavorable to them. This concession of power to the Supreme Court, as the Jeffersonians well knew, was believed to be dictated by a wish to make the state judiciaries inferior courts of the central government. The same Jefferson who embodied his theory of states' rights so clearly in the Kentucky resolutions of 1798, now in 1802 dominated both Houses of Congress. By repealing the Judiciary Act of 1789, he could have emasculated the Supreme Court. Whatever the true cause of Jefferson's inaction, it was certainly intentional. It may well be that since he was confident that states' rights were safe in his hands, he felt it would be futile to alarm the people with laws aimed at past rather than future dangers. Then, too, the threat of secession of the northern and eastern states—should they be pushed too far—was ever a factor to be contended with.[44]

John Marshall, Chief Justice of the Supreme Court of the

---

[41]C. A. Rodney to Nicholson, February 16, 1803, *Nicholson MSS.*
[42]William Plumer to George Upham, March 1, 1802, *Plumer MSS.*
[43]James A. Bayard to Andrew Bayard, January 21, 1802, *Bayard MSS.*
[44]See Henry Adams, *History of the United States,* Vol. I, pp. 247-263 for a brief discussion of this question.

United States, and his five associates on the bench were convinced that the recent Democratic repeal of the Federalist Judiciary Law of 1801 was unconstitutional. As good Federalists, they held the theory that the national judiciary had the right and power to nullify national laws, but, for the moment at least, they feared to act. Marshall begged them to overcome their fears by refusing to sit as circuit judges and "risk the consequences."[45] This they refused to do, and the Chief Justice reluctantly went along with them. Marshall and his fellow judges, by doing their circuit duty between March 3, 1802, the day of repeal, and February, 1803, the first sitting of the Supreme Court of the United States, obeyed the Democratic repeal legislation. Marshall was disappointed and fearful for the ultimate fate of his constitutional theories. He had to concede that if Jefferson's Kentucky resolutions, affirming as they did the right and power of the states to nullify national laws, were submitted to the legislatures of the states, the majority would vote endorsement.

After a year's enforced absence due to timely Democratic legislation, the Supreme Court finally convened on the second Monday in February, 1803. The case of *Marbury vs. Madison* was the first on the docket. Everyone, Federalists and Democrats alike, expected the Court to decide the case in Marbury's favor. This would mean that Madison would be ordered to deliver the withheld commissions.[46] Only four of the seventeen that had commissions withheld deemed it worthwhile to file suit. The other thirteen apparently did not consider the office of justice of the peace worth the expense of litigation. These positions were considered so unimportant that one of Adams' appointees who had actually received his commission from Madison resigned. Five others did not even take the trouble to present their credentials in order to qualify for the positions.[47] John Marshall determined, in the face of a country that was overwhelm-

---

[45]*New York Review*, Vol. III, p. 347. An unsigned article written by Chancellor James Kent of New York.

[46]Just before his term expired, Adams had appointed forty-two persons to be justices of the peace. The Federalist Senate had confirmed these nominations, and the commissions had been signed and sealed, but not delivered. When Jefferson was inaugurated, he directed Madison to issue commissions to twenty-five of these Adams appointees, but to withhold the commissions from the other seventeen. Four of these, including Marbury, applied to the Supreme Court for a writ of mandamus, compelling Madison to deliver their commissions.

[47]Albert J. Beveridge, *The Life of John Marshall* (Boston: Houghton Mifflin Co., 1919), Vol. III, pp. 114-116.

ingly Democratic, to make use of this unimportant litigation, to assert the power of the Supreme Court to declare invalid Acts of Congress that violate the Constitution.

Early in February, 1803, a few days before the Supreme Court convened to consider *Marbury vs. Madison,* President Jefferson sent a message to the House of Representatives which in effect called for the impeachment of Judge John Pickering of the United States District Court for the District of New Hampshire.[48] In Pennsylvania, a Democratic House had impeached Judge Alexander Addison, and his conviction was assured. It was clear to everybody that Pickering, due to insanity, was no longer fit to sit on the bench. The twenty-fifth section of the now defunct Judiciary Act of 1801 had made provision for such a case as Pickering's. The law had read that, whenever a district judge became unable to fulfill his duties, the circuit court should name one of its members to fill his place so long as his disability continued. The circuit court had done this very thing for Pickering in 1801. It might now in 1803 be empowered by Congress to do so again. However, that would have meant another Federalist judge, whereas impeachment would bring a Democrat to the New Hampshire court. Regarding the case of *Marbury vs. Madison,* the Democrats openly threatened to oust Marshall and his Federalist associates in case the Court decided in favor of Marbury, and the Democrats expected just this. This, too, was certain, that the Administration would not recognize Marbury and his associates, no matter what Marshall might decide. *Marbury vs. Madison,* therefore, presented only theoretical questions. As far as practical results were concerned, it was of no consequence whatever to anyone. As Jefferson was to write twenty years later, the controversy had degenerated into little more than a "moot case."[49]

Everyone but John Marshall felt that the Court would do one of two things: it would disavow its power over any branch of the Executive Department and dismiss the application, or it would assert this power, and command the Secretary of State to deliver the commissions. It was this latter course that the Jeffersonians expected the Chief Justice to take.

---

[48] Henry Adams, *History of the United States of America,* Vol. II, p. 143.
[49] Jefferson to Judge William Johnson, June 12, 1823, *Jefferson MSS.* Johnson of South Carolina served on the Supreme Court from 1803 to 1834.

If Marshall should do this, Madison would refuse to obey the Court's mandate. Since the Court had no physical means to compel the execution of its order, the Democrats would have denounced the illegality of the decision, and laughed at the plight of the Court.

If, on the contrary, Marshall dismissed the case, the Jeffersonian doctrines that the national courts could not direct executives to obey the laws, and that the Judiciary would not invalidate Acts of Congress, would have been admitted by default.

Marshall escaped both horns of his dilemma. He first convinced his five associate justices of the validity of his conclusions, and then asserted that "to withhold his commission is an act . . . not warranted by law, but violative of a vested legal right." He held that Madison's refusal to deliver Marbury's commission was "a plain violation of that right, for which the laws of his country afford him a remedy."[50] The only remaining question, continued Marshall, was whether a mandamus could issue from the Supreme Court.

In this way the Chief Justice finally arrived at the constitutionality of Section 13 of the Judiciary Act of 1789. It fitted the case "precisely," he said, and "if this court is not authorized to issue a writ of mandamus" to Madison, "it must be because the law is unconstitutional, and therefore absolutely incapable of conferring the authority."[51] February 23, 1803, was the date, therefore, that John Marshall hurled his act of defiance at Jefferson. On that day he boldly held that Section 13 of the Judiciary Act of 1789 was not "warranted by the Constitution." If Marshall had not on this occasion asserted the power of the Supreme Court to annul Acts of Congress, nearly seventy years would have passed without any question arising as to the omnipotence of Congress. After so long a period of judicial acquiescence in congressional supremacy, it seems likely that the Court would have been rendered permanently impotent.

Marshall's decision brought an immediate reaction from Democratic leadership. Judge Pickering's trial was pushed to a successful conclusion, and Marshall's associate on the Supreme Bench, Justice Samuel Chase, was quickly impeached for high crimes and

---

[50]William Cranch, *Condensed Reports of Cases in the Supreme Court of the United States,* ed. by Richard Peters (Philadelphia: J. Grigg Co., 1830), Vol. I, p. 162 and pp. 166-168.

[51]Cranch, *ibid.,* Vol. I, p. 173. The Dred Scott Decision of 1857 was the next time that the Supreme Court declared an Act of Congress unconstitutional.

misdemeanors. If the Democrats could get a verdict of guilty in Chase's case, Marshall's head might be the next to fall.

Jefferson, at least for the moment, made no comment on the *Marbury vs. Madison* decision of Marshall. He was very much concerned about the forthcoming presidential election, and for him to attack Marshall's position openly would create a political issue which might keep recruits from joining the Republican cause. Many months later, Jefferson broke his silence by writing that "nothing in the Constitution has given them [the Supreme Court] a right to decide for the Executive, more than to the Executive to decide for them." The opinion, continued the President, "which gives to the judges the right to decide what laws are constitutional, and what not . . . would make the Judiciary a despotic branch."[52] Seventeen years later Jefferson repeated his view that "to consider the judges as the ultimate arbiters of all constitutional questions . . . would place us under the despotism of an oligarchy."[53]

---

[52]Jefferson to Mrs. John Adams, September 11, 1804, *Jefferson MSS*. Democratic cohesion broke on the Chase case. The Jeffersonian-dominated Senate declared Chase "not guilty" on every count. Leaders of the party, like Randolph, Breckenridge, and Jefferson were chagrined. They pressed for an amendment which would give Congress power to expel judges. This movement failed.

[53]Jefferson to William C. Jarvis, September 28, 1820, *Jefferson MSS*. Jarvis was the author of a book called the *Republican* which made the judges the ultimate arbiters of all constitutional questions. He sent this book to Jefferson.

4
War and Secession

THE NEWPAPERS OF THE TIME were practically silent about Marshall's great decision. The bench and the bar appear to have paid little attention to it. It was buried among the thrilling events that filled the age.

The American West, rather than *Marbury vs. Madison,* profoundly troubled the Sage of Monticello, for he had been trying, unsuccessfully, to adjust our dispute with France over her purchase of Louisiana from Spain.[1] The radical West was becoming more and more insistent on a militant policy concerning the control of the Mississippi. It was imperative, so the Westerners argued, to possess New Orleans, which commanded the mouth of that great commercial highway called the Mississippi. The Federalists were egging on the Western frontiersmen, who until now had held aloft the Jeffersonian standard. Indeed, Marshall's decision, by comparison, was a very small irritant as far as Jefferson was concerned. It was essential that the Mississippi, and particularly New Orleans, be kept open for American shipping. "With respect to Spain and her control of New Orleans," Jefferson considered "her possession of the adjacent country as most favorable to our interests." He "should see with an extreme pain any other nation substituted for them."[2]

During 1801 and 1802, rumors of Napoleon's desire for Louisiana had drifted into the United States. Jefferson used his friend, Pierre Samuel DuPont de Nemours, the famous French physicist, as a medium of unofficial communication with Napoleon. Through DuPont, Jefferson warned the First Consul that the secret treaty of San Ildefonso by which France was to receive Louisiana

---

[1] On October 1, 1800, by the Treaty of San Ildefonso, France gained Louisiana from Spain in exchange for Tuscany.

[2] Jefferson to William C. C. Claiborne, July 13, 1801, *Jefferson MSS.* Claiborne was the Governor of the Mississippi Territory.

from Spain "will cost France . . . a war."[3] Faced with the necessity for action, realism triumphed over theory in the mind of the American Chief Executive. The man who had been considered by many to be a Francophile, Anglophobe, and an isolationist, admitted that we now "stand completely corrected of the error that either the government or the nation of France has any remains of friendship with us." He quickly added that the "day . . . France takes possession of New Orleans . . . we must marry ourselves to the British fleet and nation."[4]

Kentucky and Tennessee were aflame. They demanded troops at Natchez to seize New Orleans at the first sign of a French occupation. But Jefferson rejected force at this stage. He realized full well that to quiet the West without satisfying them was a delicate matter. Congress had already authorized the President to call upon the governors of the states for 80,000 militiamen. Unless something were done, the Federalists might ride into power on the Louisiana issue. At this juncture, Jefferson, a former Secretary of State himself, turned to diplomacy. He hit upon the idea of sending James Monroe to France as a special envoy to assist Robert Livingston, the regular minister. The nomination was confirmed by the Senate on January 12, 1803. Monroe owned extensive tracts of land in the West. He had identified himself with Western interests more closely than any other man of political prominence in the United States. His appointment gave the West eloquent assurance that their rights on the Mississippi would be championed with the utmost zeal. The mission was a success in its main object of quieting the West even before Monroe departed for France.[5]

Thomas Paine, intimate friend of Jefferson, and recently returned from Europe, may well have had some influence on our negotiations with France. On Christmas Day, shortly before the Monroe mission was confirmed by the Senate, Paine congratulated the Chief Executive "on the birthday of the New Sun now called Christmas day," and made Jefferson "a present of a thought on Louisiana." Before he reached his main point, Paine summed up

---

[3]Jefferson to DuPont de Nemours, April 25, 1802, *Jefferson MSS.*
[4]Jefferson to Livingston, April 18, 1802, *Jefferson MSS.*
[5]Arthur P. Whitaker, *The Mississippi Question* (New York: Appleton Century Co., 1934), pp. 207-208.

the case succinctly by remarking that "Spain has ceded Louisiana to France and France has excluded the Americans from New Orleans and the navigation of the Mississippi." The people of the Western territory had complained of it to their government. Concluding, he offered his advice that the government should "begin by making a proposal to France to repurchase the Cession made to her by Spain of Louisiana provided it be with the consent of the people of Louisiana or a majority thereof."[6] Jefferson made a long memorandum of the Paine letter for himself.[7] Yet there is nothing in the documents that reveals that Jefferson advised Monroe to follow the Paine plan. All we know is that Monroe and Livingston were instructed to offer as much as $10,000,000 for New Orleans and West Florida. Some few weeks later the President advised his envoys that should they fail to obtain their objectives at Paris they should at once open negotiations looking towards an alliance with England. Jefferson solemnly reminded Monroe that "on the event of this mission depend the future destinies of this Republic."[8]

By August of 1802, Napoleon Bonaparte realized he had lost his enormously productive sugar island of Santo Domingo. The Negro revolt there led by Toussaint L'Ouverture had already cost France fifty thousand men. Fifty thousand more men and an enormous sum of money would be needed to reconquer the island. While in this frame of mind, Napoleon received the news of Leclerc's death. He was staggered by the news. A few days later at a dinner party in the company of Madame Bonaparte, he suddenly burst out: "Damn sugar, damn coffee, damn colonies."[9] Since he had to give up Santo Domingo, he certainly had no need for the granary— Louisiana. The Peace of Amiens with England of October 1, 1802, was only a truce. War would soon break out. He would never be able to hold Louisiana against the British; therefore, it would be far

---

[6]Paine to Jefferson, December 25, 1802, *Jefferson MSS.* Paine returned from France in the summer of 1802 on the U.S.S. Maryland, put at his disposal by Jefferson.

[7]Memorandum of Jefferson, December 25, 1802, *Jefferson MSS.*

[8]Jefferson to Monroe, January 13, 1803, *Jefferson MSS.* Napoleon knew through his envoy to the United States that Jefferson was planning a British alliance aimed at France. Pichon to Talleyrand, January 24, 1803, Henry Adams, *History of the United States,* Vol. I, p. 438. Pichon was the French Charge d'Affaires in Washington.

[9]Elijah W. Lyon, *Louisiana in French Diplomacy, 1759-1804* (Norman: University of Oklahoma Press, 1934), p. 194. Leclerc was Napoleon's brother-in-law, and the general in charge of French forces in Santo Domingo.

better to sell Louisiana to the Americans for a substantial sum rather than see England conquer it. Having made his decision, Napoleon summoned his Finance Minister, Barbe-Marbois, and unexpectedly announced:

Irresolution and deliberation are no longer in season. I renounce Louisiana. It is not only New Orleans that I will cede, it is the whole colony without any reservation. I know the price of what I abandon . . . I renounce it with the greatest regret. To attempt obstinately to retain it would be folly. I direct you to negotiate this affair . . . Do not even await the arrival of Mr. Monroe: have an interview this very day with Mr. Livingston . . .[10]

Two days after that, April 13, 1803, Monroe reached Paris and joined the negotiators. A week of discussion followed. Knowing full well that they were exceeding their instructions, Monroe and Livingston bound the United States to pay $15,000,000 in cash and claims for all Louisiana. They were far from home, and the occasion called for immediate action. Our envoys acted, and Livingston solemnly declared that "we have lived long, but this is the noblest work of our lives . . . From this day the United States take their place among the powers of the first rank."[11] The acquisition of Louisiana, dazzlingly rich in natural resources, meant that the United States had more than doubled its original territory. It was the greatest real estate bargain in history—828,000 square miles of territory at nineteen dollars and twenty cents a square mile.

True to his principles, Jefferson realized that Congress had but two kinds of powers: powers expressly delegated, and powers absolutely necessary to put such as are expressly delegated into effect. The power to buy foreign soil, and to incorporate foreign nations into the Union were not expressly given to Congress. Nor was it provable that these powers of purchasing land and adding it to the United States were necessary in order to put any delegated power into effect. The President knew that to make the Louisiana Purchase Act legal, the Constitution must be amended. He drew up that amendment and sent it to his Cabinet, but his Cabinet disagreed with him. Finally, his friend, Wilson Cary Nicholas, con-

---

[10]Francois Barbe-Marbois, *The History of Louisiana* (Philadelphia: Carey & Lea, 1830), pp. 274-275.
[11]*Ibid.*, pp. 310-311. In May, 1803, the Peace of Amiens of October, 1801 was broken, and England and France were at war again.

vinced him the Constitution needed no amendment. Nicholas assured him that the treaty-making power covered the case. He concluded by begging Jefferson to keep his doubts to himself. For if the Senate learned of his doubts, they might well reject the treaty. The Chief Executive, alive to the danger, did a *volte face* and declared that "whatever Congress shall think it necessary to do should be done with as little debate as possible."[12]

The ethical problem of France's having no title to sell us Louisiana, since it was still legally owned and actually occupied by Spain, escaped Jefferson completely. Professor Edward Channing merely echoed the conclusions of a host of American and European historians when he wrote that by accepting Louisiana, the United States acted as "the accomplices of the greatest highwayman of modern history, and the goods which we received were those which he compelled his unwilling victim to disgorge."[13]

The Federalists stood on solid Jeffersonian ground in their opposition to the Louisiana Treaty. They declared it was unconstitutional. Secession, as in the debate on the repeal of the Judiciary Act of 1801, again raised its head. Senator Plumer thought the Eastern states should form a new nation. "Adopt this Western world into the Union," he said, "and you destroy at once the weight and importance of the Eastern states, and compel them to establish a separate and independent empire."[14] Fisher Ames concluded that "our country is too big for union."[15] Tapping Reeve sounded out his fellow Federalists in Connecticut, and informed Tracy that "all believe that we must separate, and that this is the most favorable moment."[16]

Gouverneur Morris summed up the real as opposed to the os-

[12]Wilson C. Nicholas to Jefferson, September 3, 1803, *Jefferson MSS.* For Jefferson's amendment, see *Jefferson MSS.,* 1803. This memo is undated. For Jefferson's conversion to Nicholas' view, see Jefferson to Wilson C. Nicholas, September 7, 1803, *Jefferson MSS.* Nicholas was a Democratic Senator from Virginia.

[13]Edward Channing, *The Jeffersonian System,* p. 79. See also, Madison to Monroe, September 29, 1803, for the fact that our Secretary of State was well aware of Spain's ethical protest, but he was sure she had not power to resist and told Monroe so. *Instructions to France, 1801-1805, Department of State.*

[14]October 20, 1803, William Plumer, Jr., *Life of William Plumer* (Boston: Phillips, Sampson & Co., 1857), p. 285.

[15]Ames to Dwight, October 26, 1803, *Works of Fisher Ames,* ed. by Seth Ames (Boston: Little, Brown & Co., 1854), Vol. I, p. 328.

[16]Reeve to Tracy, February 7, 1804, *Documents Relating to New England Federalism, 1800-1815,* ed. by Henry Adams (Boston: Little, Brown & Co., 1877), p. 342.

tensible case for the Federalists when he said, "our party . . . would have liked it well but for two things. It costs money, the greater part we to the northward must pay, and it gains territory . . . by giving strength to the Southern representatives." In fine, concluded the Senator from New York, it "diminishes Eastern influence," and "it has strengthened an administration which they abhor."[17]

Jefferson rejoiced that the "federal leaders have had the impudence to oppose it pertinaciously."[18] He consoled himself by writing his fellow philosopher, Tom Paine, that "the Executive has done an act beyond the Constitution." The President felt that "we must throw ourselves for this on our country saying that we have not hestitated to do for them what we were sure they would have done for themselves."[19]

The Senate ratified the treaty by twenty-four to seven. There were eight Federalists present, but one of them, Jonathan Dayton of New Jersey, voted in the affirmative.[20] Finally, on January 16, 1804, Jefferson's leading newspaper announced the glad tidings:

Americans! The event for which we have all looked with so much solicitude is at length realized: Louisiana is part of the Union. The acquisition is great and glorious in itself, but still greater and more glorious are the means by which it was obtained.[21]

JEFFERSON'S ONLY WAR

While Thomas Jefferson was economizing in governmental expenditures, trying to control the judiciary, and more than doubling our territory, he was also engaged in an undeclared war with Africa. The rulers of Morocco, Algiers, Tripoli, and Tunis, had long made a national industry of blackmailing. The preceding Federalist administrations had been forced to buy protection by paying tribute. During our undeclared war with France in 1798, when hundreds of Americans were shouting, "Millions for defense, but not one cent for tribute," twenty-six barrels of blackmail dollars

---

[17]G. Morris to R. R. Livingston, November 28, 1803, *Morris MSS.*
[18]Jefferson to Monroe, January 8, 1804, *Monroe MSS.* Jefferson was certain that the people applauded the purchase.
[19]Jefferson to Paine, August 10, 1803, *Jefferson MSS.*
[20]*National Intelligencer,* October 21, 1803.
[21]*National Intelligencer,* January 16, 1804.

were being shipped to the piratical Dey of Algiers.[22] Jefferson, who was pledged to economy, who disliked the navy, and who detested war, had hardly taken office when the Pasha of Tripoli, feeling neglected in the apportionment of tribute, declared war on the United States by cutting down the flagstaff at the American consulate. Jefferson did not hesitate a minute. His concern for the honor of the flag and for the safety of American seamen impelled him to send warships to Mediterranean waters.

On May 20, 1801, Jefferson ordered Commodore Dale to the Mediterranean with the *President, Philadelphia,* and the schooner, *Enterprise.* The President soon reinforced this Mediterranean squadron with the thirty-two gun frigate *Essex* under the command of Captain Bainbridge.

On August 1, 1801, the *Enterprise* captured a Tripolitan cruiser of fourteen guns, dismantled her, threw her guns and gunpowder into the sea and let her go with just enough sail to reach port.[23] Meanwhile, the *President*, with all guns showing, visited the Dey of Algiers and the Pasha of Tripoli and impressed upon these gentlemen the kind of American power they would have to face unless they mended their ways.

In the year 1802, Commodore Richard Valentine Morris was ordered to the Mediterranean with four frigates, two corvettes, and the *Enterprise,* but this impressive force was credited with little save worrying the Barbary pirates. As a result, Morris, on his return to the United States, was dismissed from the service.

The year 1803 saw Captain Edward Preble in command of our fleet. His first triumph was the capture by the *Philadelphia* of the Moorish ship *Meshboha* belonging to the Emperor of Morocco. In the winter of 1803-1804, Preble's squadron was reinforced by the *Siren, Argus, Nautilus,* and *Vixen.* With his fleet thus augmented, Commodore Preble twice bombarded Tripoli. At length, under constant American pressure, Pasha Ysuf listened to reason. The result was the 1805 treaty of peace between Tripoli and the

---

[22]Ray W. Irwin, *The Diplomatic Relations of the United States with the Barbary Powers, 1776-1816* (Chapel Hill: The University of North Carolina Press, 1931), pp. 82-91.

[23]Jefferson gave these orders to Commodore Dale: All captured Barbary ships were to be treated in the same manner. The reason for this was that only Congress could declare war, and they had not done so.

United States. It was the most favorable treaty that any nation had yet secured from Tripoli.

The Pasha agreed to live at peace with America without any tribute. The United States paid $60,000 as a ransom for captured Americans. For ten years the Barbary rulers treated the Americans with respect.[24]

Jefferson was proud of the American navy. Commodore Preble, his officers and men were honored by a special presidential citation. The Chief Executive declared that the "energy and judgment displayed by this excellent officer, through the whole course of the service lately confided to him, and the zeal and bravery of his officers and men . . . cannot fail to give high satisfaction to Congress and their country, of whom they have well deserved."[25]

Jefferson was in office about a month and a half when he fired off a note to his Chairman of the House Committee on Ways and Means that "we shall push you to the utmost in economizing."[26] Next to peace, "frugal government" was the President's passion. He followed up his letter to Macon with one to Monroe that was in effect a blueprint for saving the taxpayers' money. He assured his fellow Virginian that "we are carrying into execution all the reforms in economy we can." By partly "selling off, partly laying up . . . our navy . . . about a half million would be saved." Jefferson added that "it might have been reduced to $400,000 and still kept three frigates in the Mediterranean." Marines "will be dismissed in a few days to about 400 which will economize about 40,000 D . . ." By the discontinuance of "useless diplomatic missions . . . about the same sum is saved." In "the erection of shipyards some hundred thousands will be stopped." No doubt with his eye on the some three dozen or so midnight appointments of Adams, Jefferson concluded that the "expenses of this government were chiefly in jobs not seen . . ."[27]

---

[24]Edward Channing, *The Jeffersonian System*, Ch. III, and Henry Adams, *History of the United States*, Vol. I, p. 244 sq. and Vol. II, p. 425 sq. William Eaton, a Connecticut Yankee, raised an army of 500 men and captured the Tripolitan town of Derne in 1805. This considerably hastened the Pasha's capitulation.

[25]*American State Papers, Naval* (Washington: Gales & Seaton, 1832), Vol. I, p. 133. For an exhaustive account of Commodore Preble's actions in the Mediterranean theater for 1804, see the Commodore's own official report, *ibid.*, p. 133-138.

[26]Jefferson to Nathaniel Macon, May 14, 1801, *Jefferson MSS.*

[27]Jefferson to Monroe, June 20, 1801, *Monroe MSS.* Jefferson had his party workers check into the duties of circuit judges in Kentucky and Tennessee. His reports, used in the debate on the repeal of the Judiciary Act of 1801, showed these judges to have had very few cases.

Jefferson's preference for "those who labor in the earth" and his classification of them as "the chosen people of God" formed a basic fact of his early political thought. His abhorrence of the whole Hamiltonian system of banks, manufacturing interests, and fiscal groups was part and parcel of his pre-presidential thinking. Yet Jefferson was no mere theorist. Hamilton's characterization of him as given "to temporizing rather than a violent system" was soon shown to be valid.[28] For in the winter of 1801, he had admitted that "what is practical must often control what is pure theory." In 1789, it was possible to have kept this government "going on true principles." Unfortunately, "the contracted, English, half-lettered ideas of Hamilton, destroyed that hope in the bud." It mortified Jefferson no end "to be strengthening principles which I deem radically vicious, but this vice is entailed on us by the first error." With regard to the national debt Hamilton had contracted, Jefferson felt that "we can pay off his debts in fifteen years; but we can never get rid of his financial system." As for the "other parts of our government," our first Democratic president hoped "by degrees to introduce sound principles and make them habitual."[29]

Jefferson could do nothing about removing what he considered to be the evil Hamiltonian edifice; yet he refused to let his party suffer because of it. For example, he was "decidedly in favor of making all banks Republican," for "it is material to the safety of Republicanism to detach the mercantile interest from its enemies and incorporate them into the body of its friends." A farmer was by nature a Republican; so, too, "a merchant is naturally a Republican, and can be otherwise only from a vitiated state of things."[30]

Government expenses were reduced from $7,500,000 for the fiscal year 1800 to less than $5,000,000 for the next year. For the three succeeding years a reduction to about $4,000,000 annually was accomplished. Agrarian interests were fostered by the abolition of the hated whiskey tax. Federalists protested that a reduction might better be made in the taxes on the necessities of life, like salt, sugar, coffee, and tea. Nevertheless, the Democrats who made

---

[28]Hamilton to Bayard, January 16, 1801, *Hamilton MSS.*
[29]*The Works of Thomas Jefferson,* ed. by Paul L. Ford (New York: G. P. Putnams Sons, 1904-1905), Vol. VIII, p. 125.
[30]*Ibid.,* p. 252.

whiskey did not think it a luxury. This tax on whiskey fell on thousands of little distillers. It was keenly felt and resented; whereas the tax through the customs house was not a real source of disturbance to the majority of Jeffersonian Democrats.[31]

The public debt in 1801 stood at $83,000,000. The Democrats steadily reduced this until it stood at $57,000,000 in 1809. The largest expenditure of the Jeffersonian administration was made for the Louisiana Purchase, and even Federalist leaders like Hamilton and Morris approved of this. Democrats everywhere considered it money well spent, for not only did it mark a tremendous growth in the power and prosperity of America, but presaged—and this is what really bothered the Federalists—many more states in the Democratic column.[32]

START OF THE 1804 CAMPAIGN

The alarm caused by the tie vote in the election of 1800 convinced the Democrats that a revision of the Constitution was necessary. Therefore, on October 17, 1803, even before the Louisiana Treaty was introduced, the Twelfth Amendment was proposed by the Jeffersonians in the House. This would oblige the members of the electoral college to distinguish between the persons voted for as president and vice-president. The debate on this amendment may well be considered to be the start of the presidential campaign of 1804. The Federalists insisted that the amendment was an infringement of states' rights. They claimed that it would sweep away one of the checks on which the framers had counted to resist majority rule by the great states. The effect of this amendment, declared the Federalists, will be to strip the small states of one opportunity to have an equal vote with the large states in the election of a president. The Democrat John Randolph agreed with the Federalist Roger Griswold, that true reform required abolition of the office of vice-president.[33] Griswold added with prophetic insight that "the

---

[31]Davis R. Dewey, *Financial History of the United States* (New York: Longmans, Green & Co., 1915), p. 120.
[32]Charles A. Beard, *Economic Origins of Jeffersonian Democracy* (New York: Macmillan Co., 1915), p. 439.
[33]John B. McMaster, *A History of the People of the United States* (New York: Appleton & Co., 1928), Vol. III, pp. 184-185. Henry Adams, *History of the United States*, Vol. II, pp. 132-133.

man voted for as vice-president will be selected without any decisive view to his qualifications to administer the government." The "office will generally be carried into the market to be exchanged for the votes of some large states for president," and "the only criterion which will be regarded as a qualification for the office of vice-president will be the temporary influence of the candidate over the electors of his state."[34]

Jefferson felt the importance of the issue. He predicted that "if the amendment . . . passes R.I. . . . the election for the ensuing four years seems to present nothing formidable." He expressed his sincere "regret that the unbounded calumnies of the federal party have obliged me to throw myself on the verdict of my country for trial." His real desire had been to retire at the end of his first term.[35]

At the beginning of June, 1804, the British minister in the United States informed his Foreign Secretary that three-fourths of the states had ratified the Twelfth Amendment. He cited this as ample evidence that the "democratic party" was "extending itself in every quarter." With Delphic assurance, he concluded that the party would continue to grow until it produced "so much injustice and disorder as to occasion a revolt."[36]

The amendment business having been auspiciously launched, the Democrats held their own private presidential convention on February 25, 1804. It was a "very full meeting" of one hundred and ten Republicans of the Senate and House. Jefferson was unanimously nominated for the presidency. It was agreed that George Clinton "should be supported as vice-president, but in such a manner as not to endanger Mr. Jefferson's election." Clinton received 67 votes; Breckenridge 20; Levi Lincoln 9; Governor Langdon of New Hampshire 7; Gideon Granger 4; Samuel McClay 1.[37] William

---

[34]*Annals of the Congress of the United States* (Washington: Gales & Seaton, 1852), 8th Congress, 1st Session, p. 751.

[35]Jefferson to Elbridge Gerry, March 3, 1804, *Jefferson MSS.* He stated that if Washington had been attacked in the press the way that Jefferson was, he would have thrown up the helm in a burst of indignation. Jefferson to Sullivan, May 21, 1805, *Jefferson MSS.* Sullivan is James Sullivan, Democratic Governor of Massachusetts.

[36]Anthony Merry to Lord Hawkesbury, June 2, 1804, *British State Papers Henry Adams Transcripts.* For details see Lolabel House, *A Study of the Twelfth Amendment of the Constitution of the United States,* a thesis done at the University of Pennsylvania in 1901, p. 51.

[37]John Randolph to Monroe, February 28, 1804, *Monroe MSS.*

Plumer, Federalist Senator from New Hampshire, learned that "Burr had not a single vote." He noted that the "Virginians" wished to "elect an old man" to the vice-presidency; someone "too feeble to aspire to the presidency." Some of "the Democrats from the West were violent in their opposition to Clinton."[38] The Senator from Kentucky, John Breckenridge, was indeed the favorite of the old West for the vice-presidency. The "Western country" wanted to "claim the honor of breaking the combination between the states of Virginia and New York."[39] Even after the Democratic caucus chose Clinton, the movement for Breckenridge continued. Finally, Breckenridge sent an open letter to the Kentucy *Palladium* respectfully requesting "that the electors consider this an utter refusal that my name should be placed in the list of candidates."[40]

Meanwhile, Burr's organ in New York, under the able editorship of Dr. Peter Irving, declared that "had a ballot been taken for vice-president, free of improper influence, six weeks ago, there would have been four-fifths for Burr." Irving, who really spoke for Burr, insisted that DeWitt Clinton wanted the vice-presidency for himself and reluctantly settled for his uncle, and for his own control over the governorship of New York. The Burrites warned that "those who from motives of envy or malice have attempted to sow the seed of dissension between the President and Vice-President have much to answer for to their party and their country."[41]

The Federalists made no formal nominations. They agreed, however, to support Charles G. Pinckney and Rufus King. Before the Louisiana Purchase and the Tripolitan victory, the Federalists were talking confidently of placing King "at the head of the government of New York." It was thought that "he may do there infinitely more good than in the inefficient office of vice-president." General Pinckney "must in all events be considered as our candidate for the first office."[42] But a year later, the tone has changed to one of defeatism. The fiery Plumer, leader of the New England Federalists, was convinced that the "purchase of Louisiana," and the late "amend-

---

[38]William Plumer to Jeremiah Smith, February 28, 1804, *Plumer MSS.*
[39]Allan B. McGruder to Breckenridge, June 23, 1804, *Breckenridge MSS.*
[40]Breckenridge to Editor of *Palladium*, July 5, 1804, *Breckenridge MSS.*
[41]*New York Morning Chronicle*, March 2, 1804.
[42]Theodore Sedgwick to Hamilton, January 27, 1803, *Hamilton MSS.* King was Senator from New York.

ment to the Constitution will exclude New England from a voice in the election of president and vice-president."[43]

Even so, Plumer worked hard to save New Hampshire. Under his leadership, the Federalists of that state canvassed hard for votes. But save for this little flicker in New England, there was no contest. Seventeen states took part in the election, Ohio having been admitted into the Union on November 29, 1802. In the seven states of Vermont, New York, Connecticut, Delaware, South Carolina, Georgia, and Tennessee, electors were appointed by the legislature. They were chosen by the people on general ticket in New Hampshire, Massachusetts, Rhode Island, New Jersey, Pennsylvania, Georgia, and Ohio; and in Maryland, North Carolina, and Kentucky, they were chosen by districts.

Jefferson was elated with the results of the election. He wrote Volney that "the two parties which prevailed with so much violence when you were here are almost melted into one." Continuing, the President stated that, "at the late presidential election I have received one hundred and sixty-two votes, against fourteen only. Connecticut is still Federalist . . . and Delaware."[44]

The result was stunning to the Federalists as they watched Massachusetts and Vermont march into the Jeffersonian column. Maryland, an anti-Jeffersonian state, gave nine of her votes to Jefferson and her other two to Pinckney. Massachusetts furnished the real sensation by casting all her electoral votes for Jefferson.

Jefferson never had any doubts as to the final outcome. More than a month before the official count, he was writing that "Washington set the example of voluntary retirement after 8 years." He wrote further that "I shall follow it and a few more precedents will oppose the obstacle of habit to anyone . . . perhaps it may beget a disposition to establish it by an amendment to the Constitution." He would only consider a third term if there was "such a division about a successor as might bring in a Monarchist. But this circumstance is impossible."[45]

As early as December 12, 1796, Oliver Wolcott, Lieutenant-

---

[43]Plumer to Jeremiah Mason, January 14, 1804, *Plumer MSS.*
[44]Jefferson to Volney, February 8, 1805, *Jefferson MSS.* Volney was Count Constantin Volney, a French nobleman and friend of Jefferson.
[45]Jefferson to John G. Taylor, January 6, 1805, *Jefferson MSS.*

Governor of Connecticut, wrote to his son, then Secretary of the Treasury, that he sincerely wished "the Northern states would separate from the Southern, the moment that event [the election of Jefferson] shall take effect." It was common opinion among the Federalist leaders of New England that the acquisition of Louisiana would lead to the dismemberment of the Union. The Reverend Manasseh Cutler, Congregationalist clergyman and Member of Congress from Massachusetts, wrote that "the moment Louisiana is admitted to the Union the seeds of separation are planted." Speaking in the House of Representatives on October 25, 1803, Roger Griswold of Connecticut predicted that "the acquisition of Louisiana" with its "destruction of that balance . . . between the Eastern and Western states, threatens, at no very distant day, the subversion of our Union." One of the other causes of this secession movement was slavery. In 1803, the South had 848,000 slaves. Three-fifths of these were represented. That meant that the South acquired fifteen representatives in Congress due to her Negro population. This number was greater by one than the whole number to which New Hampshire, Connecticut, and Rhode Island were entitled. In other words, slavery gave the South fifteen extra votes in Congress, and this margin had repeatedly been found sufficient to secure legislation harmful to New England. Politicians north of the Potomac were well aware that under Article II, Section 1, of the Constitution, fifteen representatives meant fifteen more electoral votes. These votes had put the hated Jefferson in power in the election of 1800. By 1804, all New England wanted to strike out of the Constitution that provision which gave to twenty thousand owners of five thousand slaves the same voice in an election as fifty thousand free men. Representation according to free population was the purpose of the New England Ely Amendment of 1804. Proposed by Congressman William Ely of Massachusetts, the Democrats effectively blocked it. It was with this background as his framework that Senator James Hillhouse of Connecticut asserted on January 26, 1804, that while his "state . . . is yet a member of the Union, I hope I shall have as much influence, as if I were a Southern man." The cold, hard fact of adding more slave states to the Union impelled Jackson of Georgia to admit that "the settlement of Louisiana will effect, what I much deprecate, a separation of this Union." The next day Dayton of New Jersey was convinced that if "upper Louisiana is settled, the people there will separate from us; they will form a new empire, and become our enemies." On February 16, 1804, Stone of North Carolina said that "the acquisition of Louisiana will produce one of two things, either a division of the Union, or a very different government from what we have now." Senator William Plumer of New Hampshire, one of the leaders of the secession movement in 1803-1804, asserted on October 20, 1803, that if Louisiana was received into the Union it would at once "destroy . . . the weight and importance of the Eastern states, and compel them to establish a separate and independent Empire."[46]

Throughout the secession movement of 1803-1804, Jefferson was constantly informed of the proceedings. In that tireless Connecticut Yankee, Gideon Granger, his Postmaster General, he had a one-man espionage corps of the first order. Day by day, Granger, who had contact with the disunionists, reported to his Chief Executive. Yet secession was not a horrid word in 1803. We find Jefferson calmly writing Breckenridge that the Federalists are forming "a new Confederacy." If they were successful, he was prepared to accept the outcome, for "if they see their interest in separation, why should we take sides with our Atlantic rather than our Mississippi descendants?" In the President's opinion, it was a mere fraternal quarrel with "the elder and younger brother differing." Jefferson would have "God bless them both, and keep them in Union, if it be for their good, but separate them if it be better."[47]

Federalists out of Congress might be content to grumble and write gloomy letters, but those in Congress were disposed to act and act vigorously. Chief among them were Timothy Pickering, Roger Griswold, Uriah Tracy, and William Plumer.

Burr was included in the plans of the secessionist wing of the Federalist party. Three weeks before he was nominated for the governorship of New York by the discontented Democrats of that state,

---

[46]All quotations concerning the secession movement of 1803-1804 have been taken from William Plumer, Jr., *The Life of William Plumer*, pp. 283-289.
[47]Jefferson to Breckenridge, August 12, 1803, *Jefferson MSS*. Secession in 1804 was no unheard-of remedy for oppressed sectional minorities. It was urged by Rufus King in 1794, by Connecticut leaders in 1796, by John Taylor in 1798; the West threatened it constantly over the Mississippi issue; and finally thought seriously of secession in the event the United States had gone to war with France during the period from 1795 to 1799.

he had a showdown with Jefferson. Burr told the President that he thought it best to retire from politics. He requested some office that would show the world that he retired with the confidence of the Chief Executive. The request was refused.

On February 18, 1804, Burr was nominated in New York, and he accepted. Pickering and Griswold were delighted. They hastened to New York to campaign openly in Burr's behalf. Once Governor of New York, Burr would be in a position to break the New York-Virginia connection. Then they would offer him the leadership in the new confederacy, and so add New York, and perhaps New Jersey, to the five New England states.

Pickering and Griswold held long conferences with Rufus King, with Hamilton, and on one occasion with Burr. In Boston while awaiting election returns from New York, a great dinner was given in Concert Hall. The first toast was, "Virginia Dominion—may it be bounded by the Constitution or by the Delaware." Another toast stated that the "Federal virtues are obliged to swarm from the seat of government—may they find a hive in the North." The last toast of this evening was dedicated to "Aaron's Rod—may it blossom in New York, and may Federalists be still and applaud while the great serpent swallows up the less."[48]

When at last the New York gubernatorial election was over, the results showed that Burr had lost to Judge Lewis by 30,829 to 22,139. Burr carried New York City by 1414 to 1315, but the state-wide majority for Lewis was 8600.[49]

A little more than two months before this election, which saw Burr and Federalist secession schemes defeated, they sought the aid of Great Britain. The British minister reported that he had learned from the Federalist senators "that their plans and calculations . . . have been long seriously resolved." They agreed with Great Britain that in the event of a successful separation they would insist on free navigation of the Mississippi for England, and that if this were denied, they would join in a declaration of war on the United States.[50]

A little over a month after his defeat in New York, a desperate

---

[48]John B. McMaster, *History of the People of the United States*, Vol. III, pp. 49-51.
[49]*New York Morning Chronicle*, June 9, 1804.
[50]Anthony Merry to Lord Hawkesbury, March 1, 1804, *British State Papers, Henry Adams Transcripts*.

Burr approached Anthony Merry, the British Minister to the United States. Merry quickly reported to Lord Horrowby that "I have just received an offer from Mr. Burr, the actual Vice-President of the United States . . . to employ him particularly in endeavoring to effect a separation of the Western part of the United States between the Atlantic and the mountains in its whole extent."[51]

Shortly before his death, Alexander Hamilton struck his last blow for the Union. On that occasion, talking with Colonel Trumbull, he said with deep feeling: "You are going to Boston. You will see the principal men there. Tell them for me, as my request, for God's sake to cease these conversations and threatenings about a separation of the Union."[52]

Five days later, July 12, 1804, Hamilton died of a bullet wound received in a duel with Aaron Burr. Hamilton's efforts in behalf of the Union were effective. As Jefferson prepared to make his second inaugural address, he realized that the New England secessionists had failed.

---

[51] Merry to Lord Horrowby, August 6, 1804, *ibid.*
[52] *The Life and Correspondence of Rufus King,* ed. by Charles R. King (New York: G. P. Putnam's Sons, 1894-1900). Vol. IV, p. 360.

5

The President Faces Burr and England

Four years in the White House had not strengthened the President's vocal cords. Jefferson's second inaugural, like his first, was delivered "in so low a voice that not half of it was heard by any part of the crowded auditory."[1] His speech was both a hymn of praise for the triumphs of his first administration, and one of hope for the four years to come. He was aware that the acquisition of Louisiana had "been disapproved by some for a candid apprehension that the enlargement of our territory would endanger disunion." Still he was convinced that democracy could work equally well on a broad as well as a narrow scale, and added: "The larger our association the less will it be shaken by local passions." Having thus laid the groundwork for a policy of expansionism, the Chief Executive asked: "Who can limit the extent to which the federative principle may operate effectively?" At all events, Jefferson's "conscience was clear," and he was "firmly convinced . . . that with nations as with individuals our interests . . . will ever be found inseparable from our moral duties."[2]

Turning to the home front, Jefferson reminded his huge constituency that the bulk of the taxes was collected from those "who can afford to add foreign luxuries to domestic comforts." "What farmer, what mechanic, what laborer ever sees a taxgatherer of the United States?" queried Jefferson. He gave assurances that the public debt would soon be paid off and promised that the "revenue thereby liberated may be applied in time of peace to rivers, canals,

---

[1] *The Diary of John Quincy Adams,* March 4, 1805, ed. by Allan Nevins (New York: Longmans, Green & Co.), p. 36.
[2] James D. Richardson, *A Compilation of the Messages and Papers of the Presidents,* Vol. I, pp. 366-367.

roads, arts, manufactures, education, and other great objects within each state." If war should come there would be a suspension of these useful works. Then this same revenue, "aided by other resources reserved for that crisis," would meet "all the expenses of the year without encroaching on the rights of future generations by burdening them with the debts of the last."[3]

As Jefferson concluded his second inaugural address by begging "the favor of that Being in whose hands we are," he might well be proud.[4] Never before had the people been so prosperous. Jefferson's past was bright, but before him were four years crowded with such difficulties as few presidents have been called on to face.

The new presidential term began calmly enough. Upon Levi Lincoln's resignation as Attorney General, Jefferson appointed Senator John Breckenridge of Kentucky. The nomination was duly confirmed.

About a month after Jefferson's inaugural, John Randolph of Roanoke did "not like the aspect of affairs." Chairman of the powerful House Committee on Ways and Means, Randolph remarked that "Mr. J. is again seated in the saddle for four years with a prospect of selection for life." What disturbed Randolph, ardent Jeffersonian Democrat that he was, was that "the whole force of the adversaries of the man and . . . of his principles, will be bent to take advantage of the easy credulity of his temper."[5] Randolph would always insist that the Democratic revolution of 1800, in order to justify itself, must produce a "substantial reform." We "shall have little reason to congratulate ourselves on the mere change of men." We "are for a change of important principles."[6]

The blunt fact is that he could have remained Mr. Democrat on the Hill had he been content with taking directives from the Executive mansion. This Randolph refused to do. By breaking with Jefferson, he soon found himself at the head of a minority commonly called the "Quids." Old-fashioned Republicans, like Speaker Bacon of North Carolina, Joseph Hopper Nicholson of Maryland,

[3]*Ibid.*, Vol. I, p. 369. As a strict constructionist, Jefferson envisaged an amendment to the Constitution before the allocation of federal funds to state needs.

[4]*Ibid.*, Vol. I, p. 370

[5]John Randolph to Joseph H. Nicholson, April 30, 1805, *Joseph H. Nicholson MSS.*

[6]John Randolph to Joseph H. Nicholson, July 18, 1801, and December 26, 1801, *Joseph H. Nicholson MSS.*

and John Taylor of Carolina County, Virginia, the agrarian philosopher, openly joined hands with Randolph. Powerful Administration men like Samuel Smith, Senator from Maryland, and James
Monroe, secretly sympathized with Randolph's efforts. Smith wrote
a friend that Randolph was not "an apostate from principle. He
differs from the Executive on some important points. He does not
believe everything is well-conducted and he so expresses himself."[7]
Recalling the momentous event of 1787, Monroe reminded a
Quid that the "Constitution contemplates a separation of the
Executive from the Legislative branch but in the madness of the
government that principle is lost sight of. The two branches constitute virtually one body . . ."[8] But the President, ever the
masterful political tactitian, was not over-concerned. In spite of
"Randolph's popular eloquence," Jefferson informed Monroe that
the minority of Republicans voting with him has been four to six or
eight against ninety to one hundred."[9] The Sage of Monticello, with
a mixture of cautious praise and sympathy, remarked to William
Duane that "the example of John Randolph is a caution to all honest and prudent men to sacrifice a little of self-confidence and to go
with their friends, although they may sometimes think they are going wrong."[10]

However, Randolph did not know the meaning of compromise.
He could but follow his conscience. His remarks on the floor of the
House during the Yazoo debate were typical: "For this is one of the
cases, which once being engaged in, I can never desert or relinquish
till I have exercised every energy of mind and faculty of body I
possess in refuting so nefarious a project."[11]

The facts in the case were clear enough. On January 7, 1795,
the Georgia legislature, with the reluctant signature of the governor,
authorized the sale of most of the territory which comprises the
present States of Alabama and Mississippi. The land was sold to

---

[7]Samuel Smith to * * * *, February 22, 1806, *Samuel Smith MSS.* The recipient
is unidentified.
[8]James Monroe to J. Nicholson, September 24, 1808, *Joseph Nicholson MSS.*
[9]Thomas Jefferson to James Monroe, May 4, 1806, *Jefferson MSS.*
[10]Thomas Jefferson to William Duane, April 30, 1811, *Jefferson MSS.*
[11]*Annals of Congress*, 8th Congress, 1st Session, 1803-1805, Vol. XIII, p. 1104.
(Washington: Gales & Seaton, 1852). See William C. Bruce, *John Randolph of
Roanoke, 1773-1833* (New York: Knickerbocker Press, 1922), Vol. I, pp. 222-
286 for an excellent account of Randolph's break with Jefferson.

four speculating companies. It was a gross fraud against the people of Georgia. Every member of the legislature, except one, had shares of stock in the companies. William Smith, Judge of the Superior Court of Georgia, joined the ring, receiving for his service as lobbyist, $13,000. Nathaniel Pendleton, Judge of the United States Court for Georgia, handed certificates for shares to members of the legislature for their votes. Everything about the negotiation was rotten through and through.

When the foul odor of corruption finally seeped down to the people, the reaction was instantaneous. They elected a new governor and a new legislature, dedicated to the repeal of the Act of January 7, 1795. The repeal came in the winter of 1795-1796 when the Georgia legislature destroyed the Yazoo fraud. The bill denounced the land sale act as a violation of both the state and national constitutions, as the creation of a monopoly, as the dismemberment of Georgia, and as the betrayal of the rights of man.[12]

Needless to say, in the year that followed between the passage and repeal of the Yazoo bill, the four purchasers—The Georgia Company, The Georgia-Mississippi Company, The Tennessee Company, and The Upper-Mississippi Company—made millions. They had purchased thirty-five million acres of fertile, well-watered, heavily-wooded land at less than one and a half cents an acre. Opening land offices as far north as Boston, they resold their acres at tremendous profits. Nowhere in the United States were the purchases from the Yazoo companies so numerous as in New England. When the news reached Boston that the Georgia legislature had annulled the Yazoo grant, the consternation was great. Soon a large number of the New England purchasers organized the New England-Mississippi Company for the purpose of protecting their interests. They maintained a lobby at Washington headed by Gideon Granger, the Postmaster General of the United States. Eager to obtain compensation for his clients, Granger appeared on the floor of the House openly soliciting votes. In addition to Granger, three cabinet members: Madison, Secretary of State; Gallatin, Secretary of the Treasury; and Levi Lincoln, Attorney-General, favored com-

[12]*American State Papers, Public Lands.* (Washington: Gales & Seaton, 1832), Vol. I, pp. 156-158. The frauds derived their name from the Yazoo River which ran through part of the territory. The repeal enacted by the Georgia legislature was declared unconstitutional in 1810 by John Marshall in *Fletcher vs. Peck.*

pensation for the New England-Mississippi Company. Although Jefferson said nothing, it was generally understood that he supported his cabinet. Thus, in opposing Granger, John Randolph was in effect opposing Jefferson's Administration. Randolph's eloquence and logic were so effective that as long as he remained a member of Congress, compensation was prevented.[13]

After the close of the 8th Congress in 1804, it was simply a matter of time before Randolph lost the leadership of the House. Randolph did what he did with his eyes open. He knew the "whole executive government has had a bias to the Yazoo interest ever since I had a seat here." He realized that ultimately "we cannot bear up against it."[14] His opposition doomed him within his own party. Postmaster General Granger openly made plans to push Randolph out of the Chairmanship of the Ways and Means Committee. By July, 1806, Jefferson looked to Barnabas Bidwell of Massachusetts as the future leader of the House.[15]

Jefferson's first annual message, December 3, 1805, was penned at a time when Great Britain and Napoleon were engaged in a desperate struggle for the domination of the continent. English sails covered the seven seas, and French bayonets, the European harbors. America, as a profit-making neutral carrier, was more often than not molested by either the British Shark or the French Tiger. Since the loss of her lush province of Louisiana, Spain was inflicting every grievous injury that she dared upon the United States. With these insults in mind, Jefferson, after a brief reference to the scourge of yellow fever, and the dangers from George III and Napoleon, announced to the Congress that American troops were being sent to the Spanish-American frontiers of the United States.

Three days later, Jefferson sent another message to Congress, but this time a confidential one, on the subject of our relations with Spain. The document strongly hinted that France was disposed to effect a settlement of the boundary dispute between Spain and the United States. Randolph, along with Nicholson, Bidwell, John Cotton Smith of Connecticut, Gurdon S. Mumford of New York, David R. Williams of South Carolina, and Robert Brown of Penn-

[13]*Annals of Congress, 8th Congress, 2nd Session, 1804-1805*, Vol. XIV, pp. 1023-1034. Randolph retired in 1814.
[14]*Annals of Congress, 9th Cong. 1st Sess., 1805-1806*, Vol. XV, pp. 909-914.
[15]Jefferson to Bidwell, July 5, 1806, *Jefferson MSS.*

sylvania, made up the select committee appointed to deal with this secret message. After private conference with the President and the Secretary of State, Randolph discovered that Jefferson wanted to pay two million dollars to France in order to get her to pressure Spain into giving us West Florida. Randolph made his position crystal clear: we would acquire Florida honorably or not at all. When Madison told him that France would not permit Spain to adjust her differences with the United States without the payment of a bribe, Randolph replied: "Good morning, Sir. I see I am not calculated for a politician."[16] Randolph was not afraid to fight: "If war is necessary—if we have reached this point—let us have war."[17] One thing Randolph would not do: pay blackmail to any country. But like the Yazoo case, he lost this one too, only sooner. The bill to give Jefferson his way with the Florida purchase affair was passed by a large majority. And, on January 16, 1806, it was sent to the Senate for approval, but Randolph's delaying tactics proved fatal to Jefferson's desires. By the time the Senate approved the expenditure, Napoleon had changed his mind. He had now determined to seize the Spanish monarchy, colonies and all. The final disposition of Florida was postponed until the end of Monroe's first administration.

BRITANNIA WAIVES THE RULES

At precisely 4:30 p.m. on June 22, 1807, while Jefferson sputtered in anger over Chief Justice Marshall's subpoena ordering him to testify in the Burr treason trial, an event occurred at sea which was to drag the United States to the brink of war. His Majesty's frigate, the *Leopard,* fired three point-blank broadsides into the defenseless American frigate, the *Chesapeake,* killing three men and wounding eighteen. This brutal attack took place ten miles out of Norfolk, Virginia, where the *Chesapeake* was hailed by the *Leopard.* The American Commander supposed that he was going to be asked to carry dispatches to Europe.[18] He, therefore, per-

---

[16]Hugh A. Garland, *The Life of John Randolph of Roanoke* (New York: Appleton & Co., 1850), Vol. I, p. 217. See also Henry Adams, *John Randolph* (Boston: Houghton Mifflin & Co., 1882), pp. 165-169.

[17]*Annals of Congress, 9th Congress, 1st Session, 1805-1806,* Vol. XV, p. 556.

[18]Professor Burt asserts that Barron must have known what he was running into, for practically everybody on board with him was familiar with a report circulated around Norfolk that the captain of the British ship *Melamfus* had threatened to take the men from the *Chesapeake.* Alfred L. Burt, *The United States, Great Britain and British North America* (New Haven: Yale University Press, 1940), p. 242.

mitted the *Leopard* to approach without summoning his men to their proper quarters, and without having the loggerheads heated red-hot for firing guns. When the British Commander requested permission to search the *Chesapeake* for deserters, he was quite properly refused. London had never claimed the right to impress seamen from a neutral man-of-war. After helplessly enduring a savage bombardment for fifteen minutes, and after an American officer had managed to fire one gun in honor of the flag, the *Chesapeake* surrendered. A British searching party then boarded her and removed four deserters. Three of the four men seized were Americans who had been impressed into the Royal Navy. The fourth was undeniably a British subject and a deserter. He was tried by a court-martial and promptly hung from the yardarm of his own ship. The Americans were unceremoniously thrown into a British jail.[19]

When the bloody hulk of the *Chesapeake* staggered back to Norfolk, a red-blooded wave of patriotic anger swept over the country. The governor of Virginia was forced to call out the militia to maintain order as English officers on shore leave fled to their ships, and infuriated mobs destroyed the water casks of the British fleet. Writing to Albert Gallatin, Joseph Nicholson rejoiced that but "one feeling pervades the nation . . . all distinctions of federalism and democracy are vanished. The people are ready to submit to any deprivation."[20] A friend of Andrew Jackson wrote: "On my conscience and faith and honor I hope that war will take place."[21] Jackson, with pointed reference to the Burr trial then in session at Richmond cried: "Millions to persecute an American; not a cent to resist England!"[22] Even in Federalist Boston, toastmakers were demanding: "Let us whet the sword! Let us bend the bow!"[23]

War was just around the corner, and no one knew this better than Jefferson who remarked: "Never since the battle of Lexington

---

[19]British Admirality Records assert that the three Americans had volunteered and were not impressed. See Bradford Perkins, "George Canning, Great Britain, and the United States, 1807-1809," *American Historical Review*, Vol. LXIII, No. 1, October 1957. Henry Adams' chapter on the *Chesapeake* besides being scholarly is beautifully written. See Henry Adams, *History of the United States of America*, Vol. IV, pp. 1-26.

[20]Joseph Nicholson to Albert Gallatin, July 14, 1807, *Gallatin MSS*.

[21]Thomas A. Bailey, *A Diplomatic History of the American People* (New York: F. S. Crofts & Co., 1940), p. 124.

[22]*Ibid.*, p. 124.

[23]*Ibid.*, p. 124.

have I seen this country in such a state of exasperation as at present, and even then that did not produce such unanimity . . . I had only to open my hand and let havoc loose."[24] General Turreau, French Minister to the United States, reported to Talleyrand: "Jefferson . . . spoke to me about the *Chesapeake* affair and said: if the English do not give us the satisfaction we demand, we will take Canada."[25] On July 21, a month after the wanton attack of the British on defenseless *Chesapeake*, David Erskine, British Minister to the United States, wrote George Canning: "The ferment in the public mind has not yet subsided, and I am confirmed in the opinion . . . that this country will engage in war rather than submit to their national armed ships being forcibly searched on the high seas."[26] News of the *Chesapeake* affair reached London July 25. On that day Canning wrote Monroe, our minister in England: ". . . if the British officers should prove to have been culpable, the most prompt and effectual reparation shall be afforded to the government of the United States."[27] This was a private note and was in sharp contrast to the great newspapers of Foreign Minister George Canning's Tory party. Day after day, the *Morning Post,* the *Times,* and the *Courier,* abused and denounced America. On August 6, three days after Canning had admitted that Great Britain had no right to search national vessels, the *Morning Post* came out strongly for war: "Three weeks' blockade of the Delaware, the Chesapeake, and Boston harbor would make our presumptuous rivals repent of their puerile conduct." On August 5, the London *Times* defended not only the order to search the *Chesapeake* but also its manner of execution. The *Courier* put the British case succinctly, when it declared: ". . . if the laws of nations do not allow you to search for deserters in a friend's territory, neither do they allow that friend to inveigle away your troops or your seamen . . ."[28]

---

[24]Jefferson to DuPont de Nemours, July 14, 1807, *Jefferson MSS.*

[25]Turreau to Talleyrand, July 18, 1808, *French Archives, Henry Adams Transcripts.*

[26]Erskine to Canning, July 21, 1807, *British State Papers, Henry Adams Transcripts.* The British claimed the right to impress from neutral merchantmen but never from neutral men-of-war.

[27]Canning to Monroe, July 25, 1807, *American State Papers, Foreign Relations, 1807-1815,* Vol. III, p. 187. In disavowing the attack on the *Chesapeake,* Canning "acted contrary to overwhelming opinion in England." Bradford Perkins, "George Canning, Great Britain, and the United States, 1807-1809," p. 4.

[28]The three newspaper quotations are taken from Henry Adams, *History of the United States . . . the Second Administration of Thomas Jefferson,* Vol. II, p. 44.

Jefferson, whose passion was peace, could have led a united America into war with England in 1807. Besides the advantage of great popular enthusiasm, Jefferson would have had the help of Napoleon's Europe. Jefferson's plans to invade Canada indicate that he thought seriously of war. In his mind, the alternative to armed conflict was economic pressure. It was the latter weapon that he finally chose. The President only arrived at this conclusion after much careful thought and consideration. Although the *Chesapeake* was smashed on June 22, it was not until June 25 that Jefferson received word of the outrage. It took him seven days to round up his Cabinet. Finally, on July 2 he issued a proclamation. Its main points were: All armed vessels of Great Britain were required to depart from American waters. Britain must disavow the act and the principle of searching a public armed vessel. The men taken must be restored and Admiral Berkeley, the offending British officer, recalled. On July 4 at another cabinet meeting, it was agreed that Congress should convene on October 26 unless new circumstances should render an earlier call necessary. On July 5 "it was agreed to call on the governors of the states to have their quotas of one hundred thousand militia in readiness. The object is to have the portions on the sea coast ready for any emergency; and for those in the North we may look to a winter expedition against Canada."[29]

Even while America was inflamed with warlike enthusiasm, Jefferson's mind reverted to peace. His unwillingness to call Congress into immediate session showed this beyond cavil. His letters reveal it too. Writing to Democratic Congressman Bidwell on July 11, he assured him that he wanted to give England "an opportunity to disavow and make reparation."[30] Also, he wished to do "no act which might compromise Congress in their choice between war, non-intercourse, or any other measure."[31] Vice-President Clinton was reminded by Jefferson that Congress alone had the power to declare war. Jefferson would do nothing which would commit the Congress to decide for war in preference to non-intercourse.[32]

[29]*Cabinet Memorandum, The Writings of Thomas Jefferson,* ed. Paul L. Ford (New York: G. P. Putnam's Son's, 1895), Vol. I, p. 324, John Randolph was shocked that the President did not immediately convene Congress. Randolph to Joseph H. Nicholson, June 25 and 28, 1807, *Joseph H. Nicholson MSS.*
[30]Jefferson to Bidwell, July 11, 1807, *Jefferson MSS.*
[31]*Ibid.*
[32]Jefferson to George Clinton, July 6, 1807, *Jefferson MSS.*

Great Britain would, and actually did, disavow her action in the *Chesapeake* incident; but she would not under any circumstances forego what she considered her right; viz., impressments from merchant vessels. Although both Secretary of State Madison and President Jefferson wanted peace, they were not afraid to risk war. Madison's instructions to Monroe, by standing up for American rights, prevented peaceful negotiations, and in a very real sense led straight to the War of 1812:

> As a security for the future, an entire abolition of impressments from vessels under the flag of the United States . . . is also to make an indispensable part of the satisfaction.[33]

On this, England would never yield.

Jefferson's predecessor in the White House, the Federalist John Adams, put the case for America with compelling logic:

> I have said . . . to . . . Mr. Pickering, to Mr. Wolcott and McHenry . . . that there was no distinction between ships of war and merchant ships . . . If the British have a right to impress seamen from a fishing smack, they have the same right from a hundred and twenty-gun ship. The deck of a jolly boat at sea is as much the territory of its sovereign as the hold of a seventy-four . . .[34]

The British point of view was as understandable as it was pragmatic. Lord Nelson reported that in the war ending in 1801, 42,000 British sailors had deserted.[35] At the time of the *Chesapeake* affair, there were thousands of British subjects sailing the seas as members of American crews.[36] Admiral Berkeley, who ordered the capture of the *Chesapeake,* claimed that there were at least 150 English-born seamen on board the American frigate.[37] Madison's reply was: "It is impossible for the United States to view natural-born subjects of Great Britain, who have been naturalized here, in any other light

---

[33]Madison to Monroe, July 6, 1807, *American State Papers, Foreign Relations, 1807-1815,* Vol. III, p. 183.

[34]John Adams to John Quincy Adams, January 8, 1808, *John Adams MSS.* James F. Zimmerman estimates that between 1803 and 1812 at least 6,000 Americans were impressed by His Majesty's government. James F. Zimmerman, *Impressment of American Seamen* (New York: A Doctoral Dissertation at Columbia University, 1925), p. 255.

[35]Thomas A. Bailey, *A Diplomatic History of the American People,* p. 112.

[36]Alfred L. Burt, *The United States, Great Britain and British North America,* p. 234.

[37]Bradford Perkins, "George Canning, Great Britain, and the United States, 1807-1809," p. 4.

than as American citizens."[38] Jefferson's principle was that "deserters ought never to be enlisted." He instructed Madison to inform the British that "if ever such a practice prevailed, it has been without the knowledge of the government."[39] The argument of Number 10 Downing Street came to this: In England's darkest hour, when her fleet was all that stood between her and defeat, she could agree to nothing that might lessen her chances of recovering her sons of the sea.[40]

The peace parties, both in England and America, received an indirect stimulus as a result of the trial of Aaron Burr for treason. This trial, held in Richmond from March through October, 1807, claimed a major portion of the energies of President Jefferson. It was a dangerous, time-consuming political distraction for him at the very height of our crisis in foreign policy with Great Britain over the *Chesapeake*.

Since 1804 Jefferson had known of the rumors about Burr. George Morgan, Joseph H. Daveiss, and William Eaton had been his informants. These men insisted that Burr was planning a separation of the western part of the United States. Burr denied this but admitted that he intended to invade Mexico, if and when the United States found itself at war with Spain.[41] Eaton went so far as to testify that Burr had vowed to "turn Congress neck and heels out of doors, assassinate the President, seize the Treasury and Navy; and declare himself the protector of an energetic government."[42]

However, in spite of these charges, Jefferson and his Cabinet were convinced as late as October 25, 1806, that Burr was "committing no overt act against law."[43] But when mysterious warnings from Major General James Wilkinson, Commander of the United States Army, reached Jefferson, he called a special cabinet meeting

---

[38]February 8, 1808, *Madison MSS*. (Notes on Rose talks).

[39]Jefferson to Madison, August 20, 1807, *Jefferson MSS*.

[40]Alfred. L. Burt, *The United States, Great Britain and British North America*, p. 234.

[41]Walter F. McCaleb, *The Aaron Burr Conspiracy* (New York: Dodd, Mead & Co., 1903), p. 369. Colonel George Morgan lived in Pittsburgh and knew Burr at Princeton. Daveiss, brother-in-law of Chief Justice Marshall, was Federal District Attorney for Kentucky. Eaton was the hero of the spectacular Tripolitan Campaign of 1804.

[42]This is part of an affidavit made by Eaton. See William Cranch, *Condensed Reports of Cases in the Supreme Court of the United States*, Vol. II, pp. 462-467.

[43]*Cabinet Memorandum* as quoted in Henry Adams, *History*, Vol. I, p. 281.

and issued a presidential proclamation declaring that a conspiracy had been discovered. He warned all persons engaged in it to withdraw and directed that the conspirators and their "vessels, arms and military stores" be seized. Jefferson followed this up with a special message to Congress wherein he charged Burr with treason. The President contended that Burr, as the leader of the conspiracy, contemplated not only "an attack on Mexico" but also "the severance of the Union of these States beyond the Alleghany mountains." Jefferson assured Congress that Burr's "guilt is placed beyond question."[44]

Burr and his accomplices were speedily apprehended and brought to trial. Richmond, Virginia, the scene of the trial, drew thousands of spectators. If the government proved its case, it would mean the execution of two senators and a former vice-president. Winfield Scott was there, and he records that it was "President Jefferson who directed and animated the prosecution . . . hence every Republican clamored for execution . . . the Federalists . . . compacted themselves on the other side."[45] Washington Irving, then a New York newspaper reporter, thought well of Burr: "I am very mistaken if the most underhand . . . measures have not been observed towards him. He, however, retains his serenity."[46] That vigorous Democrat, Andrew Jackson, also present at Richmond, was "sorry to say that the thing has . . . assumed the shape of a political persecution . . . I am more convinced than ever that treason was never intended by Burr."[47] The Administration retaliated by branding Jackson "a malcontent."[48] George Hay, District Attorney of the United States, and lawyer for the prosecution, wrote Jefferson: "Gen. Jackson . . . has been here . . . denouncing Wilkinson in the

[44]*Annals of Congress, 9th Cong., 2nd Session*, Vol. 16, pp. 39-41. Henry Clay and leading Kentuckians thought that Burr meditated an attack on Mexico in the event of war with Spain. They were under the impression that he had governmental backing for these plans. Jefferson successfully disabused them of these ideas. See Kentucky *Gazette*, December 29, 1806 and *National Intelligencer*, January 23, 1807.

[45]*Memoirs of Lieut.-General Scott* (New York: Sheldon Co., 1864), Vol. I, p. 13. The two Senators were Dayton of New Jersey and Smith of Ohio.

[46]Irving to Mrs. Hoffman, June 4, 1807, *Life and Letters of Washington Irving*, ed. by Pierre M. Irving (New York: G. P. Putnam's Sons, 1869), Vol. I, p. 143.

[47]Jackson to Patton Anderson, June 16, 1807, James Parton, *The Life of Andrew Jackson* (New York: Mason Bros., 1860), Vol. I, p. 334. Anderson, like Jackson, came from Tennessee. They were close friends.

[48]Albert J. Beveridge, *The Life of John Marshall*, Vol. III, p. 405.

coarsest terms in every company."[49] Hay could have added, but did not, that Jackson was doing the same thing to Jefferson.[50] Fortunately for Burr, Jefferson's arch-enemy, the Federalist John Marshall was the presiding judge. The grand jury, composed of sixteen Democrats and only two Federalists, was no consolation to the defendant.

JEFFERSON AND MEXICO

In a very real sense Jefferson was also being tried at Richmond. He had publicly branded Burr a traitor, and he was determined that the jury find the New Yorker guilty. At the very moment that the grand jury was preparing an indictment for treason against Burr, Jefferson wrote a confidential letter to our minister in Spain concerning Burr:

Altho' at first he proposed a separation of the Western country . . . yet he very early saw that the fidelity of the Western country was not to be shaken and turned himself wholly toward Mexico.[51]

In this same letter, the President, in spite of his preoccupation with the Burr trial and the *Chesapeake* incident, was not unmindful of the emerging American doctrine of manifest destiny:

If we have kept our hands off her [Spain] till now, it has been purely out of respect for France . . . We expect therefore from the friendship of the Emperor [Napoleon] that he will either compel Spain to do us justice or abandon her to us. We ask but one month to be in . . . the city of Mexico.[52]

In the last week of April, 1807, the President was infuriated with what he considered to be the partisan politics of Marshall and his fellow Federalists. "The fact is," asserted Jefferson, "that the Federalists make Burr's cause their own, and exert their whole influ-

---

[49]Hay to Jefferson, June 14, 1807, *Jefferson MSS.*
[50]Albert J. Beveridge, T*he Life of John Marshall,* Vol. III, p. 457. John Adams, after recounting the story of Burr's winning the election of 1800 for the Democrats, remarked: "But what has been Burr's reward?" John Adams to Benjamin Rush, June 23, 1808, *Benjamin Rush MSS.*
[51]Jefferson to James Bowdoin, April 2, 1807, *Jefferson MSS.* According to our Constitution, treason consists in an act of levying war against the United States. This fact must be attested to by two witnesses or by a confession. See Jefferson to Breckenridge, August 12, 1803, *Jefferson MSS* for Jefferson's view that secession was legal. This view is of course pertinent to the Burr trial.
[52]Jefferson to James Bowdoin, April 2, 1807, *ibid.*

ence to shield him."[53] "It is unfortunate," he continued, "that federalism is still predominant in our judiciary department, which is consequently in opposition to the legislative and executive branches and is able to baffle their measures often."[54] The President insisted that the record bore him out: "If there ever had been an instance in this or the preceding administrations, of federal judges so applying principles of law as to condemn a federal or acquit a republican offender, I should have judged them in the present case with more charity."[55] Marshall's conduct would force a reform, warned Jefferson. The President declared that "the nation will judge both the offender and judges for themselves . . . the people . . . will see . . . and amend the error in our constitution which makes any branch independent of the nation."[56] If the Chief Justice's "protection of Burr produces this amendment, it will do more good than his condemnation would have done," concluded the Chief Executive.[57]

Joseph Nicholson's letter to John Randolph, wherein he stated: "The President's popularity is unbounded, and his will is that of the nation," neatly summed up the problem that confronted Chief Justice Marshall.[58] It is never an easy thing to fly in the face of public opinion. In the midst of the trial, Marshall admitted that "it would be difficult or dangerous for a jury to venture to acquit Burr, however innocent they might think him."[59] He was well aware that he himself had barely escaped impeachment after his *Marbury vs. Madison* decision, and now, during the Burr trial he was openly threatened.[60] As a matter of fact, after Burr was acquitted, the effigy of John Marshall was hanged by the neck until the executioner pronounced the stuffed figure to be dead. Marshall was not slow to answer the threats being made against him, and retorted:

That this court dares not usurp power is most true. That this court does not shrink from its duty is not less true . . . No man is desirous of becoming the

---

[53]Jefferson to James Bowdoin, April 2, 1807, *Jefferson MSS.*
[54]Jefferson to James Bowdoin, April 2 1807, *Ibid.*
[55]*Ibid.*
[56]*Ibid.*
[57]Jefferson to Giles, April 20, 1807, *Jefferson MSS.*
[58]Nicholson to Randolph, April 12, 1807, *John Randolph MSS.*
[59]*Blennerhassett Papers,* ed. by William H. Safford (Cincinnati: R. Clarke & Co., 1891), p. 465.
[60]Albert J. Beveridge, *The Life of John Marshall,* Vol. III, p. 500.

peculiar subject of calumny. No man, might he let the bitter cup pass from him without self-reproach, would drain it to the bottom. But if he have no choice in the case, if there be no alternative presented to him but a dereliction of duty or the opprobrium of those who are denominated the world, he merits the contempt as well as the indignation of his country, who can hesitate which to embrace.[61]

In his final charge to the jury, Marshall was to admonish them to "find a verdict of guilty or not guilty as their own consciences shall direct."[62]

Major General James Wilkinson, Commander of the Army of the United States, reached Richmond on Saturday, June 13. He was Jefferson's star witness. Unfortunately, he was nothing less than a cheap spy in the employ of the Spanish government. The Spanish minister to the United States reported to his government that Wilkinson "is entirely devoted to us. He enjoys a considerable pension from the King . . . and the separation of the Western states has been his favorite plan."[63] As early as September 28, 1806, Wilkinson had sent word to Senator Adair of Kentucky that the hour had come for "subverting the Spanish Government in Mexico" and for carrying "our conquests to California and the Isthmus of Darien."[64] John Randolph, as foreman of the grand jury, felt that Burr "supported himself with great fortitude," but "the mammoth of iniquity . . . Wilkinson . . . escaped." Wilkinson, continued Randolph, "is the only man that I ever saw who was from the bark to the very core a villain . . . It was once a matter of astonishment to me that the administration should choose to embark its reputation in the same bottom with Wilkinson's—now nothing surprises me."[65] Wilkinson had actually cooperated with Burr until he realized it would be more lucrative to turn on him.[66] Much to Jefferson's chagrin, his Commander-in-Chief barely got out of the Richmond courtroom alive. Seven of the sixteen members of the jury voted to indict him

[61]*Reports of the Trials of Colonel Aaron Burr*, taken in shorthand by David Robertson (Philadelphia: Fry & Kammerer Co., 1808), Vol. II, pp. 444-445.

[62]*Ibid.*, p. 441.

[63]Yrujo to Cevallos, January 28, 1807, *Spanish Archives, Henry Adams Transcripts.*

[64]Wilkinson to Adair, September 28, 1806, Bernard Mayo, *Henry Clay: Spokesman of the New West* (Boston: Houghton Mifflin Co., 1937), p. 232.

[65]John Randolph to Joseph H. Nicholson, May 31 and June 25, 1807, *Joseph H. Nicholson MSS.*

[66]James R. Jacobs, *Tarnished Warrior: Major General James Wilkinson* (New York: Macmillan Co., 1938), pp. 231-233.

for treason.[67] Expressing his misgivings to the President, the tarnished warrior wrote: "I had anticipated that a deluge of testimony would have poured forth . . . to overwhelm him . . . to my astonishment I found the traitor vindicated and myself condemned."[68]

One of the reasons why Jefferson did not allow Congress to consider the *Chesapeake* outrage until four months after its occurrence was a letter from Wilkinson that he received during the Burr proceedings:

The late outrage by the British has produced . . . a degree of emotion bordering on rage. I revere the honorable impulse but fear its effects . . . The present is no moment for precipitancy or a stretch of power—on the contrary, the British being prepared for war and we not, a sudden appeal to hostilities will give them a great advantage . . .[69]

At long last it came time for Marshall to charge the jury. The Administration's case against Aaron Burr had begun on March 30, 1807. Now on August 31, the Chief Justice reminded the jurors "that the difficulty of proving a fact will not justify conviction without proof . . ." and "certainly it will not justify conviction without one direct and positive witness in a case where the constitution requires two." And finally, "to advise or procure a treason is not treason in itself."[70] The jury retired on September 1, 1807, and soon after returned with the verdict:

We of the jury say that Aaron Burr is not proved to be guilty under this indictment by any evidence submitted to us. We therefore find him not guilty.[71]

On September 15, the jury returned another verdict. This one cleared Burr of the guilt of any misdeameanor. On October 20, Marshall delivered his last opinion in the case of Aaron Burr:

If those whose duty and province it is to prosecute offenders against the laws of the United States shall be of the opinion that a crime of a deeper dye has been committed, it is at their choice to act in conformity with that opinion.[72]

Jefferson, beside himself with rage over the verdict, declared: "We

[67]Walter F. McCaleb, *The Aaron Burr Conspiracy*, p. 335.
[68]Wilkinson to Jefferson, June 17, 1807, *Jefferson MSS*.
[69]Wilkinson to Jefferson, June 29, 1807, *Jefferson MSS*.
[70]Albert J. Beveridge, *The Life of John Marshall*, Vol. III, p. 512.
[71]*Ibid.*, p. 513.
[72]*Ibid.* p. 528.

- If there never had been an instance in this or the preceding administrations of federal judges so applying principles of law as to condemn a federal, or acquit a republican offender, I should have judged them in the present case with more charity. All this however will work well. The nation will judge both the offender & judges for themselves. if a member of the Executive or Legislature does wrong, the day is never far distant when the people will remove him. they will then see, & amend the error in our constitution which makes any branch independent of the nation. they will see that one of the great coördinate branches of the government, setting itself in opposition to the other two, and to the common sense of the nation, proclaims impunity to that class of offenders which endeavors to overturn the constitution, and are themselves protected in it by the constitution itself: for impeachment is a farce which will not be tried again. if their protection of Burr produces this amendment it will do more good than his condemnation could have done. against Burr personally I never had one hostile sentiment. I never indeed thought him an honest frank-dealing man, but considered him as a crooked gun or other perverted machine whose aim or shot you could never be sure of. still while he possessed the confidence of the nation, I thought it my duty to respect in him their confidence, & to treat him as if he deserved it: and if his punishment can be commuted now for an useful amendment of the constitution, I shall rejoice in it. — my sheet being full I perceive it is high time to offer you my friendly salutations and assure you of my constant & affectionate esteem & respect

29321-9

Th: Jefferson

1. Jefferson to Giles, April 20, 1807

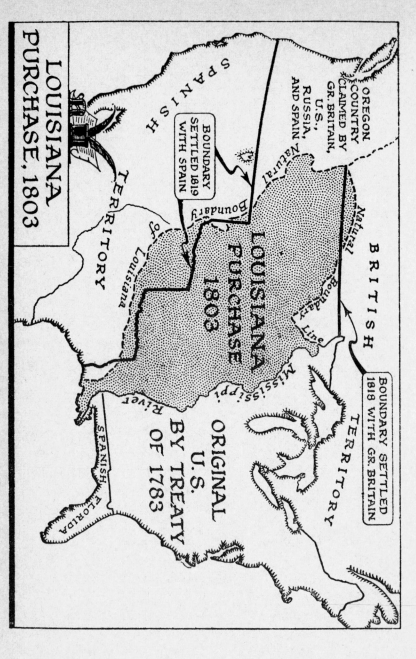

LOUISIANA PURCHASE, 1803

OREGON COUNTRY CLAIMED BY GR. BRITAIN, U.S., RUSSIA, AND SPAIN

SPANISH

BOUNDARY SETTLED 1819 WITH SPAIN

BRITISH

Natural Boundary

BOUNDARY SETTLED 1818 WITH GR. BRITAIN

TERRITORY

LOUISIANA PURCHASE 1803

of Louisiana

Boundary Line

BRITISH TERRITORY

Mississippi River

SPANISH FLORIDA

ORIGINAL U.S. BY TREATY OF 1783

3. James Madison

Bonaparte siezes every American vessel, that has been so unfortunate as to enter the ports of France, and declares that he will not restore either ships or cargoes, unless our government will consent to join him in the war. And yet, say Duane, Irvine and every other democratic editor in the country, "Bonaparte is our good friend and is fighting our battles."

Bonaparte arrests and imprisons all such American seamen, as are so unhappy as to land upon his inhospitable coasts; and yet, if we believe the democratic editors, "he is our good friend, & we ought to wish him success."

Samuel Smith and all his minions exert themselves as much as possible to involve the country in a war with England. Why? Because Smith has always been a French partisan, and he wishes to get back four hundred thousand dollars, now in the possession of Bonaparte.

The democratic faction in this country have always been a French faction. Their object, since the war between England and France commenced in 1793, has uniformly been, to join the force of the United States to the force of France. They were formerly defeated in their designs by the firmness of Washington suported by the virtue of the people. Now they flatter themselves that this aim will be accomplished. But we think, that the good sense and virtue of the people will again disappoint them. When we speak of the democratic faction, we do not mean the great mass of those who vote for democratic candidates; but we mean the leaders, such as Sam and Robert Smith, &c. The great majority of those who support these men, are actuated by the best of motives; but they are deceived by false information. Unfortunately, they read only democratic papers and therefore have not the means of hearing the truth.

"France has been treated by this country with shameful ingratitude," says the abandoned Duane and his co-adjutors. Ingratitude for what? For confiscating our property and imprisoning our seamen? Or is it for the Berlin, Milan and Bayonne decrees, that we should be grateful?

"We ought to conciliate France," says the Boston Cronicle. Aye, that's the cry. Let us have an alliance with France and then our democrats will be satisfied. Now, we say, let us endeavour to obtain an amicable settlement with both France and Great Britain. Let us not rashly rush into war; but let us maintain our rights firmly against the encroachments of every foreign nation. If Jefferson had been governed by these maxims, we should now enjoy peace and commerce. But by always meanly submitting to the demands of France and by throwing every obstacle in the way of negociation with England, he has brought the country into its present situation. Now our only prospect of relief must be from the good sense of the people. If they wish to have a return of prosperous times, they must abandon the advocates of Jefferson's policy.

4. From the *Federal Republican*, Sept. 13, 1809

had supposed we possessed fixed laws to guard us equally against treason and oppression. But now it appears we have no law but the will of the judge."[73] He strongly suggested that Congress impeach Marshall. The two leading Democratic newspapers, the Philadelphia *Aurora* and the *Enquirer,* called out in loud tones for the immediate impeachment of the "impostor," Marshall.[74] Had it not been for the fact that we were on the verge of war with Great Britain, the Administration might well have punished the Chief Justice.

After a careful study of all the available documents, Professor Abernethy concludes that the Burr conspiracy was "so portentous that it seems reasonable to say that next to the Confederate War it posed the greatest threat of dismemberment which the American Union has ever faced."[75] Burr died on September 14, 1836. In the early part of June of that same year, it was thought that he was dying, and the question was asked of him: "Whether in the expedition to the southwest he had designed a separation of the Union?" His reply in no way unravelled the mystery: "No, I would as soon have thought of taking possession of the moon, and informing my friends that I intended to divide it among them."[76]

PRELUDE TO EMBARGO

As Burr slipped into oblivion the focus was set once again on the titanic struggle between the Union Jack and the Tricolor. This upheaval, which was to last for twenty-two years, presented our eighteen-year-old republic with both a boon and a challenge. The boon came in the form of trade. The total value of our exports for the years 1805, 1806, and 1807, came to $307,696,365.[77] The United States, as the most important neutral carrier, was enjoying

---

[73]Jefferson to William Thompson, September 26, 1807, *Jefferson MSS.*
[74]Beveridge, Albert J., *The Life of John Marshall,* Vol. III, p. 532.
[75]Thomas P. Abernethy, *The Burr Conspiracy* (New York: Oxford University Press, 1954), p. 274.
[76]Walter F. McCaleb, *The Aaron Burr Conspiracy,* Vol. III, p. 369. John Randolph saw Burr as a "man . . . enveloped in mystery," who if he did hang for treason would "contrive to make posterity doubt whether he was ever executed." Randolph to Joseph H. Nicholson, March 25, 1807, *Joseph H. Nicholson MSS.* Jefferson allocated $8,737.11 for the prosecution of Burr. He turned this over to the Attorney-General. Jefferson's Memorandum to the House and Senate, January 8, 1808, *Jefferson MSS.*
[77]Timothy Pitkin, *A Statistical View of the Commerce of the United States of America* (Hartford: Charles Hosmer & Co., 1816), p. 136.

a lush prosperity. The challenge came when the theories of Grotius and Vattel succumbed to the rule of claw and fang. Starting with the summer of 1806, international law took an extended vacation. American merchant ships were made to run the gauntlet between the English Orders in Council, and Napoleon's Continental System. Any ship of the United States that attempted to trade with Great Britain, or even allowed herself to be searched by the English, was fair game for French warships. Any American vessel that attempted to trade with forts under Napoleon's control without first having paid tribute to Albion, was subject to seizure by British frigates.

With an ineffective navy lopsided with gunboats, and an army commanded by a spy, Jefferson could hardly retaliate in a manner commensurate with the dignity of Old Glory. On December 17, 1807, a little less than two months after Marshall had delivered his last opinion in the Burr case, Jefferson submitted to his cabinet the gist of his embargo plan which would be contained in his forthcoming message to Congress:

The whole world is thus laid under interdict by these two nations, and our vessels, their cargoes and crews are to be taken by the one or the other . . . If therefore on leaving our harbors we are certainly to lose them, is it not better . . . to keep them at home? This is submitted to the wisdom of Congress, who alone are competent to provide a remedy.[78]

Jefferson, unlike his predecessor, was the master of his party. And in the 10th Congress which convened on October 26, 1807, the Democrats controlled the Senate by 29 to 5 and the House by 110 to 30. The support of Jefferson's embargo became an act of faith for all good Democrats.[79]

Before the message reached the Congress, Gallatin, Secretary of the Treasury, was the sole cabinet member who sought to restrain his chief. He wrote Jefferson that he thought that

---

[78]Henry Adams, *History of the United States During the Second Administration of Thomas Jefferson* (New York: Charles Scribners & Sons, 1921), Vol. II, pp. 87, 169.

[79]Louis M. Sears, *Jefferson and the Embargo* (North Carolina: Duke University Press, 1927), p. 239. The Essex decision, handed down by the Lords Commissioners of Appeal on June 22, 1805, marked a deterioration in Anglo-American affairs. For example, American merchantment could no longer carry wine from Barcelona, land it at Salem, pay duty, reload it and sail for Havana. This was a drastic change, for the British had decided in the Polly case of 1800 that the above example of broken voyage legalized the trade. See Bradford Perkins, "Sir William Scott and the Essex," *William and Mary Quarterly*, April 1956, Vol. XIII, pp. 171-179.

an embargo for a limited time will at this moment be preferable in itself and less objectionable in Congress. In every point of view privations, sufferings, revenue, effect on the enemy, politics at home . . . I prefer war to a permanent embargo . . . As to the hope that it may have an effect on the negotiation with Mr. Rose, or induce England to treat us better, I think it entirely groundless.[80]

Out of deference to Gallatin, Jefferson called an emergency cabinet meeting for ten o'clock in the morning. No notes were kept, but by twelve noon of the same day, December 18, 1807, Jefferson's original message, without the Gallatin amendment, was read to the Congress. The Senate passed the President's embargo by a vote of 22 to 6, that very day. The House concurred three days later by an 82 to 44 decision.

Jefferson signed the Embargo Act on December 22. Four days later, Henry Rose arrived in the United States on a special mission. He came well-instructed. George Canning, His Majesty's Foreign Minister, had authorized him to state that:

Admiral Berkeley has been recalled from his command . . . that His Majesty is prepared to discharge those men who were taken by this unauthorized act out of the American frigate . . . but he requires a formal disavowal of . . . Commodore Barron . . . in encouraging deserters from His Majesty's Service . . .[81]

This Jefferson refused to do. Since Rose's instructions were inflexible, he remained here three months, returning to England in March of 1808. Before he left, Secretary of State Madison gave him a confidential report:

Madison observed that since England has thus publicly disclaimed the right of search of national ships for deserters, and Admiral Berkeley has been recalled . . . although a more formal mode of terminating the business would have been more acceptable to this Government, it would consider itself as satisfied on the restoration of the seamen . . .[82]

No sooner had Jefferson signed the Embargo Act, than loopholes to its enforcement appeared. As a result, Congress passed two sup-

---

[80]Gallatin to Jefferson, December 18, 1807, *Gallatin MSS.*
[81]Instructions to G. H. Rose, October 24, 1807, *British Archives, Henry Adams Transcripts.* John Adams thoroughly agreed with Gallatin's view of limited embargo. John Adams to John Quincy Adams, January 8, 1808, *John Adams MSS.*
[82]Rose to Canning, March 22, 1808, *British State Papers, Henry Adams Transcripts.*

plementary acts, one of January 9, the other on March 12, 1808. The meaning of the Embargo was now lucidly clear: it prohibited sending out of the United States, by sea or by land, any goods either the produce of the United States or re-exportations. In the debate on the supplementary acts, Barent Gardenier, a member of the House of Representatives from New York, accused Jefferson of a pro-French bias:

I ask the intelligent and candid men of this House whether to prevent the farmers of Vermont from selling their pigs in Canada is calculated to increase or diminish our essential resources; whether the object which the President professed to have in view is counteracted by a traffic of this kind . . . stop your present course. Do not go on forging chains to fasten us to the imperial Conqueror . . . [83]

The accusation that Jefferson was a Francophile, so thoroughly advertised by the Federalist press as well as by Timothy Pickering, Josiah Quincy, and the entire Essex junto, is not demonstrable in the extant documents. Minister Turreau reported that the embargo was but another proof of the United States' "falsity in regard to France." He was sure that "the United States, whatever insults they may have to endure, will never make war on Great Britain unless she attacks them." The French minister concluded that "the federal government intends today more than ever to hold an equal balance between France and England."[84]

Senator Timothy Pickering now entered into secret negotiations with Great Britain. On March 13, 1808, Pickering advised the Court of St. James: ". . . to bear patiently the wrongs we do ourselves. In one word, amidst the irritations engendered by hatred and folly, to maintain a dignified composure, and to abstain from war, relying on this, that whatever disposition exists to provoke, there is none to commence a war on the part of the United States."[85]

---

[83]*Annals of Congress, 10th Cong., 2nd Sess. 1808*, Vol. XVIII, p. 1654.
[84]Turreau to Champagny, May 20, 1808, *French Archives, Henry Adams Transcripts*.
[85]Pickering to Rose, March 13, 1808, Henry Adams (ed.), *Documents Relative to New England Federalism* (1800-1815), p. 366. The Essex junto was a group of New England ultra-Federalists, most of whom resided in Essex County, Mass. They talked in terms of nullification and secession. By some sort of historical irony, the Logan Act, which prohibited unauthorized persons to negotiate with foreign countries, was passed in 1799 under Pickering's inspiration.

Two days before Pickering penned the above words, Jefferson had written in quite a different vein to his Secretary of State:

I take it to be an universal opinion that war will become preferable to a continuance of the embargo after a certain time. Should we not then avail ourselves of the intervening period to procure a retraction of the obnoxious decrees peaceably, if possible?[86]

Persuading himself that Jefferson was bound by a secret treaty with Napoleon to effect the ruin of England, Pickering forged ahead in his efforts to form a British party in New England.[87] On February 16, 1808, he wrote a letter to the Governor of Massachusetts, intended for official communication to the state legislature:

Has the French Emperor declared that he will have no neutrals? Has he required that our ports, like those of his vassal States in Europe, be shut against British Commerce . . . our country is in imminent danger . . . it is essential to the public safety that the blind confidence in our rulers should cease . . .

The Senator from Massachusetts, in words reminiscent of Federalist schemes in 1804, stated that it was essential that:

The state legislatures should know the facts and the reasons on which important general laws are founded, and especially that those states whose farms are on the ocean and whose harvests are gathered in every sea, should immediately and seriously consider how to preserve them.[88]

Henry Adams is certain that to "those Federalist leaders who had been acquainted with the plans of 1804, the meaning of this allusion to the commercial states could not be doubtful."[89] With the publication of the Pickering letter on the eve of the Massachusetts election, the issue between the British and American party was sharply drawn. James Sullivan, Democratic governor, who charged Pickering with sedition and rebellion, was reelected by a majority of 1200 in a total vote of 81,000, but in the state legislature, the Federalists gained a decided majority. They immediately elected James Lloyd

---

[86]Jefferson to Madison, March 11, 1808, *Jefferson MSS.*
[87]Jefferson admitted that the "Embargo which appears to hit France and England equally is for a fact more prejudicial to the latter." Turreau to Champagny, June 28, 1808, as quoted by Lawrence S. Kaplan, "Jefferson, the Napoleonic Wars, and the Balance of Power," *William and Mary Quarterly,* April, 1957, Vol. XIV, p. 201.
[88]Henry Adams, *History of the United States,* Vol. IV, pp. 238-239.
[89]*Ibid.,* p. 239. James Sullivan, a Democrat, and Governor of Massachusetts at the time, refused to communicate the Pickering letter to the legislature.

to the Senate to succeed John Quincy Adams. Resolutions were adopted condemning the Embargo.[90]

LETTERS FROM HENRY

In seven years American politics had undergone a revolution. In 1801 the Federalists were the national party of the United States. In 1808 they were a British faction in league with George Canning. The progress of Rose's alliance with Timothy Pickering and his Essex junto was highlighted by the reports of John Henry who visited New England in March, 1808. Henry, an Englishman, sent his dispatches to the Governor of Lower Canada, Sir James Craig. Craig forwarded them to the British War Secretary, Lord Castlereagh. Craig assured Castlereagh that Henry was "a gentleman of considerable ability, and, I believe, well able to form a correct judgment on what he sees passing." Besides, Henry had "resided for some time in the United States, and is well acquainted with some of the leading people of Boston." Henry, after attending "a private meeting of several of the principal characters of Boston," reported on March 18 that the fear of war had vanished. Jefferson meant to rely solely on the Embargo. However, continued Henry:

It is . . . to be expected that the evil will produce its own cure, and that in a few months more of suffering and privation of all the benefits of commerce the people of the New England states will be ready to withdraw from the confederacy, establish a separate government, and adopt a policy congenial with their interests and happiness . . ."[91]

If New England had been as loyal as the Middle states and the South in enforcing the Embargo, it is possible that it would have been successful. Debates in Parliament, private correspondence and articles in English reviews, all bear witness to the effectiveness of Jefferson's Embargo. All the above sources show that the centers of manufactures and commerce were the first to suffer. Parliament

---

[90]*Ibid.*, p. 242. John Quincy Adams had gone over to the Democrats and supported the Embargo Act. As soon as John Quincy Adams was ousted as Senator, Governor Sullivan asked Jefferson to give him a "foreign appointment of respectability." Adams was sent in 1809 as our minister to Russia. Governor Sullivan to Jefferson, June 3, 1808, *Jefferson MSS.*

[91]Sir James Craig to Lord Castlereagh, April 10, 1808, *British Archives, Henry Adams Transcripts.* John Quincy Adams kept Jefferson informed of the goings-on of Henry. Jefferson to John Adams, April 20, 1812, *Jefferson MSS.*

received heartrending protests from London, Liverpool, and Manchester. In Yorkshire, sixty thousand looms were reported to be idle. In the Embargo year, the poor-rate rose in Manchester from an average of £4000 to £49,000. The chart of British exports for 1808 shows a loss of £6,604,774 over the 1807 trade to the United States. Unfortunately for the effectiveness of the Embargo, the opening up of South America in 1808 enabled Great Britain to make up this trade deficit at least to some extent.[92]

Southern patriotism in refusing to export cotton produced real tension in the English cotton industry. This tension was reflected in parliamentary petitions from thousands of His Majesty's cotton-weavers. One feels a new respect for Jefferson's Embargo when it is realized that it curtailed the manufacture of liquor in Great Britain. This was something that all the Kaiser's submarines were to fail to achieve. The fact is that British corn, grain, and meal imports diminished from 920,435 pounds in 1807 to 146,119 in 1808, and English distillers were restricted in the manufacture of grain and malt liquors.

In spite of Latin American trade and smuggling operations in Canada, the United States was still Great Britain's richest export market. British goods to the value of £12,000,000 entered America in 1807. In 1808, the exports shrunk to £5,000,000, a deserving tribute to the Embargo as a weapon of economic warfare. In the parliamentary debates of May, 1808, George III's loyal opposition made the point that since the Orders in Council "the diminution of our commerce may fairly be estimated at £14,000,000."[93] The editors of the *Edinburgh Review* felt the pressure of the Embargo. They remarked that were it not for "the increased communication with Brazil and Spanish America . . . our loss of trade in consequence of the orders would probably have been more than double."[94]

---

[92]British North America actually benefited from the embargo. Vermont and New York poured their produce into the Canadas so that the exports from the St. Lawrence in 1808 were doubled from the average of the previous five years. Alfred L. Burt, *The United States, Great Britain, and British North America*, pp. 240-241.
[93]Louis M. Sears, *Jefferson and the Embargo*, p. 299. This material on the effectiveness of the embargo has been taken from Sears. See Chapters VI, VII, VIII. Since the British controlled the sea lanes, the effect of the Embargo on France was nil. Southern states were hit the hardest but were the most loyal. The Middle states were lukewarm as regards loyalty. New York and Delaware were just behind New England in disloyalty.
[94]*Edinburgh Review*, July, 1809, Vol. XIV, p. 450.

Henry Adams' researches brought him to the conclusion that:

Probably at least five thousand families of workingmen were reduced to pauperism by the embargo and the decrees of Napoleon; but these sufferers, who possessed not a vote among them and had been in no way party to the acts of either government, were the only real friends of Jefferson could hope to find among the people of New England; and his embargo ground them into the dust in order to fatten the squires and shipowners who had devised the Orders in Council. If the English laborers rioted, they were shot; if the West Indian slaves could not be fed, they died. The embargo served only to lower the wages and the moral standard of the laboring classes throughout the British empire, and to prove their helplessness.[95]

The Federalists claimed that the Embargo was ruining America: "Our merchants complain of the embargo as a serious evil; it oppresses our seamen, many of whom are in want of bread, and our farmers feel its pressure in the reduced price of the produce of their lands."[96] George Cabot wrote his friend Timothy Pickering on April 5, 1808 that ". . . although our people now begin to suffer very much from the Embargo, yet it appears that other feelings are stronger, and other passions govern them."[97] Cabot demanded that ". . . our government . . . raise the embargo, and leave commerce free; but this they know would offend France, and therefore they refuse to do it."[98]

Shipping interests were dealt a severe blow by the Embargo. On April 1, 1808, there were 108 ships, 117 brigs, and 71 schooners tied up in New York harbor. In ports south of New York, there were 123 ships, 140 brigs, and 150 schooners; and in ports east of New York, 50 ships, 109 brigs, and 100 schooners. The number of men, apart from seamen, who lost their businesses as a result of the above tie-up, came to 8,712. On September 1, 1808, 29 Boston-owned ships, 31 brigs, and 11 schooners were embargoed in that city. These vessels would have employed 600 seamen. According to the American Register there were on January 1, 1809, a total of 625 ships lying in the harbors of Boston, Charleston, Salem, and New Bedford.

---

[95]Henry Adams, *History of the United States*, Vol. IV, p. 330.
[96]William Plumer, Jr., *The Life of William Plumer*, pp. 364-365.
[97]George Cabot to Pickering, April 5, 1808, Henry C. Lodge, *Life and Letters of George Cabot* (Boston: Little, Brown & Co., 1877), p. 391.
[98]*Ibid.*, p. 391.

The cost of the Embargo can never be definitely known. After six months, the Carlisle, Pa. *Herald* and the New England *Palladium* computed the loss to be $48,000,000. The Federalist James A. Bayard declared in the Senate on February 14, 1809, that the national treasury had lost at least $15,000,000 as a result of the Embargo. He calculated the country's loss to be $40,000,000. Congressman Edward Livermore of Massachusetts estimated the annual loss to be $150,000,000, but the cost of war is also very high. Neither can be accurately determined. When war finally did come, it had the same effects as the Embargo: the ruin of commerce, the stimulation of manufacture, and hindrance to agriculture. A point of interest is that in every year of the War of 1812, save one, the value of exports from the United States was greater than in 1808. The exceptional year was 1814 when exports sank to $6,927,441, or about a third of the $22,430,960 in 1808.[99]

A presidential election during the embargo crisis was not at all to the liking of the Democrats. In August of 1808, the Secretary of the Treasury warned the President:

There is almost an equal chance that if propositions from Great Britain, or other events, do not put it in our power to raise the embargo before the first of October we will lose the presidential election. I think that at this moment the Western states, Virginia, South Carolina, and perhaps Georgia are the only sound states, and that we will have a doubtful contest in every other.[100]

In the tradition of George Washington, Jefferson announced, after his second inauguration, that he would not run for a third term. From then on, he made no secret of his wish that Madison should be his successor. On January 21, 1808, the Virginia legislature held two caucuses. The first, attended by 119 members, unanimously recommended Madison. The other, attended by 60, gave all but ten votes to Monroe. On January 23, 1808, Democratic members of both Houses of Congress held a caucus in the Senate chamber. Although 94 Senators and Representatives attended, only

---

[99]American losses due to the Embargo Act are taken from Walter W. Jennings, *The American Embargo: 1807-1809* (Iowa City: Iowa University Press, 1921), pp. 222-230.

[100]Gallatin to Jefferson, August 6, 1808, *Jefferson MSS.* Three months before he received the above letter, Jefferson wrote: ". . . there will be no question who is to be my successor, of this be assured whatever may be said by newspapers and private correspondence." Jefferson to DuPont de Nemours, May 2, 1808, *Jefferson MSS.* Jefferson meant Madison.

89 votes were cast. Madison received 83 votes, George Clinton 3, and Monroe 3. On the first ballot for a candidate for vice-president, George Clinton received 79, John Langdon of New Hampshire 5, Henry Dearborn, Secretary of War, 3, and John Quincy Adams 1. Madison and Clinton were formally declared nominated.[101]

Some twenty-five or thirty Federalist leaders from seven states north of the Potomac, plus South Carolina, held a secret conference in New York during August. The question at issue was whether they should support George Clinton as the best means of defeating Madison. Rufus King's view prevailed, and the decision was made to nominate Charles Cotesworth Pinckney and King.[102]

The number of states in 1808 was the same as in 1804— seventeen. Electors were chosen by the legislature in Vermont, Massachusetts, Connecticut, New York, Delaware, South Carolina, and Georgia. In New Hampshire, Rhode Island, Pennsylvania, Virginia, and Ohio, they were chosen by the people on a general ticket. In Maryland, North Carolina, Kentucky, and Tennessee, they were selected by districts in a popular vote.

When the Federalists met with DeWitt Clinton in New York during August they soon realized that he would not cooperate with them. Thus all hope of a coalition was given up by the Federalists. Madison had nothing to fear as soon as it became apparent that his opponents were divided. Another factor that worked to the advantage of Madison was that the majority of the state legislatures had been chosen in the spring or summer when the Embargo was still comparatively popular. In New York the opponents of the Embargo were very strong. It is conceivable that in a popular election the nineteen electoral votes of that state might have been taken

---

[101]Edward Stanwood, *A History of the Presidency,* pp. 86-96. Randolph and the Quids backed Monroe. Monroe's treaty of 1805, since it did not contain a British promise to forego impressment, was not even submitted to the Senate by Jefferson. For copy of the Treaty, see Monroe and Pinckney to Madison, January 16, 1807, *Dispatches, Department of State.* William Pinckney had been sent to London to help Monroe negotiate the Treaty of 1806. The Quids and Monroe had the feeling that both the Pinckney mission and Jefferson's withholding the treaty from the Senate, were intended to hurt Monroe's presidential chances. Monroe remained a "spectator" during the campaign of 1808. Jefferson having placated Monroe, received a letter from him wherein Monroe stated that he was "perfectly satisfied that you never meant to injure me." Monroe to Jefferson, March 22, 1808, *Jefferson MSS.*

[102]Samuel E. Morrison, "The First National Nominating Convention, 1808," *American Historical Review,* Vol. XVII, July, 1912, pp. 744-763.

from Madison. In this event, Pennsylvania would have decided the election. Eighty-eight electoral votes were needed to win. New England, New York, and Delaware represented sixty-seven. North Carolina and Maryland were so uncertain that if Pennsylvania had gone Federalist, they would probably have followed her.[103]

The wave of Federalist success was stopped short when it reached New York. DeWitt Clinton was able to garner six of New York's nineteen electoral votes for his uncle, George Clinton. Although George Clinton was running as vice-presidential candidate on Madison's ticket, he was also the presidential candidate of certain Northern Democrats who opposed a perpetuation of the Virginia Dynasty. The presidential election of 1808 was, therefore, unique in the fact that "Clinton remained Madison's vice-presidential running-mate while campaigning against him for the presidency."[104] The remaining thirteen of New York's electoral votes went to Madison. At the October gubernatorial election in Pennsylvania, Duane's candidate, Simon Synder, won out by a majority of twenty thousand votes. Synder's triumph enabled Madison's followers to drive hesitant Democrats back into the fold. All of Pennsylvania's twenty electoral votes were captured by Madison.

The final results of the contest were decisive. Madison received 122 electoral votes, Charles C. Pinckney 47, and George Clinton, 6. Pinckney took all of Delaware's 3 and picked up 2 of Maryland's 11, and 3 of North Carolina's 14. In the contest for the vice-presidency, Clinton received 113, James Madison 3, John Langdon 9, James Monroe 3, and Rufus King 47. Thirty-nine of Pinckney's 47 votes came from New England.

The Embargo had been in effect a little over a year when Jefferson "saw the necessity of abandoning it, and instead of effecting our purposes by this peaceful weapon, we must fight it out or break the Union."[105] The Administration had done its very best to

---

[103]Henry Adams, *History of the United States*, Vol. IV, pp. 284-286. Both Wilson C. Nicholas, Democratic Congressman from Virginia, and David Erskine, British Minister to the United States, felt that there was a good chance that New York and Pennsylvania would desert Madison. Philip N. Nicholas to W. C. Nicholas, March 17, 1808, *W. C. Nicholas MSS.* Erskine to Canning, November 15, 1808, *British State Papers, 1808-1814, Henry Adams Transcripts*, Vol. II.

[104]Irving Brant, *James Madison: Secretary of State, 1800-1809* (New York: Bobbs Merrill Co., 1953), p. 431.

[105]Jefferson to William B. Giles, December 25, 1825, *Jefferson MSS.*

develop opinion in support of the Embargo by favorable newspaper accounts which exalted its beneficial effects on manufactures. It had at times lightened the operation of the Embargo through permits granted to influential men. Party discipline had accounted for hundreds of town and state resolutions favorable to the Embargo. But the opposition made even better propaganda. Federalists organized meetings of sailors, fishermen, and other sufferers. Vehement petitions were drawn up at these gatherings. Smuggling developed into armed opposition. Distinguished Americans declared the Embargo unconstitutional. Public opinion supported violations of the law. Governors refused to enforce the Embargo. Town meetings condemned the measure. Newspapers advised resistance, and threats of disunion came thick and fast from New England.[106]

Jefferson never forgot the violence of the last few months of his administration:

How powerfully did we feel the energy of this organization in the case of the Embargo. I felt the foundations of the government shaken under my feet by the New England townships.[107]

Sixteen years later, Jefferson wrote that his conversation with John Quincy Adams in 1809 was still too "deeply engraved in my mind . . . ever to be forgotten." Adams, recalled Jefferson,

Spoke then of the dissatisfaction of the Eastern portion of our confederacy with the restraints of the Embargo . . . that certain citizens of the Eastern states . . . were in negotiation with agents of the British government . . . that without formally declaring their separation from the Union of the States, they should withdraw from all aid and obedience to them . . . I then recommended to yield to the necessity of a repeal of the Embargo, and to endeavor to supply its place by the best substitute, in which they could procure a general concurrence.[108]

On March 1, 1809, three days before Jefferson turned over the keys of office to Madison, Congress repealed the Embargo. A non-intercourse law was substituted which legalized American commerce

---

[106]Samuel E. Morison, *The Life and Letters of Harrison Gray Otis: Federalist 1765-1848* (Boston: Houghton Mifflin Co., 1913), Vol. I, pp. 323-325. Otis was a member of the Massachusetts State Legislature in 1808. He was a prominent member of the Essex Junto. He was for nullification of the Embargo, and looked on secession only as a last resort.
[107]Jefferson to J. C. Cabell, February 2, 1816, *Jefferson MSS.*
[108]Jefferson to William B. Giles, December 25, 1825, *Jefferson MSS.*

with all parts of the world except those under British and French control. The British Minister to the United States, David M. Erskine, was delighted with the non-intercourse bill and informed the British Foreign Office that

I conceive that great advantages may be reaped from it by England as she has the command of the seas, and can procure through neutrals any of the produce of this country . . . whereas France will obtain but little, and at a great expense and risk . . . it is thoroughly understood that the whole measure is a mere subterfuge to extricate themselves from the embarrassments of the embargo system, and is never intended to be enforced.[100]

---

[100]Erskine to Canning, February 10 and 13, 1809, *British Archives, Henry Adams Transcripts,* Canning was the British Foreign Secretary. Gallatin realized the ineffectiveness of a non-importation act. Gallatin to Joseph H. Nicholson, October 18, 1808, *Joseph H. Nicholson MSS.* In the repeal of the Embargo, Jefferson was conscious of the economic motive: "We have taken off the Embargo . . . because 50 millions of exports annually sacrificed are the treble of what war would cost us." Jefferson to Du Pont de Nemours, March 2, 1809, *Jefferson MSS.*

6

America Fights Britain Again

Jᴀᴍᴇs Mᴀᴅɪsᴏɴ ᴘᴀɪᴅ a silent tribute to the Embargo when, "dressed in a full suit of cloth of American manufacture," he took the presidential inaugural oath on March 4, 1809, before a crowd of ten thousand people. A large audience gathered in the new and beautiful House of Representatives to hear Madison's address. They were disappointed, for his speech was totally inaudible. Those who read it in the newspapers were informed that the depression caused by the Embargo could in no way be charged to the Democratic party. Furthermore, it "has been the true glory of the United States to cultivate peace by observing justice, and to entitle themselves to the respect of the nations at war by fulfilling their neutral obligations with the most scrupulous impartiality." How long the unjust edicts of the belligerents would be prolonged "cannot be anticipated." The United States, continued Madison, desired "to cherish peace and friendly intercourse with all nations having corresponding dispositions; and to prefer in all cases amicable discussion and reasonable accommodation of differences to a decision of them by an appeal to arms." The co-author of the Virginia and Kentucky resolutions concluded by promising "to respect the rights and authorities reserved to the states."[1]

On March 1, Wilson Cary Nicholas warned the president-elect that a cabal headed by William Leib, Samuel Smith, and William B. Giles were determined to block his appointment of Gallatin as Secretary of State. Bent on avoiding a party schism, Madison was told that if Robert Smith, brother of Samuel, received the Treasury, Gallatin could be Secretary of State. Madison was agreeable to this, but when Gallatin learned that, although Secretary of State, he would still, in effect, have to manage the Treasury Department, he de-

---

[1]*The Diary of John Quincy Adams,* March 4, 1809, p. 544.

98

clined. The result was that Robert Smith became Secretary of State, and Gallatin retained his post as Secretary of the Treasury.[2] The fifty-six-year-old William Eustis of Boston, who had served in Congress during Jefferson's first administration, was chosen to serve as Secretary of War in place of Henry Dearborn. The latter had retired in February to become Collector of the Port of Boston. Paul Hamilton, one-time Governor of South Carolina, succeeded Robert Smith in the Navy Department.

No sooner was the cabinet business settled than Madison was confronted with the news of the vigorous advance of Federalism in New England. The gubernatorial election in Massachusetts saw the Federalist Christopher Gore triumph over the Democrat, James Sullivan, by a majority of three thousand. The new legislature was even more Federalist than the old one had been.

New Hampshire, Rhode Island, New York, and Maryland elected Federalist legislatures. The legislatures of Massachusetts and Connecticut declared Acts of Congress unconstitutional and refused to execute them. The legislature of Pennsylvania authorized Governor Synder to resist by armed force a mandate of the Supreme Court.[3] Nevertheless, the Union was secure, at least for the time. The Federalist leaders, rejoicing over the Embargo repeal, were no longer contemplating secession. Secret agent John Henry, reported that "an unpopular war . . . can alone produce a sudden separation of any section of this country from the common head."[4]

In spite of Federalist newspapers that asserted that the Nonintercourse Act was just as ruinous as the Embargo, New England shipping was getting on its feet again. The markets at Lisbon, Gothenburg, Riga, and the Spanish ports in America were almost as convenient as London or Havre for the sale of American produce. Massachusetts alone owned more than a third of the American-registered tonnage, and the returns for 1809 proved that her profits were enormous. The manufactures of New England, created by the Embargo, brought even more wealth to that section than its commercial enterprises. In 1807, the Embargo year, New England pos-

---

[2]Gallatin to Jefferson, November 8, 1809, *Jefferson MSS*. Caesar A. Rodney of Delaware continued as Attorney General and Gideon Granger of Connecticut as Postmaster General.
[3]Henry Adams, *A History of the United States of America*, Vol. IV, pp. 12-13.
[4]Henry to Craig, March 13, 1809, *John Henry MSS*.

sessed 8,000 spindles. In less than two years the number was increased to 80,000. The Middle and Southern states were obliged to buy New England manufactured articles or go without them. There is no doubt that the economic motive played a vital role in cementing the Union in 1809.[5]

MADISON AND NAPOLEON

Two weeks after Madison was sworn in as America's fourth president, Turreau reported to his Minister for Foreign Affairs that

You will have judged from my last dispatches that the Embargo Law would be repealed. It has been so despite my efforts to maintain it . . . I have informed your Excellency of the disunion projects shown by some of the Northern states. Their avowed opposition to the continuance of the embargo, and their threats to resist its execution, terrified Congress to such a degree that the dominant party became divided, and the feebleness of Mr. Jefferson sanctioned the last and most shameful act of his Administration . . . I am convinced there is nothing to hope from these people.[6]

The British minister, whose conciliatory efforts had something to do with the action of Congress, made Turreau's anger the subject of a special dispatch to Canning. He doubtless hoped it would move the British Foreign Secretary in the direction of a *modus vivendi* with the United States. He recorded in his dispatch that the

French Minister it seems is so much offended at the Non-intercourse Law which has been lately passed, and is so little pleased with the general disposition, as he conceives it, of the new Administration of the United States towards France, that he has quitted the city, having previously given up his house and removed all his furniture, without calling either upon the new President or any members of the Administration, as was his uniform custom in former years, and as is always done by foreign ministers.[7]

Robert Smith informed David Erskine that if Britain would repeal her Orders in Council, the United States would restore intercourse with His Majesty's government, and assert its rights against France. During the rest of March, Turreau disconsolately watched the work-

[5] *American State Papers, Commerce and Navigation* (Washington: Gales & Seaton, 1832), Vol. VII, p. 812, pp. 897-898.
[6] Turreau to Champagny, March 19, 1809, *French Archives, Henry Adams Transcripts.* Louis Turreau was the French Minister in Washington and Jean Champagny was the French Minister for Foreign Affairs.
[7] Erskine to Canning, March 17, 1809, *British Archives, Henry Adams Transcripts.*

5. James Monroe

NILES' WEEKLY REGISTER.

No. 25 OF VOL. VII.]·   BALTIMORE, SATURDAY, FEBRUARY 18, 1815.   [WHOLE NO. 181.

Hæc olim meminisse juvabit.—VIRGIL.

Printed and published by H. NILES, South-st. next door to the Merchants' Coffee House, at $5 per ann.

Glorious News!

Orleans saved and peace concluded.

"The star spangled banner in triumph shall wave
"O'er the land of the free and the home of the brave."

The matters detailed and recorded in the present number of the REGISTER, are of incalculable importance. The enemy has retired in disgrace from New-Orleans, and peace was signed at *Ghent* on the 24th December, on honorable terms: At least, so we believe from the *dolefuls* of the British ministerialists. For particulars, see the several heads.

In our next paper, as we hope by that time to be a little more composed under those joyful tidings, we shall endeavor to arrange a great mass of interesting matter that lies over for insertion.

Who would not be an American? Long live the republic! All hail! last asylum of oppressed humanity! Peace is signed in the arms of victory!

§·The present number was held back on the hope of obtaining a copy of the TREATY. See page 397.

New Orleans preserved.

Copy of a letter from major-general Jackson to the secretary of war, dated

Head-quarters, 7th military district,
Camp 4 miles below New-Orleans, 19th Jan. 1815.

Last night at 12 o'clock, the enemy precipitately decamped and returned to their boats, leaving behind him, under medical attendance, eighty of his wounded including two officers, 14 pieces of his heavy artillery, and a quantity of shot, having destroyed much of his powder. Such was the situation of the ground which he abandoned, and of that through which he retired, protected by canals, redoubts, entrenchments and swamps on his right, and the river on his left, that I could not without encountering a risk, which true policy did not seem to require, or to authorize, attempt to annoy him much on his retreat. We took only eight prisoners.

Whether it is the purpose of the enemy to abandon the expedition altogether, or renew his efforts at some other point, I do not pretend to determine with positiveness. In my own mind, however, there is but little doubt that his last exertions have been made in this quarter, at any rate for the present season, and by the *next* I hope we shall be fully prepared for him. In this belief I am strengthened not only by the prodigious loss he has sustained at the position he had just quitted, but by the failure of his fleet to pass fort St. Philip.

His loss on this ground, since the debarkation of his troops, as stated by the last prisoners and deserters, and as confirmed by many additional circumstances, must have exceeded four thousand; and was greater in the action of the 8th than was estimated, from the most correct data then in his possession, by the inspector-general, whose report has been forwarded to you. We succeeded, on the 8th, in getting from the enemy about 1000 stand of arms of various descriptions.

Since the action of the 8th, the enemy have been allowed very little respite—my artillery from both sides of the river being constantly employed, till the night, and indeed until the *hour* of their retreat, in annoying them. No doubt they thought it quite time to quit a position in which so little rest could be found.

I am advised by major Overton, who commands at fort St. Philip, in a letter of the 18th, that the enemy having bombarded his fort for 8 or 9 days from 13 inch mortars without effect, had, on the morning of that day, retired. I have little doubt that he would have been able to have sunk their vessels had they attempted to run by.

Giving the proper weight to all these considerations, I believe you will not think me too sanguine in the belief that *Louisiana* is now clear of its enemy. I hope, however, I need not assure you, that wherever I command, such a belief shall never occasion any relaxation in the measures for resistance. I am but too sensible that the moment when the enemy is opposing us, is not the most proper to provide for them.

I have the honor to be, &c.
ANDREW JACKSON,
Maj. gen. comd'g.

P. S. On the 18th our prisoners on shore were delivered us, an exchange having been previously agreed to. Those who are on board the fleet will be delivered at Petit Coquille—after which I shall still have in my hands an excess of several hundred.

20th—Mr. Shields,* purser in the navy, has to-day taken 54 prisoners; among them are four officers.

A. J.

*I have the honor to claim the gallant *Shields* as one of my most respected friends. I have letters from him of the 16th and 17th ult. He says, "the day after the gun-boats were taken I was sent down under a flag of truce to ascertain the fate of our officers and men, with power to negociate an exchange, especially for the wounded. But the enemy would make no terms—they treated the flag with contempt, and myself and the surgeon, who was with me, as prisoners, until the 17th inst. He is now lowered his tone, and begs the exchange that we offered. Defeat has humbled the arrogance of the enemy, WHO HAD PROMISED HIS SOLDIERS FORTY-EIGHT HOURS PILLAGE AND RAPINE OF THE CITY OF NEW-ORLEANS!!"

"Our beloved Jackson deserves immortality. He was always in the hottest and thickest of the fight; and although his health is much impaired he still sticks to his post. We pray the Almighty to spare him.

"Every movement of the enemy indicates a retreat. I am just starting on a secret business to avenge myself. If I succeed, the affair will be creditable to me—if I fail, the world, at least, shall say "there lived a man."

We have not yet the particulars of Mr. Shields' successful enterprize; but, I flatter myself when they come to hand, they will redound no little to the honor of my generous high-minded friend, and perhaps add a ray of glory to the blaze that encircles the American navy. Mr. S. was a volunteer.

He states that our five gun-boats had a complement of 200 men—they were attacked by forty-five boats carrying 1200 men. The fight against such fearful odds lasted one hour and fifty minutes—we had only five killed and thirty wounded; the enemy acknowledge a loss of 100; but Mr. Shields adds "we may with perfect safety double that number."   [Ed. Reg.

6. From the *Niles Weekly Register*, Feb. 18, 1815

7. Andrew Jackson

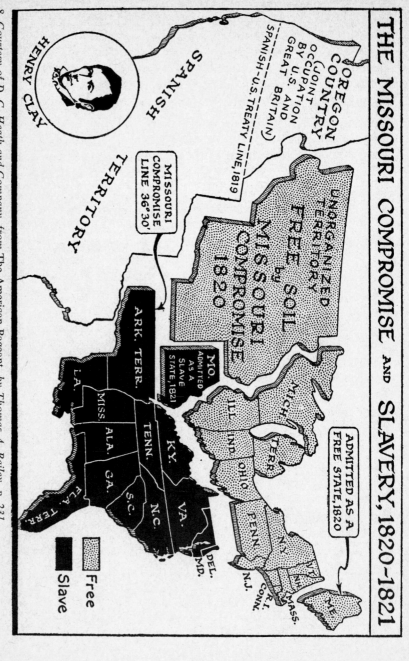

THE MISSOURI COMPROMISE AND SLAVERY, 1820–1821

OREGON COUNTRY (JOINT OCCUPATION BY U.S. AND GREAT BRITAIN)

SPANISH-U.S. TREATY LINE, 1819

SPANISH

TERRITORY

HENRY CLAY

MISSOURI COMPROMISE LINE 36°30'

UNORGANIZED TERRITORY FREE SOIL by MISSOURI COMPROMISE 1820

MO. ADMITTED AS A SLAVE STATE, 1821

ADMITTED AS A FREE STATE, 1820

ARK. TERR.

LA.

MISS. ALA.

TENN.

KY.

GA.

S.C.

N.C.

VA.

FLA. TERR.

MICH. TERR.

ILL. IND. OHIO PENN.

N.Y.

VT. N.H. MASS.

R.I. CONN. N.J.

DEL. MD.

ME.

Free

Slave

8. Courtesy of D. C. Heath and Company, from The American Pageant, by Thomas A. Bailey, p. 231.

ings of the Non-intercourse Act. In a somber report he wrote that: "the French government may rest assured that among a hundred ships leaving the ports of the Union . . . ninety of them will have the real object of satisfying the wants and demands of England." Turreau expected a break in relations between France and the United States. He had some hopes of delaying it until autumn. He believed "it would be well to await the result of the next session . . . before taking a severer course against the Americans." He expressed this opinion "only with doubt." Yet, he felt it was "warranted by advices . . . which have been given by men who know the Executive intentions, and who at least till now have not deceived me."[8]

Turreau was right. An Anglo-American rapprochment began on January 13, 1809, when the London *Times* sounded a new note of conciliation:

If America will withdraw her Embargo and Non-importation Acts as far as they relate to England provided we rescind the Orders in Council we cannot consider this as a disgraceful concession in our part.[9]

Less than a fortnight later, Foreign Secretary George Canning instructed David Erskine, British Minister in Washington, to attempt a reconciliation with America. Canning offered to repeal the Orders in Council if the United States formally and publicly endorsed three stipulations: British trade should be admitted to American ports while that of Napoleon remained excluded; the United States should recognize the validity of the Rule of 1756; and Madison should permit the Royal Navy to seize American ships violating their own country's prohibition on trade with France. Both Madison and Smith gave Erskine their solemn word that America would abide by the three conditions. Forestalling a protracted congressional debate, Madison got Erskine to drop the "formal and public" endorsement requirement. Erskine felt he was adhering to the spirit of his instructions when he chose to accept this informal agreement.[10]

---

[8]Turreau to Champagny, April 20, 1809, *French Archives, Henry Adams Transcripts.*

[9]London *Times,* January 13, 1809.

[10]Bradford Perkins, "George Canning, Great Britain, and the United States, 1807-1809," *American Historical Review,* Vol. LXIII, October, 1957, pp. 15-16. The Rule of 1756 meant that trade not open in time of peace could not be permitted in time of war.

An exchange of notes then took place between the American Secretary of State Robert Smith and the British minister. In his note of April 18, 1809, Erskine asserted that His Majesty would recall the Orders in Council if the President would issue a proclamation renewing intercourse with Great Britain. When Madison immediately promised to comply, Erskine on April 19 said he was "authorized to declare that His Majesty's Orders in Council of January and November, 1807, will have been withdrawn as respects the United States on the 10th of June next." Robert Smith assured Erskine that Madison would immediately issue his proclamation. On April 21, the *National Intelligencer* published the four notes and the proclamation.[11]

The headline in the New Hampshire *Patriot:* "Great and Glorious News: Our Differences with Great Britain Amicably Settled,"[12] reflected the joy not only of New England but of the entire country. Without waiting for June 10, over a thousand American vessels rushed to sea carrying raw materials and foodstuffs which England sorely needed. Not a voice was heard in protest about impressments, or about the fact that war with France must follow reconciliation with England. Turreau remonstrated with Gallatin, who replied: "The offers could not be refused." Turreau rebutted: "But you have only promises, and already twelve hundred vessels, twelve thousand sailors, and two hundred million francs of property have left your ports." Napoleon's minister warned: "May not the English take all this to serve as a guarantee for other conditions which their interest might care to impose?" Gallatin replied: "We would like it! Perhaps our people may need such a lesson to cure them of British influence and the mania of British Commerce."[13]

The Democrats, speaking through the pages of the *National Intelligencer,* claimed credit for the newly founded peace and prosperity:

Thanks to the sage who now so gloriously reposes in the shades of Monticello, and to those who shared his confidence . . . it may be boldly alleged that the revocation of the British Orders is attributable to the Embargo.[14]

---

[11]*National Intelligencer,* April 21, 1809.

[12]New Hampshire *Patriot,* April 9, 1809.

[13]Turreau to Champagny, June 1, 1809, *French Archives, Henry Adams Transcripts.*

[14]*National Intelligencer,* April 26, 1809.

However, the Federalists and their newspapers were certain that their efforts against the Embargo had disposed Great Britain to think in terms of the Erskine arrangement. They also asserted that the removal of Jefferson's sinister influence made Madison's brilliant success possible. For the moment, James Madison was the most popular president that ever faced a Congress.[15]

On May 22, 1809, Erskine's dispatches were received by Canning. The next day the *Morning Post* printed the news with obvious satisfaction: "Upon this pleasing event we sincerely congratulate the public."[16] However, the very next day the London *Times* with "considerable pain though but little surprise" announced that Canning had disavowed Erskine.[17] The news of this seemingly surprising *volte face* on the part of the British Foreign Secretary reached the United States so slowly that our merchants enjoyed three months of unrestricted trade with England. From April 21 until July 21 our ships carried the accumulations of nearly two years' produce, and when on July 21 the news of Canning's repudiation reached America, merchants still had time to rush their last cargoes to sea before the Non-intercourse Act was restored. The *National Intelligencer* echoed the Administration's feelings: "The late conduct of the British ministry has capped the climax of atrocity toward this country."[18] Three days after the news reached Washington, the ever practical Gallatin revealed that since the treasury was "exhausted we must begin our plan of resistance with considerable and therefore unpopular loans."[19] Madison heard the news with as much perplexity as anger. On August 3, 1809, he wrote Jefferson:

The intricate state of our affairs with England produced by the mixture of fraud and folly in her late conduct . . . are thought by the heads of departments to require that I should join them . . . you will see by the instructions to Erskine, as published by Canning, that the latter was as much determined that there should be no adjustment as the former was that there should be one.[20]

---

[15]Henry Adams, *History of the United States,* Vol. IV, pp. 77-79.
[16]*Morning Post,* May 23, 1809.
[17]London *Times,* May 24 and 25, 1809.
[18]*National Intelligencer,* July 26, 1809.
[19]Gallatin to Montgomery, July 27, 1809, in Henry Adams, *History of the United States,* Vol. I, p. 3.
[20]Madison to Jefferson, August 3, 1809, *Madison MSS.*

The President charged Canning with fraud as freely as Canning credited Madison with connivance. On August 9, Madison signed a proclamation reviving the Non-intercourse Act against Great Britain. He also authorized the collectors of customs not to enforce the law against vessels entering American ports on the faith of Erskine's arrangement.[21]

On June 23, 1809, William Pinckney, United States Minister at the Court of St. James, informed Robert Smith that Canning was replacing Erskine with "Copenhagen" Jackson. Whatever good qualities Francis James Jackson possessed, his reputation was permanently marred by his role in the savage destruction of Copenhagen in September of 1807. In the chancelleries of the world, his name was a threat of violence. His temper and manners were notorious. Canning's selection of Jackson was so singular as to suggest that Great Britain had substituted terror for negotiation. Jackson's first instruction charged bad faith against the American government: "The American government cannot have believed that such an arrangement as Mr. Erskine consented to accept was conformable to his instructions."[22] The rest of the instructions authorized Jackson "to renew the negotiation and to conclude it on the terms of my instructions to Mr. Erskine." He was "at liberty to receive for home any proposal which the American government may tender to you; but it is only in the case of that proposal comprehending all the three conditions which Mr. Erskine was instructed to require."[23] Gallatin's view on the Jackson mission was soon to become the Administration's: "He is probably sent out like Mr. Rose to amuse and to divide; and we shall, I trust, by coming at once to the point, bring his negotiations to an immediate close.[24]

Jackson arrived in Washington on September 8, 1809. He immediately set himself to reading Erskine's correspondence and rapidly concluded that:

---

[21]The British reciprocated and promised protection to American ships selling in good faith. Henry Adams, *History of the United States,* Vol. IV, p. 114.

[22]Canning to F. J. Jackson, July1, 1809, *British Archives, Henry Adams Transcripts.*

[23]*Ibid.*

[24]Gallatin to Montgomery, July 27, 1809, Henry Adams, *History of the United States,* Vol. IV, p. 3.

Erskine is really a greater fool than I could have thought it possible to be and it is charity to give him that name . . . To be obliged to wade through such a mass of folly and stupidity, and to observe how our country had been made, through Erskine's means, the instrument of these people's cunning, is not the least part of my annoyance. The tone which Erskine had accustomed them to use with him . . . is another great difficulty I have had to overcome. Every third word was a declaration of war.[25]

Jackson regarded Madison as a "plain and rather mean-looking man," and his wife Dolly as "fat and forty but not fair." To him Americans were "all alike," except that some few were "less knaves than others."[26] When Jackson had been sent to Copenhagen, he was accompanied by twenty ships of the line, forty frigates, and thirty thousand regular troops. At Washington, he was equipped with but verbal armament. After a series of caustic interchanges, Robert Smith formally sent to the British legation the note which closed Jackson's diplomatic career in the United States:

Finding that in your reply of the 4th instant you have used a language which cannot be understood but as reiteration and even aggravating the same gross insinuation, it only remains, in order to preclude opportunities which are thus abused, to inform you that no further communications will be received from you . . .[27]

Great Britain, refusing to disapprove Jackson's conduct, did not replace him until nearly two years after his dismissal. The legation was left with a *chargé d'affaires*. This episode, coming so soon after the Erskine debacle, further jeopardized the chances for peace. In taking leave of Washington, Mrs. Jackson epitomized the attitude of England toward the United States: "Francis, being accustomed to treat with the civilized courts and governments of Europe, and not with savage Democrats, half of them sold to France, has not succeeded in his negotiation."[28]

---

[25] F. J. Jackson to Mrs. Jackson, October 7, 1809, Henry Adams, *History of the United States,* Vol. IV, pp. 119-120.

[26] Thomas A. Bailey, *A Diplomatic History of the American People,* p. 127.

[27] Henry Adams, *History of the United States,* Vol. I, p. 132. Jackson spent "seven hundred pounds for newspaper propaganda during his year of residence in the United States." Josephine Fisher, "Francis Jackson and Newspaper Propaganda in the United States, 1809-1810," *Maryland Historical Magazine,* Vol. XXX, June 1935, No. 2, p. 113.

[28] Henry Adams, *History of the United States,* Vol. IV, p. 157.

NAPOLEON'S INTRIGUE

The Emperor had been partial to the Embargo, but he violently disliked our Non-intercourse Act. In retaliation he issued the Rambouillet decree of March 23, 1810. As a result, scores of American ships in Holland, in France, and in Italy, which Napoleon claimed were smuggling for the British, were confiscated. Official American protests fell on deaf ears. As a desperate measure to avert war, the Congress passed Macon's bill No. 2. This measure was Congress's last legislative act to counteract by commercial means the encroachments of France and Great Britain. The bill reopened intercourse with both France and England. It also provided that if Great Britain repealed her Orders in Council, non-intercourse would be renewed against France, and that if France repealed her decrees, non-intercourse would be renewed against England. This experiment created a situation made to order for Bonaparte. On August 5, 1810, he had his Foreign Minister, Duc de Cadore, send a vaguely worded communication to William Armstrong, the American Minister to Paris. The letter ostensibly announced the repeal of the French decrees. The string attached either required England to revoke her Orders in Council, or the Americans would have to "cause their rights to be respected" by establishing non-intercourse against her. These conditions were impossible, for Britannia ruled the waves. The Cadore letter committed France to nothing. Madison acted identically as he had in the Erskine affair. He accepted the word of Napoleon and issued a proclamation on November 2, 1810, indicating that non-intercourse would be renewed against England if she did not cancel her Orders within three months. This was violative of Macon's bill which demanded convincing proof of French repeal. On the very day of the Cadore letter, the French Emperor was engaged in selling captured American ships. That American vessels were being daily seized and scuttled at Napoleon's orders was apparent from every letter arriving in Washington from Europe. His Majesty's government was not fooled by the Cadore deceit, and therefore, the British Orders in Council remained in effect against the United States. Anglo-American enmity received a new impetus when on March 2, 1811, Congress passed a new measure renewing non-intercourse against Great Britain.[29]

Meanwhile the hammer blows that Napoleon dealt Madrid shook the entire Spanish empire. In the spring of 1810 both Buenos Aires and Caracas, under British influence, separated themselves from Spain. Madison now began to put into action the Jeffersonian view of the Floridas:

We have some claims . . . to go eastwardly . . . These claims will be a subject of negotiation with Spain, and if as soon as she is at war, we push them strongly with one hand, holding out a price with the other, we shall certainly obtain the Floridas, and all in good time.[30]

In the summer of 1810, just prior to the reception of the Cadore letter, Madison began to connive at a separatist movement in West Florida. Numerous Americans settled in the Spanish province within sight of Fort Adams across the American border. The examples of Buenos Aires and Caracas assured them that Spain could safely be defied. Assembling all the armed men they could muster, they accused the Spanish governor of perfidy and assaulted the fort at Baton Rouge. The young Spanish Commander Louis Grandpré rejected the summons of surrender. With but a handful of soldiers, Grandpré defended the citadel. When the Americans swarmed over the ruined remains, they found him almost alone defending his flag. He was killed in the ensuing conflict.

On September 26, 1810, the Americans in West Florida issued a proclamation: ". . . appealing to the Supreme Ruler of the World for the rectitude of our intentions, We do . . . declare . . . West Florida to be a free and independent State." A few days later, West Florida requested annexation to the United States. On October 27, 1810, Madison issued a proclamation announcing that Governor Claiborne would take possession of West Florida to the Perdido

---

[29]*American State Papers*, Vol. III, pp. 390-393. Madison knew that Napoleon was still capturing American ships, but he went along with the fiction that the Cadore letter created a contract with France. The majority of Democrats in the House followed this fiction. As late as January 14, 1812, Jonathan Russell, American *chargé d'affaires* in London, was hopeful that he might be able to relay some evidence of the discontinuance of the French decrees, but he could find no tangible proof. Russell to James Monroe, January 14, 1812, *Dispatches to the Department of State.*

[30]Jefferson to Breckenridge, August 12, 1803, *Jefferson MSS.* By the summer of 1810, Cordova and Seville had fallen to the French, and the American minister to Spain returned to the United States. George W. Erving to Robert Smith, July 7, 1810, *Dispatches, Department of State.*

River in the name and on behalf of the United States.[31]

The British *chargé* at Washington, J. P. Morier, wrote the American Secretary of State, Robert Smith, expressing the official opinion of His Majesty's government:

Would it not have been worthy of the generosity of a free nation like this, bearing, as it doubtless does, a respect for the rights of a gallant people at this moment engaged in a noble struggle for its liberty—would it not have been an act on the part of this country dictated by the sacred ties of good neighborhood and friendship which exist between it and Spain, to have simply offered its assistance to crush the common enemy of both, rather than to have made such interference the pretext for wresting a province from a friendly Power, and that at a time of her adversity?[32]

John Quincy Adams, American Minister at St. Petersburg, attempted somewhat shamefacedly to explain the Florida affair to Czar Alexander I. The Czar bowed, and with an obvious reference to Napoleon's continental conquests, genially remarked: "Everybody is getting a little bigger nowadays."[33] The 11th Congress convened in December, 1810, and passed a bill which in effect approved what Madison had done in West Florida. Then it went into secret session and authorized the President to take possession of East Florida. Madison immediately appointed George Matthews and John McKee as commissioners to carry the law into effect.[34]

THE END OF THE BANK

In the midst of these troubles with France and Spain, the Democrats were confronted with the domestic issue of the Bank of the United States. Early in 1791, in spite of Jefferson's opposition, Congress had approved a twenty-year charter for the Bank of the

---

[31]*American State Papers,* Vol. III, pp. 396-397.

[32]Morier to Robert Smith, December 15, 1810, *American States Papers,* Vol. III, p. 399. Professor Cox asserts that the United States resorted to dishonesty and bribery to attain the Floridas. Isaac J. Cox, *The West Florida Controversy, 1798-1813* (Baltimore: Johns Hopkins Press, 1918), pp. 660-663.

[33]Thomas A. Bailey, *A Diplomatic History of the American People,* p. 164. R. R. Stenberg feels that Madison's acceptance of the Cadore letter was a bribe to secure Napoleon's acquiescence in the American annexation of West Florida. R. R. Stenberg, "Louisiana and West Florida: A Few Notes," *The Southeastern Social Science Quarterly,* Vol. XVIII, December, 1937, No. 3, pp. 249-254.

[34]Henry Adams, *History of the United States,* Vol. IV, p. 327. Jefferson wished Congress to authorize the president "to take possession of East Florida immediately." Jefferson to Eppes, January 5, 1811, *Jefferson MSS.* John Eppes was Jefferson's brother-in-law and a member of Congress from Virginia.

United States. It was to have a capital of $10,000,000, one-fifth of it owned by the federal government. By the beginning of 1811, as the charter was about to expire, two-thirds of the bank stock was owned in England.[35] All the five thousand shares originally held by the United States government had been sold to England. In many states, private banks were applying for charters. They were preparing to issue notes in the expectation of receiving their share of the profits of the United States Bank. These new corporations induced one state legislature after another to instruct their senators to vote against charter renewal. The burden of defending the bank fell to Gallatin. Madison refrained from using his influence. The Secretary of the Treasury did what he could in the House, but the debate ended there on January 24, 1811, with a vote of 65 to 64 in favor of indefinite postponement. Three days later Nathaniel Macon "was at Gallatin's," and "found him mortified at the indefinite postponement of the bill to renew the charter of the bank of the U.S."[36] By common consent all factions looked to the Senate to decide. William Henry Crawford of Georgia was Gallatin's man in the Senate. Samuel Smith and Henry Clay opposed him. On February 20, 1811, 17 Senators voted for the Bank, and seventeen voted against it. Vice-President George Clinton remarked that: ". . . the power to create corporations is not expressly granted; it is a high attribute of sovereignty, and in its nature not accessorial or derivative by implication, but primary and independent." He then voted against the bill. So perished the first Bank of the United States.[37]

Gallatin, irked by the fact that Robert Smith had cooperated with his brother Samuel in disposing of the bank, threatened to resign. In March, 1811, he wrote Madison that in

. . . a government . . . a perfect heartfelt cordiality . . . among its members . . . is . . . essentially necessary to command the public confidence . . . Meas-

---

[35]A majority of the directors of the bank were Federalists, and the Federalists supported the recharter of the bank. Democratic antipathy to the British-owned bank, and to the British allies, the Federalists, was a major factor in the defeat of the recharter resolution. Bray Hammond, *Banks and Politics in America from the Revolution to the Civil War* (Princeton: Princeton University Press, 1957), p. 224.
[36]Nathaniel Macon to Joseph H. Nicholson, January 28, 1811, *Joseph H. Nicholson MSS.* For an excellent analysis of the collapse of the first Bank, see, Davis R. Dewey, *Financial History of the United States* (New York: Longmans, Green & Co., 1931), pp. 126-128.
[37]*Annals of Congress, 11th Cong., 3rd Sess., 1810-1811,* Vol. XXII, p. 346.

ures of vital importance have been and are defeated . . . I clearly perceive that my continuing a member of the present Administration is no longer of any public utility.[38]

Gallatin was obviously referring to his disagreement with Smith. Madison, realizing this, refused to accept Gallatin's resignation, and at once authorized him to sound out James Monroe as a successor to Smith. When the President was informed that Monroe would accept the post of Secretary of State, he told Smith that "the want of harmony and unity . . . was exclusively chargeable to him."[39] Smith protested without avail. Madison offered to send him to St. Petersburg to succeed John Quincy Adams. After consideration, Smith refused the Russian post, and retired to private life. John Taylor of Carolina had persuaded Monroe to accept the State Department on the ground that he might possibly change Madison's pro-French policy. In Monroe's letter of acceptance, he informed Madison that "it was for the interest of our country to make an accommodation with England."[40] Six days before the declaration of war against England, Monroe wrote a letter of explanation to Taylor explaining how he had tried for peace but Great Britain demanded "unconditional surrender."[41] Monroe began his duties as Secretary of State on April 1, 1811. Thus Gallatin's threat to resign led directly to Secretary of State Robert Smith's dismissal and the appointment of Monroe in his place.

THE LITTLE BELT

In the very month that James Monroe became Secretary of State, the British, claiming the renewal of Franco-American trade as justification, renewed their blockade of New York. The *Melampus* and the *Guerrière,* both flying the Union Jack, lay off Sandy Hook capturing American vessels, and impressing American seamen at will. Apprised of the situation, the South Carolinian Secretary of the Navy, Paul Hamilton, ordered Commodore John Rodgers

[38]Gallatin to Madison, March, 1811, *The Writings of Albert Gallatin,* ed. by Henry Adams (Philadelphia: J. B. Lippincott & Co., 1879), Vol. I, pp. 495-496.

[39]Memorandum by Madison, March 23, 1811, *Madison MSS.* On May 25, 1810, Jefferson advised Madison that Monroe was "with us again." Jefferson to Madison, May 25, 1810, *Jefferson MSS.*

[40]William P. Cresson, *James Monroe* (Chapel Hill: University of North Carolina Press, 1946), pp. 245-246.

[41]Monroe to John Taylor, June 13, 1812, *Monroe MSS.*

with his flagship, the twenty-two gun frigate *President,* to proceed at once from Annapolis to New York. Rodgers received orders "to vindicate the injured honor of our navy and revive the drooping spirits of the nation . . . to maintain and support at any risk and cost the honor" of the American flag. Hamilton underlined his commands by citing the "inhuman and dastardly attack on our frigate *Chesapeake*—an outrage which prostrated the flag of our country, and has imposed on the American people a cause of ceaseless mourning."[42]

At noon on May 16, 1811, Rodgers, bound for New York, but still about thirty miles from Cape Charles and eighteen miles from the coast, espied what eventually turned out to be the twenty-gun British corvette, the *Little Belt.* Believing the ship to be His Majesty's frigate the *Guerrière* with an impressed American seaman on board, Rodgers gave chase for some eight hours. When the *President* drew within pistol shot of the *Little Belt,* the opposing captains greeted each other with: "What ship is that?" There are conflicting reports as to who fired the first shot. But both British and American sources agree as to the final outcome. The *Little Belt* was terribly crippled and lost 9 killed and 23 wounded. Only one of the *President's* crew was wounded, and aside from a little damage to her rigging she came out unscathed.[43] The *Chesapeake* had been more than revenged.

A few weeks after the *Little Belt* incident, the new British Minister to the United States, Augustus John Foster, arrived in Norfolk, Virginia. He was no stranger to Washington, having served as secretary of the legation there. Foster had none of Jackson's truculence. Everyone spoke well of him. His affiliations were Whig, and therefore, a distinct asset in Washington. His instructions authorized him to settle the *Chesapeake* outrage, but when he discovered that Commodore Rodgers had killed four men for every one killed by Captain Humphries, he felt himself obliged to seek redress

---

[42]Secretary Hamilton to Commodore Rodgers, June 9, 1810, Henry Adams, *History of the United States,* Vol. V, p. 26.
[43]Albert L. Burt, *The United States, Great Britain, and British North America,* p. 292. The feeling of America was expressed by Jefferson a few days before the *Little Belt* incident: ". . . it can no longer be doubted that Great Britain means to claim the ocean as her conquest." Jefferson to John Hollins, May 5, 1811, *Jefferson MSS.* The American minister in Paris reported that Napoleon personally congratulated him on the *Little Belt* affair. Barlow to Madison, December 19, 1811, *Madison MSS.*

instead of giving it. The outraged London *Courier* reflected the initial feelings of the British government with regard to the *Little Belt:* "The blood of our murdered countrymen must be revenged, and war must ensue . . . We have behaved towards America with unexampled forbearance; but that forbearance has produced insolence, and that insolence must be punished."[44] By November 1, 1811, after the United States had complied with Foster's request that a court of inquiry be held on the *Little Belt* incident, the British minister closed the *Chesapeake* account. Of the four seamen taken from the *Chesapeake* in 1807, one had been promptly hanged as a British deserter. Another died in a hospital in Halifax in 1809. The two survivors were finally placed back on the deck of the *Chesapeake* in Boston harbor on July 11, 1812. Since the war had already commenced, special arrangements had to be made for this ceremony. The war also prevented the United States government from accepting payment of damages. The Baltimore *Whig* echoed the sentiments of most Americans when it remarked that the reparation was "like restoring a hair after fracturing a skull."[45]

AN IMPASSE

There is more than a grain of truth in Alfred Thayer Mahan's statement that "Conditions were hopeless, and war assured, even when Foster arrived in Washington in June, 1811."[46] The heart of Wellesley's instructions to Foster dealt with the Orders in Council. Foster was to require proof that the French decrees were repealed. By Madison's proclamation, and the passage of the Non-intercourse Act of March 2, 1811, the United States was committed to the contention that Napoleon had revoked his decrees. But the decrees were not revoked, for seizures were still made under them. Four months after Foster's arrival in Washington, Monroe wrote to the American minister in Paris: "It is not sufficient that it should appear that the French decrees are repealed, in the final decision of a case brought before a French tribunal. An active, prohibitory policy should be

---

[44]Thomas A. Bailey, *A Diplomatic History of the American People, op. cit.,* p. 130.
[45]*Ibid.,* p. 130.
[46]Alfred T. Mahan, *Sea Power in its Relations to the War of 1812* (London: Sampson Low, Morston & Co., 1905), Vol. I, p. 255. Charles Carroll of Carrollton felt that the only explanation of Madison's conduct was "a secret understanding between our government and that of France." Charles Carroll to Robert G. Harper, February 6, 1811, *Robert G. Harper MSS.*

adopted to prevent seizures on the principle."[47] After his blunder in the Erskine case, it proved too difficult a task for Madison to admit that he had been duped again. In London, Wellesley came to feel that the impasse could have been avoided. When the war was five months old, the British Foreign Secretary accused his colleagues of misleading him during the entire time of Foster's stay in America:

This disposition of the American government was quite evident; and therefore common policy should have urged ministers to prepare fully for the event; and they should have made adequate exertion either to pacify, to intimidate, or to punish America.[48]

Up until 1811, Massachusetts had been an effective instrument in preventing a British war, but in April of that year, Elbridge Gerry, a Democrat, defeated the Federalist Christopher Gore in the gubernatorial election by a majority of 3,000 votes. In the State House of Representatives, which consisted of 650 members, a Democratic speaker was chosen by a majority of 31 votes. In the State Senate, the Democrats, by a majority of 1, won control for the first time. Timothy Pickering lost his seat in the United States Senate. The Democrat, Joseph B. Varnum, Speaker of the House, won it. These Democrats in Massachusetts were prepared to move with Madison for war against England. In fact, by September, 1811, Democratic newspapers were calling for war. Impressment, the *Little Belt*, Pinckney's return from London, the battle of Tippecanoe, and Foster's refusal to withdraw the Orders in Council, all these and others were cited as causes for war. On November 4, 1811, as the tempo increased in the press, the 12th Congress convened. It contained seventy new members. One of them, Felix Grundy, reported to General Jackson that at a meeting "of the Committee on our Foreign Relations, of which I am a member" it was determined "to report in favor of actual war."[49] Besides Grundy, the other leaders were: Henry Clay, Richard M. Johnson of Kentucky, Wil-

---

[47]*American State Papers, Foreign Relations*, Vol. III, p. 514. In an instruction of March 21, 1812, Monroe complained to the American minister in Paris of the destruction of several American merchant vessels by a French squadron. Monroe to Joel Barlow, March 21, 1812, *Instructions, Department of State.* Richard Wellesley was British Foreign Secretary in 1811.

[48]Henry Adams, *History of the United States*, Vol. VI, p. 24.

[49]Felix Grundy to Andrew Jackson, November 28, 1811, *Andrew Jackson MSS.* Grundy was from Tennessee and was one of the leaders of the War Hawks. British weapons were found on the battlefield of Tippecanoe.

liam Lowndes, John C. Calhoun, David R. Williams, Langdon Cheves of South Carolina, and Peter B. Porter of New York. All were under forty. These men gave a new energy and decisiveness to the government. In time they came to be known as the War Hawks.[50]

Secretary Gallatin's report, sent to the House on November 22, expected war. For the past year, the receipts from customs and other revenue exceeded $13,500,000. The current expenses were only $8,000,000. If war should be declared, Gallatin asked only for an increase of 50 percent in the duties.[51] The French Minister in Washing, Serurier, was informed by Secretary Monroe of Madison's plan:

Ten thousand regulars were to be raised and placed at the disposition of the Executive, with a great number of volunteers; that the posts would be put in a state of defense, the navy increased, and merchants authorized to arm for the protection of their commerce . . . the Administration in taking this resolution had perfectly seen where it led.[52]

It is certain that the impetus for a rupture with Great Britain came from the hot-blooded West, under the ardent leadership of the War Hawks. They elected their champion, Henry Clay, as Speaker of the House. He, in turn, organized the committees for war. Foreign Relations was entrusted to Porter, Grundy, and Calhoun. Ways and Means went to Ezekiel Bacon, and Langdon Cheves. David R. Williams was placed in charge of Military Affairs. Cheves was appointed Chairman of the Naval Committee. These men were keenly patriotic. They bitterly resented the degradation to the Stars and Stripes as a result of impressment. A day before the House voted for war, the War Hawk House Committee on Foreign Affairs reported regarding impressments: ". . . while this practice is continued, it is impossible for the United States to consider themselves an independent nation."[53] Shortly after Tippecanoe, Felix Grundy

---

[50]Henry Adams, *History of the United States,* Vol. VI, pp. 115-116. The British minister in Washington had been somewhat calm until "the insolence of the War Party . . . passed all bounds". . . until Speaker Clay "the head of the advocates for war," forced a decision. Bernard Mayo, *The Life of Henry Clay,* p. 471.
[51]Henry Adams, *History of the United States,* Vol. VI, p. 126.
[52]Serurier to Maret, November 28, 1811, *French Archives, Henry Adams Transcripts.* Clay urged Monroe to urge Madison to declare an embargo and to follow it up with a war message. Henry Clay to Monroe, March 15, 1812, *Monroe MSS.* Jefferson wrote to Madison that his "declaration of war is expected with perfect calmness"; as to the Essex junto, this "is as good a time for trying them as we can expect." Jefferson to Madison, May 25, 1812, *Jefferson MSS.*
[53]*American State Papers, Foreign Relations,* Vol. III, p. 569. (June 3, 1812).

of Tennessee, three of whose brothers had been butchered by the Indians, exclaimed in a fighting speech: "We shall drive the British from our Continent. They will no longer have an opportunity of intriguing with our Indian neighbors, and setting on the ruthless savage to tomahawk our women and children."[54] Two weeks before Madison signed the declaration of war, Andrew Jackson's heart bled "on the receipt of the news of the horrid cruelty and murders committed by a party of Creeks, on our innocent wives and little babes."[55] As early as 1810, Henry Clay had issued a call for action: "The conquest of Canada is in your power . . . is it nothing to extinguish the torch that lights up savage warfare? Is it nothing to acquire the entire fur trade connected with that country . . . ?"[56] While Northern War Hawks demanded Canada, Southern War Hawks clamored for Florida: "Florida and Canada, a fee simple in the one, a mortgage upon the other,"[57] ran a Kentucky toast. The Federalist Josiah Quincy, lampooned what he termed Western greed: "We want West Florida. Our Western brethren will have West Florida. By G . . . we will take West Florida. By G . . . it is in the title deed."[58] John A. Harper, a New Hampshire War Democrat, declared on the floor of the House: "To me, Sir, it appears that the Author of Nature has marked our limits in the south, by the Gulf of Mexico; and on the north by the regions of the eternal frost."[59] The editor of the Nashville *Clarion* pointedly asked: "Where is it written in the book of fate that the American republic shall not stretch her limits from the Capes of the Chesapeake to Nootka Sound, from the Isthmus of Panama to Hudson Bay."[60]

On June 1, 1812, Madison sent his memorable war message to Congress. The President made four definite charges. The first was

---

[54]*Annals of Congress, 12th Cong., 1st Sess.* (December 9, 1811), Vol. I, p. 426. On November 7, 1811, William Henry Harrison engaged the Indians at Tippecanoe near the Wabash River. The battle was indecisive. When the Indians were finally beaten off, they left behind newly marked British arms. James A. Green, *William Henry Harrison* (Richmond: Garrett & Massie, 1941), p. 115-140.

[55]Andrew Jackson to Governor William Blount, June 4, 1812, *Andrew Jackson MSS.*

[56]*Annals of Congress, 11th Cong., 1st Sess.* (February 22, 1810), *op. cit.,* Vol XX, p. 580. (Washington: Gales & Seaton, 1853).

[57]Thomas A. Bailey, *A Diplomatic History of the American People*, p. 133.

[58]*Ibid.,* p. 134.

[69]*Annals of Congress, 12th Cong., 1st Sess.* (January 4, 1812), Vol. 1, p. 657.

[60]Quoted in Julius W. Pratt, *Expansionists of 1812* (New York: Peter Smith, 1949), p. 14.

impressment. The second was that the British navy violated the peace of our coasts by harassing incoming and outgoing commerce. The third was the use of pretended blockades to plunder American merchantmen. The fourth was the ever-hated Orders in Council. After a short paragraph which gave credence to the charges of the British tampering with the Indians, Madison put the question of war or peace squarely up to Congress. The bellicose House promptly passed a war resolution on June 4 by a vote of 79 to 49. The Federalists and fifteen Democrats opposed the war. Among the Democrats were the Quids and six New York Clintonians. Federalist and Eastern influence was stronger in the Senate. The debate there was prolonged. Finally on June 17, the Senate voted, 19 to 13, for immediate and unrestricted war. The only Democrats in opposition were Thomas Worthington of Ohio, Obadiah German of New York, and Nicholas Gilman of New Hampshire. That evening the British minister visited Madison. He recorded that the President "looked ghostly pale." As for pallor, concluded Foster, the Chief Executive "very naturally felt all the responsibility he would incur."[61] On June 18, the House accepted minor Senate amendments, and the declaration of war was signed that day by Madison. In the Senate, the vote for war against France was 15 for it and 17 against it. Monroe was sure that both Houses would have included France in the declaration of war had it not been for a recent letter from the American minister in Paris. This letter gave assurances that from now on the French really would stop seizing American ships.[62]

It is just possible that peace might have been preserved if a number of purely fortuitous occurrences had not helped defeat the work of the diplomats. In November, 1810, George III went completely insane. American affairs received scant attention while several precious months elapsed during the formation of a regency. By the first of May, 1812, British manufacturing and mercantile groups had high hopes of effecting a repeal of the Orders in Coun-

---

[61]Irving Brant, *James Madison: The President* (New York: Bobbs-Merrill Co., 1956), pp. 474-477. The British minister to the United States felt that the reading of the John Henry letters to Congress on March 9, 1812, was a contributory cause of the war. Henry, the British secret agent, sold his correspondence to the Federalists to Madison for fifty thousand dollars. He deleted most of the important names. See Ernest A. Cruckshank, *The Political Adventures of John Henry* (Toronto: Macmillan Co., 1936), pp. 126-127.

[62]Monroe to Joel Barlow, June 16, 1812, *Instructions, Department of State*.

cil. But more delay followed when on May 11, 1812, Prime Minister Perceval was assassinated by a madman.

Just about a week after the American declaration of war, Monroe fired an instruction off to our *chargé* in London. Peace was still possible, said Monroe. The President would, if necessary, even go to the summit to arrange the details. Monroe saw "no reason why hostilities should not cease . . . if the Orders in Council are repealed . . . and orders are given to discontinue the impressment of seamen on our vessels." As an incentive for Britain to yield on impressments, Monroe gave "assurance that a law will be passed (to be reciprocal) to prohibit the employment of British seamen in the public or commercial service of the United States."[63] In London the British Foreign Secretary, Lord Castlereagh, was also thinking about the possibility of peace. On June 16, the day before the United States Congress voted for war, he announced in the House of Commons that the Orders in Council would be immediately suspended. They were officially revoked on June 23. Since war had been declared before the revocation order of June 23 reached the United States, Castlereagh felt confident that Madison, upon learning of it, would induce Congress to recall its declaration of war. Admiral Warren, commanding the British fleet in American waters, was therefore authorized by His Majesty's government to propose an armistice to the American government. Warren immediately contacted James Monroe, our Secretary of State, informing him of his power to agree to a cessation of hostilities. Monroe received him cordially, but respectfully informed him that unless the British yielded on impressment the war would continue. Experience has shown, insisted Monroe, "that no peace can be durable unless this object is provided for."[64] Warren relayed this *sine qua non* to London. Castlereagh was adamant. Speaking to the American *chargé*, Jonathan Russell, he declared: "You are not aware of this great sensitivity and jealousy of the people of England on this subject; and no administration could expect to remain in power that should consent to renounce the right of impressment."[65]

---

[63]Monroe to Russell, June 26, 1812, *Instructions, Department of State.*
[64]Monroe to Warren, October 27, 1812, as quoted in Frank A. Updyke, *The Diplomacy of the War of 1812* (Baltimore: Johns Hopkins University Press, 1913), p. 142.
[65]*American State Papers, Foreign Relations,* Vol. III, p. 594.

Some historians of diplomacy adhere to the view that if the United States had been represented at the Court of St. James by a minister plenipotentiary of the ability of Albert Gallatin, instead of by a mere *chargé d'affaires* in the person of Jonathan Russell, it would have been possible to avoid war.[66] Perhaps. No one will ever know. This much is certain: impressment was the rock that wrecked the last hope of peace.

About a month before the declaration of war, the Democratic caucus for the nomination of candidates for the president and vice-president was held. The War Hawks dominated here also. Madison was assured of their support by his pro-war stand. Of the 133 Democratic senators and members of the House, only 83 attended the caucus. Madison received 82 votes for president. John Langdon, of New Hampshire, the first President *pro tempore* of the Senate, received 64 votes for vice-president. When Langdon declined on the ground of age, a second caucus was held. Elbridge Gerry of Massachusetts was speedily nominated by 74 votes to 3. Those present who had not attended the first caucus were permitted to vote for a presidential candidate. Madison received 10 votes. He now had the support of 92 out of 133 members of Congress.[67]

On May 28, a Democratic convention was held in Albany, New York. DeWitt Clinton was nominated unanimously. The convention recommended him to the party throughout the Union as New York's candidate for the presidency. Clinton opposed war. He did not believe the United States was militarily prepared for war at this juncture. Many Democrats, fearing a split in party ranks, deplored the action of the Clintonian meeting. In general, the Federalists approved it, since, in effect, it opposed the war, and they had already insisted that war with England was no more called for than war against France.[68]

Thus the New York-Virginia alliance, which had monopolized

---

[66]Frank A. Updyke, *The Diplomacy of the War of 1812*, p. 125.

[67]Edward Stanwood, *A History of the Presidency*, p. 99. The caucus was held on May 12, 1812. The followers of DeWitt Clinton absented themselves.

[68]Dorothie Bobbe, *DeWitt Clinton* (New York: Minton, Balch & Co., 1933), pp. 185-186. Sometime in August of 1812, DeWitt Clinton met with Gouverneur Morris, John Jay, and Rufus King. He assured them that if elected president he would administer the government on the principles of Alexander Hamilton. Dixon R. Fox, *The Decline of Aristocracy in the Politics of New York* (New York: Columbia University Press, 1918), pp. 168-169.

Democratic nominations for the presidency since 1796, was broken by DeWitt Clinton's insurgency. In early September, a decisive conference was held in New York City by the elder statesmen of Federalism. Some seventy persons, representing eleven states, convened to endorse a candidate. South Carolina was the only state south of the Potomac that sent delegates. Rufus King proved to be the stumbling block in the way of outright endorsement of Clinton. He favored a separate Federalist ticket. King felt that the Federalists, by allying with the Clintonians, might place a Caesar Borgia in the White House. The majority, however, influenced by Harrison Gray Otis of Massachusetts, opposed King. Without giving a formal endorsement, the meeting adjourned, understanding that DeWitt Clinton would get Federalist support in each state. Robert G. Harper, Federalist Senator from Maryland, attended the meeting, and rejoiced that Clinton "looks with abhorrence on a French alliance in any form . . . and . . . thinks a peace with England on honorable terms is easily attainable."[69]

Eighteen states participated in the election of 1812, Louisiana having been admitted to the Union on April 8, 1812. The method of choosing the electors was the same as in 1808. It was a very close election. Clinton had 89 electoral votes to Madison's 128. Pennsylvania's 25 saved the day for the Virginia Dynasty. If Clinton had received Pennsylvania's 25, he would have been our fifth president by 114 to 103. The South and the West were not enough to elect Madison. He needed, and received, Pennsylvania's vote. DeWitt Clinton captured all New England save Vermont. He also won New York, New Jersey, Delaware, and 5 of Maryland's 11. His coalition had almost triumphed.[70]

---

[69]Robert G. Harper to Clement Dorsey, September 25, 1812, *Robert G. Harper MSS*. See also, Samuel E. Morison, *The Life and Letters of Harrison Gray Otis*, Vol. I, p. 310. John S. Murdock, "The First National Nominating Convention," *American Historical Review*, Vol. I, (October 1895-July 1896), pp. 680-683.

[70]Eugene H. Roseboom, *A History of Presidential Elections* (New York: Macmillan Co., 1957), pp. 68-69. Gouverneur Morris' remark that: ". . . the friends of peace . . . will . . support the election of Mr. Clinton," was typical of many who voted for Clinton. Gouverneur Morris to Aaron Ogden, August 20, 1812, *Gouverneur Morris MSS*.

7

Wartime Diplomacy

On OCTOBER 23, 1809, JOHN QUNCY ADAMS began his duties as our minister at St. Petersburg. The successful wartime diplomacy of the Democratic party would owe much to this astute New Englander. Six months before the American declaration of war, he could see what Madison seemed determined not to see: that Bonaparte's real purpose was to "rivet upon us the fetters of France" in order to get us into the conflict as his ally.[1] Fearing that war might breed secession, he wrote to his mother from Russia in the summer of 1811: if the Federalists "are not effectively put down in Massachusetts . . . the union is gone."[2] In the second year of the war, these Federalists that Adams feared so much predicted that "if Bonaparte is effectively humbled, his minion must bite the dust, and Mr. Madison will not long stickle about terms." On the other hand "if any event should occur to re-establish the tottering fortunes of his master, the Vice-Roy in Washington will remain true to his allegiance."[3] Depressed by the commencement of hostilities, Adams saw hopes for a short war when negotiations for peace started simultaneously with the firing of guns.

On June 22, 1812, four days after the American declaration of war against England, Napoleon attacked Russia. By September 14 of the same year, his army entered Moscow. On September 21, Czar Alexander I authorized his Chancellor, Count Roumanzoff, to sound out Adams on the acceptance of Russian mediation to end the Anglo-American war. Alexander naturally wished to see the American war ended. With a good segment of his country occupied by French troops, Madison's war not only directed Britain's strength

---

[1]John Quincy Adams to Thomas B. Adams, November 6, 1811, *John Quincy Adams MSS*. Thomas B. was John Quincy's brother.
[2]John Quincy Adams to Abigail Adams, June 30, 1811, *John Quincy Adams MSS*.
[3]*Boston Daily Advertiser,* January 13, 1814.

from the common effort against France, but was closing off much desired Russian commerce with the United States. Confronted with the Russian chancellor's proposal, Adams realized that he had no authority to say anything. He must refer the question to his government, but that would have meant six months of war before an answer would reach St. Petersburg. Striking a blow for peace, the American minister replied that although he was not authorized to say so, he was certain that his government would look upon the Czar's offer as new evidence of his friendship, and that he personally did not know any difficulty in the way of accepting the offer. "I lament the war," Adams confided to Roumanzoff, especially since it will "affect unfavorably the interests of Russia . . . I can see no good results likely to arise from it to anyone."[4]

By the time the Czar's offer reached the President, the international scene had changed ominously. The failures of the initial American campaigns against Canada and Florida, Napoleon's defeat in Russia, plus the opposition of New England to the war, made Madison anxious for peace. Canada was particularly worrisome to the President. After an inept attempt to invade that territory, General William Hull, on August 16, 1812, surrendered Detroit, and 2300 American effectives, to the lieutenant-governor of Upper Canada, General Isaac Brock. Jefferson, who had said the conquest of Canada would be a "mere matter of marching," now accused Hull of treason, and wanted him hanged immediately without benefit of court-martial.[5] Henry Clay agreed with Jefferson.[6] Actually Hull was court-martialed and found guilty of cowardice and neglect of duty. Ordered to be shot, he was pardoned by Madison, who, though he agreed with the verdict, felt Hull should be spared because of his Revolutionary War record.

After the Canadian debacle, William Eustis resigned as Secretary of War. Monroe, while still retaining his position as Secretary

---

[4]John Quincy Adams to James Monroe, September 30, 1812, *John Quincy Adams MSS*. Instead of reproof for acting on his own, Adams received commendation from Monroe. Monroe to John Quincy Adams, April 13, 1813, *John Quincy Adams MSS*.
[5]Jefferson to Duane, August 4, 1812, and Jefferson to Madison, November 6, 1812, *Jefferson MSS*.
[6]Glydon G. Van Deusen, *The Life of Henry Clay* (Boston: Little, Brown & Co., 1937), p. 91.

of State, took over as Acting-Secretary of War. After Madison's re-election, Monroe was relieved of this extra duty, and John Armstrong of New York was appointed Secretary of War. The antagonism between Monroe and Armstrong was of long standing. For one thing, Armstrong, together with his fellow New York Democrats, wanted to end the Virginia Dynasty. Monroe was well aware that military success might create a political rival for him in 1816. After Armstrong's appointment by Madison, Monroe somewhat plaintively informed Jefferson that he "would not have hesitated a moment" in accepting the office of Secretary of War if only the President had requested it.[7]

Among the various strategems proposed to turn defeat into victory in Canada, was one suggested by the famous Irish rebel, John Binns. Born in Ireland, Binns was by 1813 an American citizen as well as the editor of Pennsylvania's most powerful newspaper, the *Democratic Press*. The Binns plan was to make an open appeal to the Irish troops in Canada to desert the British and seek asylum under the Stars and Stripes. Richard Rush, the Attorney General of Pennsylvania, agreed with Binns that "if the Irish troops she may send to Canada were to turn their arms against her or come over the line to a free country ready to protect them, it would be but the reaction of eternal justice upon most unrelenting cruelty." However, Rush, who was very close to the Administration in Washington, ultimately found the plan too bold. He hesitated "at openly inviting them, or at taking, or hinting at any measures to break their enlistments."[8] Rush's influence with Madison proved sufficient to kill Binns' plan.

Meanwhile Madison had not changed his mind about the need for peace. In fact, he snapped up the Russian proffer of mediation without even waiting to see if England would do so. Two special plenipotentiaries: Albert Gallatin, Secretary of the Treasury, and Senator James A. Bayard of Delaware, a Federalist, were appointed to join Adams in negotiating a peace under Russian auspices. Gallatin, in view of the "dangers of the first magnitude both at home and abroad," felt impelled to take part in "the negotiation con-

---

[7]Monroe to Jefferson, June 7, 1813, *Jefferson MSS.*
[8]Richard Rush to John Binns, February 24, 1813, *Richard Rush MSS.* In 1817, Rush became our minister to England.

templated under the mediation of Russia." The Secretary of the Treasury was convinced that "Peace, provided we obtain security on the subject of impressment, gives us everything we want . . . the . . . organization of our naval and armed forces . . . will put us beyond the reach of insult." On the home front, Gallatin foresaw that "Peace . . . will defeat the Eastern plan of a separation of the union."[9] On this last point of secession, the Governor of New Hampshire went along with Gallatin by exclaiming: "What deed is too vile for some men in the Eastern States to attempt?"[10] However, Senator Charles Cutts, Federalist Senator from New Hampshire, questioned Gallatin's motives in leaving Washington. Writing to Governor Plumer, he informed him that "everybody blames him for quitting the country at this time . . . it is freely imputed to him that he fled to avoid the odium of the system of taxation . . . which he himself reported necessary to be adopted."[11]

Lord Castlereagh, British Foreign Secretary, responded to Madison's hopes for negotiation. However, His Majesty's government preferred not to use Russia's good offices. England refused to submit such issues as impressment and blockade to the mediation of the Czar who had proclamed to the world the principles of the Armed Neutralities of 1780 and 1800.[12] Castlereagh wrote to Monroe that Great Britain would negotiate directly with the United States. Madison was as quick to accept England's offer for direct discussions as he had been to grasp at Russian mediation. He nominated a new peace commission of five men. Henry Clay of Kentucky, Speaker of the House of Representatives, and Jonathan Russell, our recent *chargé* in London, were to join Adams, Gallatin, and Bayard.

GHENT

The appointment of such a distinguished American commission was a political achievement of the first order. The Democrats could well be proud of it. Any peace agreed to by these men

---

[9]Gallatin to William Few, May 9, 1813, *Gallatin MSS*. Few was the Director of the Bank of Manhattan in New York City.

[10]William Plumer to John A. Harper, January 19, 1813, *Plumer MSS*. Harper, a Democrat, was a Representative from New Hampshire. Plumer, Governor of New Hampshire, left the Federalists in 1808 and supported Madison.

[11]Charles Cutts to Plumer, June 8, 1813, *Plumer MSS*.

[12]These Armed Neutralities were designed to improve the position of the neutrals in time of war and weaken the preponderant sea power of England.

would be sure to get overwhelming approval both in the Senate and from the people. Any compromise they refused would be almost certain to unite the country in a desperate war of defense. It was finally agreed that the negotiators should meet in Ghent, in Dutch Flanders. It was not until August 8, 1814, that the Americans faced their opposite numbers across the familiar green baize peace table. The first meeting was held at the Hotel des Pays Bas. The British Foreign Office did not think it necessary to send its best men to Ghent. Outstanding leaders like Canning, Wellington, and Castlereagh were needed to settle the general peace of Europe at Vienna; therefore, the plenipotentiaries sent to Ghent by England, Lord Gambier, Henry Goulburn, and Dr. William Adams, were little more than messenger boys from the British Foreign Office. The real decisions would be made by the British Cabinet. The Cabinet left the chores of diplomatic dinners, notetaking, and verbal fencing to their subordinates at Ghent. Gambier, a naval officer, had received a peerage for his part in the bombardment of Copenhagen in 1807. Goulburn had been a member of Parliament, and successively an Undersecretary of State for Home Affairs, for War, and for the Colonies. Dr. Adams was an expert in international and maritime law.

The European war ended at least three months before the first conference at Ghent took place. In 1813, Germany had drawn the sword, and, with the help of British money and Russian manpower, drove Napoleon back across the Rhine. The French Emperor's disasters at the hands of the Russians gave Charles Carroll of Carrollton high hopes of an early peace with England. For Britannia, rid of Napoleon, would have no need to impress American seamen.[13] In the same year, 1813, the Duke of Wellington successfully concluded the peninsula campaign by ridding Spain of French troops. Paris was occupied by allied troops on March 31, 1814. Napoleon abdicated on April 8, 1814. Great Britain had finally emerged in complete triumph from her twenty-year struggle for existence and power. France lay humbled at her feet. So unchallenged was her supremacy on the high seas that her allies agreed

---

[13]Charles Carroll to Robert G. Harper, February 15, 1813, *Robert G. Harper MSS.* Harper, originally a Democrat, was a Federalist from 1803 on. He was elected to the U.S. Senate from Maryland in 1816.

to forego the discussion of maritime questions at the Congress of Vienna.

Lord of the continent, the high seas, and firmly entrenched in substantial parts of the United States, Lord Castlereagh based his diplomatic strategy at Ghent on the principle of *uti possidetis*. This meant that Great Britain intended to keep what she had according to the war map at the time of the negotiation, and also get as much more as possible. The British Foreign Secretary had high hopes that the war map in North America would look better and better as the year 1814 progressed. The Union Jack already flew over Fort Michilimackinac, Fort Niagara, and Astoria on the Northwest Coast, and all the country east of the Penobscot. While London deliberately dragged its diplomatic feet at Ghent, the Royal Navy was convoying two massive military expeditions, recently released from European wars, to the United States. One of these would sail into the St. Lawrence for the invasion and conquest of the Champlain and Hudson Valleys, and the other would engage in operations against the Eastern Seaboard states as well as New Orleans and the Mississippi Valley. If all went well with British arms, Louisiana and the old Northwest would be taken from the United States. In Maine, all territory east of the Penobscot would then change its allegiance from Washington to London. In New York, the south bank of the St. Lawrence would become British territory. Other changes in the map would provide England with a military road from Quebec to Halifax. Downing Street also wanted to terminate American liberty to the inshore fisheries. With regard to impressment, William H. Crawford of Georgia, our Minister to France in 1814, informed Henry Clay that he believed the British would "insist upon the unqualified admission of their right to impress on board American vessels at sea." The Georgian pleaded with the Kentuckian never to concede this right. Crawford stated that "it would be better to return to our colonial relations with our mother country than submit to this condition." Not at all sanguine about our chances at Ghent, Crawford ended his plea by declaring that if the right to impress "must be conceded, a federal President must make the concession."[14] Crawford had correctly divined the general intentions of the British. Indeed, Lord Castlereagh

[14]Crawford to Clay, June 10, 1814, *Henry Clay MSS.*

fairly exuded confidence. He was in no hurry to begin negotiations at Ghent. He would wait for good news from the forthcoming battles in North America. He could then make unlimited demands.[15]

In the spring and summer of 1814, the London *Times* accurately reflected the British official mind with reference to the Ghent Conference:

As we urged the principle, no peace with Bonaparte: so we must maintain the doctrine of no peace with James Madison . . . Mr. Madison's dirty swindling manoeuvres in respect to Louisiana and the Floridas remain to be punished . . . He must fall a victim to the just vengeance of the Federalists . . . Our demands may be couched in a single word—submission . . .[16]

Other British newspapers like the *Sun,* the *Morning Post,* and the *Courier* followed the *Times* in demanding unconditional surrender.[17] Backed by the vigorous support of the British press as well as the excellent British military position, the British commissioners on August 19, 1814, issued what was practically an ultimatum. Guided by Castlereagh's instructions of July 28 and August 14, Goulburn demanded the whole Northwest Territory of the United States for Britain's Indian allies. In other words, the country now represented by the states of Michigan, Wisconsin, Illinois, three-fifths of Indiana, and one-third of Ohio, was to be set apart forever as a sort of Indian barrier between the United States and Canada. This demand was made as a *sine qua non.* Goulburn insisted that the Indian boundary was not primarily for the sake of the Indians, but for the protection of Canada. When Gallatin expressed concern for the 100,000 Americans living in this territory, Goulburn cheerfully added that the "the 20,000 or so savages would treat their white wards well; he knew an Indian who was very intelligent."[18] After this audacious beginning, Goulburn pressed on. The Canadian frontier was to be rectified to give the British a line from Lake Superior west to the Mississippi, and a direct communication between Halifax and Quebec. The treaty right of the British to the navigation of the

---

[15]Alfred L. Burt, *The United States, Great Britain and British North America,* pp. 345-372. Excellent for British objectives at Ghent.
[16]London *Times,* February 4, 10; April 27; May 17, 1814.
[17]Henry Adams, *History of the United States,* Vol. IX, pp. 2-5. These newspapers were published in London.
[18]Thomas A. Bailey, *A Diplomatic History of the American People,* p. 148.

Mississippi was to be continued while American treaty rights regarding the fisheries were to be discontinued. Finally, the United States must keep no armed vessel or naval force on the Great Lakes from Ontario to Superior, inclusive. We must also agree neither to build new fortifications along these lakes nor to maintain such fortifications as are already there. Goulburn added that disarmament by the United States in the Great Lakes, like the creation of an Indian buffer-state, was essential for Canada's safety.

These oral demands were formalized in a written document and sent by the British delegation to their American counterparts on August 20, 1814. John Quincy Adams, as head of the American commission, replied in the name of his colleagues on August 25, that the British demands were "dishonorable to the United States."[19] On the same day, he confided to his diary that the American reply "will bring the negotiations very shortly to a close."[20] He grimly informed his mother that the "British . . . have . . . disclosed their intentions of reducing again to subjection as large a portion of the United States as they can occupy."[21] The Americans now began making preparations to leave Ghent. The British waited for further instructions from London. When President Madison finally received the terms, and read them to his Cabinet, he got the response he wanted: ". . . our Ministers were all present and in perfect harmony of opinion on the arrogance of such demands."[22] The demands of Great Britain aroused great popular indignation in the United States. More than one newspaper pointed out that the land claimed by Great Britain comprised 233,000,000 acres, an extent of territory larger than England, Wales, Ireland, and Scotland. The value of such real estate was conservatively estimated at $500,000,-000. The Philadelphia *Aurora* correctly mirrored American public opinion by stating:

It is impossible that our Commissioners can listen to such terms without indignation, and we feel warranted in saying, that to restrain the United States from treating with the Indians; that to despoil them through Massachusetts, Michi-

---

[19]*American State Papers, Foreign Relations,* Vol. III, p. 711.
[20]Diary of John Quincy Adams, August 25, 1814, *John Quincy Adams MSS.*
[21]John Quincy Adams to Mrs. John Adams, October 25, 1814, *John Quincy Adams MSS.*
[22]Madison to Jefferson, October 10, 1814, *Madison MSS.*

gan, Ohio, and the Lakes of their natural frontier and soil; to admit Great Britain into an exclusive right to arm the lakes and to a military occupation of both shores; to erect an independent savage power on our confines and within our domain; and to curtail our fisheries, sacred by the Treaty of 1782, are demands, attempts, or pretensions which the United States will never submit to, but with the loss of her freedom.[23]

The Essex Junto was the lone dissenting voice. The reaction of Governor Caleb Strong of Massachusetts was perfectly British. He, along with Timothy Pickering and other leading Federalists of New England, felt that England's offer was moderate. They blamed the American negotiators and Madison for rejecting such a just peace.[24]

The gloom that enveloped the American diplomats at Ghent was complete save for a ray of hope afforded by Henry Clay. He alone felt that London might be bluffing. Britain's ever-shifting interests on the continent might make her wish to liquidate the American war. A general peace had to be made at Vienna. The great problems of Germany and Poland were still unsettled. Defeated France would seek the first opportunity to throw off foreign shackles. The current American campaigns might turn the tide in favor of the United States. Soon the capture and burning of Washington would dampen even the Great Pacificator's optimism.

Both the British Prime Minister, the Earl of Liverpool, and the Foreign Secretary, Viscount Castlereagh, were incensed at what they regarded as the bungling work of their diplomats. Writing to Castlereagh, Liverpool berated his Ghent negotiators, and thought that it was "of the utmost importance that the rupture of the negotiation, if it is to take place, should be thrown upon the American Commissioners, and not upon us."[25] He was convinced that "if the negotiation had been allowed to break off upon the two notes already presented . . . the war would have become quite popular in America."[26] The firm stand of John Quincy Adams and company seemed to be paying dividends. Castlereagh felt that "the substance

---

[23]Philadelphia *Aurora*, October 24, 1814.

[24]Henry Adams, *History of the United States*, Vol. VIII, pp. 287-288.

[25]Liverpool to Castlereagh, September 2, 1814, *Supplementary Dispatches, Correspondence and Memoranda of Field Marshall Arthur, Duke of Wellington* (London: John Murray, 1862), Vol. IX, p. 214.

[26]Liverpool to Castlereagh, September 2, 1814, *ibid*.

of the question," was: "Are we prepared to continue the War for territorial arrangements?"[27] "Looking to a continuance of the American war," sighed Liverpool, "our financial state is far from satisfactory." We "shall want a loan for the service of the year of £27,000,000 or £28,000,000, and the American war will not cost us less than £10,000,000." The Prime Minister fully expected "to hear it said that the property tax is continued for the purpose of securing a better frontier for Canada."[28]

By the end of September, 1814, British flexibility was evident in the new instructions from Castlereagh to his commissioners at Ghent. Goulburn and company were now authorized to give up their *sine qua non* demand of an Indian buffer state. The door to compromise and peace was at last partially opened. It was opened still more when in mid-October London received the distressing news that the American Captain MacDonough had defeated and killed the British Captain Downie on Lake Champlain. American hopes soared on learning of this important victory. Reporting the event to President Madison, the Secretary of the Navy fairly exuded joy: "'Tis glorious news and nothing could have been better timed . . . this will tend to diminish the lustre of our burning capital."[29] After the destruction of Washington and the burning of our capital by British troops on August 24, 1814, Madison needed the consolation of the Plattsburgh triumph. Just about the time the good news of Mac-Donough's victory reached the ruins of the White House, Madison was reading a stinging editorial in the *Federal Republican* entitled, "The Bladensburg Races." His blood must have boiled as this Federalist Washington newspaper "had him and his select crew of War Hawks . . . at least one mile out of danger," and still going before the first shot was fired on Washington.[30] No one could accuse the editors of a lack of a sense of timing, for as their fellow Federalists convened at Hartford to adopt what many were predicting would be a secessionist resolution, they boldly proclaimed that "Mr. Madison's resignation alone will save the nation."[31] Crawford's dispatch

---

[27]Castlereagh to Liverpool, August 28, 1814, *ibid.*, p. 192.
[28]Liverpool to Castlereagh, October 28, 1814, *ibid.*, p. 383.
[29]William Jones to James Madison, September 12, 1814, *Madison MSS.* This naval battle of Plattsburgh was fought from 9:30 a.m. until 11 a.m. on Sept. 11, 1814.
[30]*Federal Republican,* October 7, 1814.
[31]*Federal Republican,* October 21, 1814.

from Paris assuring the President that the conduct of the British in Washington "has excited universal disgust in Europe,"[32] was balm to Madison, and acted somewhat in the nature of an antidote to the steady diet of Federalist criticism. Besides, Crawford agreed with the President that Monroe's efforts to thwart the British attack on Washington, merited for him his new post of Secretary of War. Our minister to France concluded his lengthy dispatch by remarking that since John Armstrong had not lived up to his expectations as head of the War Department, it was well that he had resigned after the Washington debacle.[33]

The burning of Washington thrilled the British, but the Plattsburgh defeat depressed them. General George Prevost had been hammering away unsuccessfully at Plattsburgh from September 6 to September 14, 1814. Since Downie's defeat on September 11 deprived Prevost of naval support, he decided to retreat into Canada and give up the invasion of the Champlain Valley area. Depressed by these reverses, the British cabinet in early November offered the Duke of Wellington "the chief command in America . . . with full powers to make peace, or to continue the war."[34] The Iron Duke's answer is famous. Upon its receipt the British ministry had no choice but to abandon its claims for territory. The Duke felt

no objection to going to America, though I don't promise to myself much success there . . . that which appears to me to be wanting in America is not a general, or a general officer and troops, but a naval superiority on the lakes . . . in regard to your present negotiations, I confess that I think you have no right, from the State of War, to demand any concession of territory from America . . .[35]

Perry's victory on Lake Erie at the end of 1813, followed by MacDonough's on Lake Champlain the following year, were decisive factors in Wellington's thinking. His thinking so impressed his superiors that less than three weeks after his answer to the Prime Minister, the British commissioners at Ghent presented the American commissioners with the note that ended the war. In essence it

---

[32]Crawford to Monroe, October 21, 1814, *Dispatches, Department of State.*
[33]*Ibid.* Monroe remained Secretary of State while taking over the duties of the War Department.
[34]Liverpool to Wellington, November 4, 1814, *op. cit.,* p. 406.
[35]Wellington to Liverpool, November 9, 1814, pp. 425-426.

read: ". . . the undersigned have foreborne to insist upon the basis of *uti possidetis,* to the advantage of which they consider their country fully entitled."[36]

PEACE

The British government, following Wellington's advice, had found it "desirable to bring the American war if possible to a conclusion."[37] They had "been led to this determination by the consideration of the unsatisfactory state of negotiations at Vienna, and by that of the alarming situation of the interior of France."[38] Then "the state of finances, and . . . the difficulties in continuing the property tax . . ." also inclined the cabinet towards peace.[39] The judgment of the Iron Duke had been the determining one. His letter ended the war in a few weeks by forcing the British to drop their *uti possidetis* for the American *status quo ante bellum.*

Great was the rejoicing in the American lodgings at Ghent on November 27, 1814, when the news of the British change of heart arrived. They were pleased beyond measure with the very real prospect of ending the war without loss of territory. Now that the main obstacle to peace—*uti possidetis*—was removed, the negotiators were not long in coming to terms. After conferences on December 1 and again on December 23, the envoys finally agreed to the terms of the peace. The treaty was signed at the residence of the British commissioners on Christmas Eve, 1814. Lord Gambier said that he hoped the treaty would be a permanent one.[40] John Quincy Adams remarked: "I hope it will be the last treaty of peace between Great Britain and the United States."[41] It was. Adams' diary for the evening records a prayer of thanksgiving: "I cannot close the record of this day without a humble offering to God for the conclusion to which it has pleased Him to bring the negotiations for peace . . . and a fervent prayer that its result may be propitious to the welfare, the best interests, and the union of my country."[42]

---

[36]*American State Papers, Foreign Relations,* Vol. III, pp. 740 sq.
[37]Liverpool to Castlereagh, November 18, 1814, *op. cit.,* p. 438.
[38]*Ibid.*
[39]*Ibid.*
[40]Diary of John Quincy Adams: December 24, 1814, *John Quincy Adams MSS.*
[41]*Ibid.*
[42]*Ibid.*

The treaty contains eleven articles. The first contains the essence of the agreement: "All territory, places, and possessions whatsoever taken by either party from the other during the war . . . shall be restored without delay."[43] The treaty in effect meant simply a cessation of hostilities and a return to the *status quo ante bellum*. After the defeat of Napoleon, Jefferson sagely remarked that although the war had been "undertaken on both sides to settle the questions of impressment and the Orders in Council . . . these are now done away by events."[44] Bonaparte's downfall rendered British wartime maritime practices unnecessary. Neither Britain nor America had won the war or desired to continue it. Neither nation could enforce its will upon the other. Exercising a legitimate flexibility both governments had dropped their *sine qua non* demands: the British, the Indian buffer state; the Americans, their demand that London renounce impressment. The rights and privileges that the Indians enjoyed in 1811 were to be restored to them. Fishes, rivers, and arms on the Great Lakes were assigned to arbitral commissions.

The American negotiators rushed three copies of the treaty to the United States. In London, the Prince Regent immediately ratified the treaty. In the United States, the Senate would merely have to advise and consent by a two-thirds majority of senators present before the President could ratify. The British Prime Minister informed his Foreign Secretary that "even if peace is signed, I shall not be surprised if Madison endeavors to play us some trick in the ratification of it." Therefore, he continued, "it will be stipulated . . . that hostilities shall not cease till after the exchange of ratifications at Washington."[45] It was so agreed, and Bayard wrote: "We have this day concluded and signed a treaty of peace . . . hostilities do not however cease till it be ratified by our Government."[46]

HARTFORD VS. GHENT

While John Quincy Adams fought to preserve the rights of

---

[43]*Treaties and Other International Acts of the United States of America,* ed. by David Hunter Miller (Washington: United States Government Printing Office, 1931), Vol. II, pp. 574-575.

[44]Jefferson to Madison, October 15, 1814, *Madison MSS.*

[45]Liverpool to Castlereagh, December 24, 1814, *op. cit.,* p. 495.

[46]James A. Bayard to Andrew Bayard, December 24, 1814, *James A. Bayard MSS.* Andrew was James A. Bayard's nephew. Jackson's New Orleans victory took place a good month before the exchange of ratifications.

Massachusetts at Ghent, at Hartford in Connecticut, twenty-three delegates were assembling from Massachusetts, Connecticut, and Rhode Island to threaten rebellion if their recommendations were not complied with. The total number attending eventually reached twenty-six when three new members, one representing the county of Windham in Vermont, and two appointed by popular meetings in New Hampshire, were given seats. This Hartford Convention, as it came to be called, was a culmination of a whole series of disloyal acts by leading Federalists and their followers in New England. These unpatriotic men loaned the enemy money, traded with him, refused to use the militia to fight him, and we have every reason to believe, even sent him tentative proposals of armistice and alliance.[47] Colonel Thomas Hart Benton, fighting on the Canadian border in the winter of 1813, apprised Henry Clay of this rotten spirit. Southern Federalists, he wrote, "will be filled with horror when I tell them what I have seen here for they have no idea of treason." Benton urged Clay "to press on vigorously . . . make the war successful and glorious, and the people will bear with pride all the bothers it imposes." Britain's main object, according to Benton, was to keep the conflict alive as a means of "dividing the union."[48] Although large numbers of New Englanders supported the war, the voice of New England came to be the voice of extreme Federalism. This extreme view was epitomized by Timothy Pickering, Senator from Massachusetts:

a separation of the Northern section of the states would be ultimately advantageous, because it would be temporary, and because in the interval the just rights of the states would be recovered and secured . . . The Southern states would earnestly seek a reunion, when the rights of both would be defined and established on a more equal and therefore more durable basis . . .[49]

Gouverneur Morris, one of the Founding Fathers, stood four-square with Pickering: "The traitors and madmen assembled at Hartford will, I believe, if not too tame and timid, be hailed hereafter as the patriots and sages . . . may the blessing of God be upon

---

[47]George Dangerfield, *The Era of Good Feelings* (New York: Harcourt, Brace & Co., 1952), p. 87.
[48]Benton to Clay, January 22, 1813, *Henry Clay MSS.*
[49]Timothy Pickering to Gouverneur Morris, October 21, 1814, in Henry Adams, *Documents Relating to New England Federalism*, p. 401.

them, to inspire their counsels and prosper their resolutions."[50] Moderate Federalists, like Senator Charles Cutts of New Hampshire, were "happy to learn that New Hampshire does not join in the Convention at Hartford." Cutts expressed the sincere "hope that another election will place her out of the reach of the mad schemes of the Essex Junto."[51] Another moderate, the Federalist Senator Samuel W. Dana of Connecticut, expressed confidence in the belief that "all Federalists So. of the Hudson are ready to go with the Adm. in a vigorous prosecution of the War."[52]

As the voice of the Essex minority grew in power, it tended more and more to advocate disunion. Probably only a small fragment of the Federalist peace party wished to end the war by an act of treason, but this fragment was composed of wealth and learning. It was backed by the influential Congregationalist clergy, and it exercised an unfortunate magnetic effect upon the unorganized masses around it.

The major concession to be demanded of the federal government by the ambassadors from the Hartford Convention was that of surrendering to Massachusetts, Connecticut, and Rhode Island "a reasonable portion of taxes collected within said states." Also Washington was to consent to some arrangement "whereby the said states may, separately or in concert, be empowered to assume upon themselves the defense of their territory against the enemy." If the United States government should refuse such a request, the state legislatures were to send delegates to another convention to meet at Boston, June 15, "with such powers and instructions as the exigency of a crisis so momentous may require."[53]

The Governor of New Hampshire was one of those who were deeply disturbed by the impending crisis. He poured out his fears to Jefferson:

We are, in the Eastern states, threatened with insurrection and rebellion by the Hartford Convention now in session . . . their object is dismemberment, which will injure the South, but ruin the North. Your flour, cotton, rice,

---

[50]Morris to Pickering, December 22, 1814, ibid., p. 419.
[51]Charles Cutts to William Plumer, November 6, 1814, Plumer MSS..
[52]Samuel W. Dana to William Eustis, November 2, 1814, William Eustis MSS. Eustis, Secretary of War in 1812, was in 1814 our minister to Holland.
[53]Henry Adams, History of the United States, Vol. VII, p. 298.

and tobacco are necessary to us—without them our commerce could not subsist . . . [54]

On the other hand, the Federalist Gouverneur Morris was so disgusted with the Union he had done so much to form, that he rejoiced that at Hartford "Events may take place to open a commerce between . . . the United Kingdom . . . and the Northern States."[55] With regard to taxes, he saw "one consolation . . . they will not long be paid. The war must end soon or a separation of the States will take place."[56]

Fortunately the Governor's fears and Morris' hopes were soon dissolved by American military victory and diplomatic success, for when the Hartford commissioners enroute to Washington reached Baltimore, on February 12, 1815, they were greeted with the news of the "miraculous success" of General Andrew Jackson at New Orleans.[57] General Pakenham's British troops had marched against the city, only to be thrown back and their commander killed in Jackson's magnificent triumph of January 8, 1815. Thus were British plans to return Louisiana and West Florida to "the protection of the Spanish Crown" finally thwarted. Prior to Jackson's smashing victory, the British Secretary for Colonial Affairs had instructed his commanding officer in the New Orleans theater that American rule in Louisiana and West Florida "can be regarded only as usurpation."[58]

Sections of the Federalist press had gone so far as to assert that the fall of New Orleans to the British was to be the signal for a general demand that Madison resign. Jackson's feat stilled this Essex newspaper propaganda. Hard on the heels of the news of New Orleans came the information that the Treaty of Ghent had been signed. The Hartford Convention was now turned into a pitiful

---

[54]Plumer to Jefferson, December 30, 1814, *Plumer MSS.*

[55]Morris to J. B. Delauncey, January 31, 1814, *Morris MSS.* Delauncey, a merchant in Schenectady, was a Federalist and a friend of Morris.

[56]Morris to Leroy de Chaumontfils, November 18, 1814, *Morris MSS.* Chaumontfils was one of the many friends Morris made in Paris. Morris was our minister to France in 1795.

[57]Harrison Gray Otis to Mrs. Otis, February 12, 1815, in Samuel E. Morison, *Life and Letters of Harrison Gray Otis,* Vol. II, p. 164.

[58]Lord Bathhurst to Major General Robert Ross, September 6, 1814, *Henry Adams Transcripts of British Documents.*

farce. Its ambassadors, the defeatists of 1814, slunk home in obscurity pursued by the jeers of the press. They were soon to become forgotten men. The future belonged to new nationalists, men like Jackson, Adams, and Clay.

Jefferson had seen a direct relationship between Hartford and Ghent. It was his contention that the British were holding on to *uti possidetis* as "a thread . . . until they can hear the result, not of the Congress of Vienna, but of Hartford. When they shall know, as they will know, that nothing will be done there, they will . . . complete the peace of the world, by agreeing to the *status quo ante bellum.*"[59]

The Treaty of Ghent reached Washington on February 14, 1815. As soon as the senators had read it along with a summary of the diplomatic record, they unanimously ratified it on February 17, 1815. They were thrilled with both Jackson's brilliant conquest of a veteran British army and with the peace that yielded not a single inch of American territory. At eleven o'clock that very evening, February 17, James Monroe exchanged final ratifications with Anthony St. John Baker, Secretary of the British Legation. Next morning, February 18, 1815, the President announced the good news. Practically everyone, North, South, East, and West was happy with the peace. The minority, represented by such papers as the Federalist New York *Evening Post,* saw no cause for celebrating. The *Post* claimed that by involving America in war, Madison won a second term, $25,000 a year, a marbled mansion fitted out at the expense of $14,000, and "the prerogative of naming his successor from the State of Virginia." Whereas, how can the people ever be "recompensed for the death of thousands and the expense of millions." When the terms are disclosed, concluded the editor, it will be found that Madison and his cohorts have not "obtained one single avowed object, for which they involved the country in this bloody and expensive war."[60] However, in a very real sense, even the Essex Junto had to like Ghent. For peace, peace at any price, was what they had been demanding. The Democrats had

---

[59]Jefferson to Correa de Serra, December 27, 1814, *Jefferson MSS.* Correa de Serra was minister to the United States from Portugal.
[60]New York *Evening Post,* February 13, 1815.

brought them peace with honor. After two years of galling humiliations, the honor of the Stars and Stripes had been redeemed in diplomatic circles and on the battlefield. Rejoicing over the peace that his son had so much to do with, John Adams wrote that "the town of Boston was last night all in flames, and the day before yesterday all the bells in New England I suppose rang from morning to night."[61]

Jefferson, in a congratulatory letter to the President, injected elements that would soon help to form the Monroe Doctrine: "I sincerely congratulate you on the peace; and more especially on the éclat with which the war was closed. The affair of N. Orleans . . . will show . . . the nations of Europe . . . we mean to take no part in their wars and count no odds when engaged in our own."[62] Not at all optimistic about the duration of the peace, Jefferson viewed the treaty "as an armistice only because no provision is made against the practice of impressment." The founder of the Democratic party believed that impressment "would revive in the first moment of a war in Europe," and "its revival will be declaration of war here." Therefore, argued the Sage of Monticello, "our whole business in the meantime ought to be a sedulous preparation for it, fortifying our seaports, filling our magazines . . . disciplining our militia . . . and above all, establishing a sound system of finance."[63]

In England the treaty was greeted with feelings of mixed satisfaction and anger. The British were annoyed with the terms of the treaty, but somewhat satisfied over having at last attained peace, but British wrath over Ghent soon disappeared with the news of the crushing defeat at New Orleans and Napoleon's escape from Elba.[64] The Emperor's return to Paris led to Waterloo, and in the glory of that day, England found compensation for her American peace without victory. Goulburn of Copenhagen and Ghent fame, wrote Clay, expressing hope "that our joint work is approved in America. I assure you it is in England . . . whatever may be said in the newspapers."[65]

[61]John Adams to Mrs. Catherine E. Rush, February 23, 1815, *John Adams MSS.*
[62]Jefferson to Madison, March 23, 1815, *Madison MSS.*
[63]Jefferson to DuPont de Nemours, February 28, 1815.
[64]James Maury to Madison, April 19, 1815, *Madison MSS.* Maury, a friend of Madison, in England on business, reported on British reaction.
[65]Henry Goulburn to Clay, March 8, 1816, *Henry Clay MSS.*

HARTFORD, GHENT, AND POLITICS

For the Federalists, the peace of Ghent was the kiss of death. Their wartime conduct destroyed them as a political party. Possessing the bulk of the nation's financial resources, they had refused to finance the war. They not only would not provide militia for the conquest of Canada, but they rejoiced in the news of British victories. Their use of blue light signals on dark nights to warn British war vessels of the presence of American blockade runners, won them the opprobrious sobriquet of Blue Light Federalists. So sure were the British of their sympathy that they did not even attempt to blockade their coast until almost the end of the war. Then, too, the British encouraged secession, but fortunately for the Union, the moderate George Cabot headed the Massachusetts delegation at Hartford. When asked by a young friend what he intended to do at Hartford, Cabot replied: "We are going to keep you young hotheads from getting into mischief."[66] Unfortunately for the Federalist party, the great majority of Americans made no distinction between the Cabot moderates and the Pickering fanatics. All Federalists were damned as plotters and disunionists. The Administration newspaper in Washington naturally did nothing to encourage the people to make distinctions between Federalists. It called upon all Democrats and their supporters to rejoice because "by the unsurpassed exploits of your Army and Navy, and the consummate wisdom of your statesmen, you have achieved an honorable peace with one of the most powerful nations on the globe." Federalists were asked to rejoice in that "your opposition has been unavailing in checking the measures of your government . . . that your Hartford Convention, your plots . . . have not arrested the march of the Republic to the heights of fame and glory."[67]

After Hartford and Ghent, the once powerful party of Hamilton was reduced to ashes. Nothing remained but the funeral service. These obsequies were to get under way on March 16, 1816, when 119 Democratic senators and representatives were due to convene in the House of Representatives to choose Madison's successor. Just a week before, Governor Plumer, in an attempt to bring

---

[66]Henry Adams, *History of the United States,* Vol. VIII, p. 292.
[67]*National Intelligencer,* February 16, 1815.

his friend John Quincy Adams up-to-date on domestic politics, ventured a prediction: "Monroe, Crawford, and Tompkins are the prominent candidates; the first I think will be elected. The other two are not sufficiently known."[68] Plumer proved to be right, but it was a very close race between Monroe and Crawford.

A month before the caucus, Alexander C. Hanson, Federalist editor of the *Federalist Republican,* quoted Monroe as saying: "A caucus is an unfair way of getting to the will of the people." Feeling that Monroe spoke for the Democrats, Hanson and his friends looked in vain for "a denunciation of caucuses in the *National Intelligencer,* the Administration newspaper in Washington." As Hanson mingled among the politicians on Capitol Hill, he was given assurances that "Crawford . . . has agreed to stand against Monroe. An agent has gone to New York to get Tompkins to serve as vice-president. It is confidently expected that they will succeed."[69] They almost did. Because of the actions of Hanson and other Federalists, some Crawford Democrats started a rumor that Crawford was more acceptable to the Federalists than Monroe. Hanson scotched this as "altogether erroneous and fallacious."[70] Congressman Samuel R. Betts of New York gives us an inside picture of the March 16 caucus in one of his many reports to Van Buren. Betts records that the Monroeites feared a showdown. During the caucus, "Mr. Clay moved a resolution that it was inexpedient at this time to make any nomination." When this resolution was finally defeated after a lengthy discussion, Betts was confident of Crawford's chances. However, when eight Congressmen from the Southwest "who had always declared their decided preference for Crawford, voted for Monroe . . . the decision was made . . . 65 for Monroe, 54 for Crawford, 85 for Tompkins, vice-pres., 30 for Synder." Since 19 of New York's 23 Democratic members of the House and Senate voted in the caucus, Betts' penultimate sentence is revealing: "Four of our delegates voted Monroe." These four, in addition to the four absentee New Yorkers, had it in their power to give the crown to Crawford.

---

[68]Plumer to John Quincy Adams, March 6, 1816, *Plumer MSS.*
[69]Alexander C. Hanson to Robert G. Harper, February 1, 1816, *Harper MSS.*
[70]*Federal Republican,* March 15, 1816. This Federalist newspaper was published in Washington, D.C.

Some historians have given the impression that Van Buren swung the New York delegation to Monroe. The Betts-Van Buren correspondence does not support this view. Originally, Van Buren worked hard to make Tompkins president, but dropped this when it became evident that Tompkins did not have sufficient support outside of New York. Actually the "Little Magician" remained neutral as between Crawford or Monroe. This is revealed in a conversation between New York's Congressman Jabez D. Hammond and Van Buren.[71] Actually Crawford had unselfishly withdrawn from the caucus and afterwards maintained that the presidency "was clearly in my reach if I had been ambitious of it."[72] Congressman Betts ends his succinct account of the March 16 caucus on a note of assurance and cooperation: "We shall now support the ticket as nominated."[73] The Virginia Dynasty was still intact. The nomination of the energetic Governor Daniel D. Tompkins of New York for the vice-presidency restored the Virginia-New York alliance of earlier years. The election of Monroe was virtually assured.

No candidates were nominated by the Federalists. The Boston *Daily Advertiser* remarked the obvious: "We do not know, nor is it very material, for whom the Federal electors will vote."[74] Gouverneur Morris' remark to Rufus King that "it seems to be acknowledged that no Federal character can run with success," reflects the general feeling of helplessness among Federalists. King, distinguished Federalist Senator from New York, not only agreed with Morris, but contended that the Federalists were "out of the question as a rival party." In his judgment, former Federalists would "be able to assist the true interests of freedom and of justice, by

---

[71]Jabez D. Hammond, *The History of Political Parties in the State of New York* (Syracuse: Hall, Mills & Co., 1852), Vol. I, p. 411. Hammond voted for Crawford in the caucus of March 16, 1816.

[72]Crawford to Charles Tait; September 4, 1821, as quoted in J. E. D. Shipp, *Giant Days or the Life and Times of William H. Crawford* (Americus, Ga.: Southern Printers, 1909), p. 149. Tait was a Senator from Georgia. For Crawford's voluntary withdrawal from the caucus see Robert V. Remini, "New York and the Presidential Election of 1816," *New York History*, Vol. XXXI, July 1950, pp. 320-322.

[73]Samuel R. Betts to Martin Van Buren, March 17, 1816, *Van Buren MSS*. Van Buren was Attorney General of New York at this time. Synder is Simon Synder, Governor of Pennsylvania. See Edward Stanwood, *A History of the Presidency*, p. 109, and DeAlva S. Alexander, *A Political History of the State of New York* (New York: Henry Holt & Co., 1906), Vol. I, pp. 240-247 for the view that Van Buren influenced the New York delegation in favor of Monroe.

[74]Boston *Daily Advertiser*, December 3, 1816.

giving their influence to the least wicked section of the Republicans."[75] Monroe was such a sure thing, that a good two months before the election, Jefferson, after asking him to provide a White House job for a fellow Virginian, concluded with the benediction: "God bless and preserve you for the next eight years to come especially."[76]

The result at the polls was just what the Federalists and everyone else expected. Monroe received 183 votes to Rufus King's 34. The electors of Massachusetts, Connecticut, and Delaware, who had been chosen by the legislatures, cast the 34 votes for Rufus King. Daniel Tompkins won the vice-presidency with 183 votes. His Federalist runners-up were: John F. Howard of Maryland, 22; James Ross of Pennsylvania, 5; John Marshall of Virginia, 4; and Robert G. Harper of Maryland, 3. In December, 1816, the public heard the news of the overwhelming Democratic victory with an apathy in keeping with the onesidedness of the contest. The surprise, if there was any, was that King got any votes at all. The vigorous criticism of the caucus system of choosing presidential nominees, led by such prominent citizens as Roger B. Taney, was the only stimulating phase of the entire campaign. The Democrats admitted the inherent difficulties in nomination by caucus. Jefferson's followers were willing to settle for another method "if any preferable mode of concentrating the sentiments of the different sections of the union can be devised."[77]

Nineteen states had participated. The state legislatures had, for the most part, chosen the electors. Monroe was unopposed from Virginia southward. Rhode Island, Vermont, New York, Pennsylvania, and Ohio also voted for the Virginian. Since the election of 1812, Indiana had been the only state admitted into the Union. The Hoosiers chose Monroe.

The election of James Monroe ushered into American history what the Boston *Sentinel* termed the "Era of Good Feelings."[78] Without Madison's successful presidential years, this era would never have been born. John Adams' comment on those preparatory

---

[75]Morris to King, March 15, 1816, and King to Edward King, May 21, 1816, *Rufus King MSS.*
[76]Jefferson to Monroe, October 9, 1816, *Jefferson MSS.*
[77]*National Intelligencer,* September 13, 1816.
[78]Boston *Sentinel,* July 12, 1817.

years is pertinent: "Notwithstanding a thousand faults and blunders, his administration has acquired more glory, and established more union, than all his three predecessors, Washington, Adams, and Jefferson, put together."[79] Patriotism, somewhat quiescent during the war, now burst out all over. The young nation, proud of having smashed the British at Plattsburgh and New Orleans, set itself to the task of remedying the national weaknesses revealed by the war. Congress, controlled by the War Hawks, now called the Young Republicans, speedily passed measures for a larger peacetime army and navy, for the creation of a second Bank of the United States, and for an increase in tariff rates. The initial defeats in the recent war made the military bills imperative. Jefferson's remark to Monroe concerning the "general bankruptcy" and the total absence of all other medium of payment save the worthless paper money of state banks, demonstrated a need for a second Bank of the United States.[80] With regard to industrial growth, Jefferson's wartime exultation that "our manufactures are spreading with a rapidity that could not have been expected," pointed up the need for more protection.[81] The war bequeathed to the American people a powerful drive for economic self-sufficiency. Under the vitalizing influence of an intense nationalism, the followers of Thomas Jefferson outstripped Alexander Hamilton and his Federalists as advocates of a broad construction of the Constitution. Typical of the new mood of the Democratic party was the opinion of John C. Calhoun that a discussion of the constitutionality of chartering a second Bank of the United States would be a "useless consumption of time."[82] Jefferson's historic opinion against the chartering of the first bank was given the *coup de grace* by his own disciples when they dredged up the Federalist arguments of 1791, and used them in arguing for a second Bank of the United States. When Webster and other Federalists opposed the new bank by using Jefferson's 1791 arguments, the topsy-turviness of politics was apparent. At this point, Josiah Quincy, an outstanding Federalist leader, lamented that the Democrats had "out-Federalized Fed-

[79]John Adams to Jefferson, February 2, 1817, *Jefferson MSS.*
[80]Jefferson to Monroe, September 24, 1814, *Jefferson MSS.*
[81]Jefferson to David B. Warden, December 29, 1813, *Jefferson MSS.* At this time Warden was the American consul in Paris.
[82]Wilfred C. Binkley, *American Political Parties*, p. 98.

eralism."[83] Before his retirement, Madison attempted an answer to Quincy by arguing that there had been a great change of circumstances which reconciled the Democrats to "certain measures and arrangements which may be as proper now as they were premature and suspicious when urged by the champions of Federalism."[84] Gouverneur Morris analyzed the new look in Jeffersonian politics somewhat differently: "By downright demonstration it is shown that the Republican party were not dissatisfied because the power of the Government was too great, but because it was not in their hands."[85]

Madison, ever the practical statesman, and aware of the "difficulties . . . in which . . . finances were left by the war . . .," advocated "the establishment of a National Bank and a continuance of a large portion of the war taxes."[86] He also backed the higher tariff of 1816 as a "very important provision . . . for fostering our manufactures."[87] Having gracefully presided over the metamorphosis of his party, Madison had but a few months wait before relinquishing his authority to his Secretary of State.

---

[83]Wilfred C. Binkley, *American Political Parties,* p. 98.

[84]Roseboom, *A History of Presidential Elections,* p. 74.

[85]Morris to H. W. Livingston, November 25, 1803, *Gouverneur Morris MSS.*

[86]Madison to William Eustis, May 12, 1816, *Madison MSS.*

[87]Madison to William Eustis, May 12, 1816, *Madison MSS.* The Tariff of 1816 was the first in our history that was primarily protective. Its rates were 20 percent to 25 percent on the value of dutiable imports. Jefferson agreed with Madison on the bank and tariff questions. See Jefferson to Benjamin Austin, January 9, 1816, *Jefferson MSS.* Austin, a Democrat, was commissioner for loans to Massachusetts.

8

Foreign Policy and Slavery

As James Monroe, the last of the "Virginians," took his oath to uphold the Constitution, his resemblance to George Washington was striking. More than a few of the eight thousand people that gathered in front of the Capitol noted the similarities. The grayish-blue eyes, the broad shoulders, the finely chiselled features, and above all the severe expression of his face, reminded the audience of the founder of the "Virginia Dynasty."[1]

The clear, blue sunshiny day that was March 4, 1817, was almost a necessity for the District of Columbia's first outdoor inaugural. Heretofore, the exercises had been held in the House of Representatives. The break in precedent had been caused by Henry Clay, Speaker of the House. Clay, deeply disappointed over Monroe's failure to appoint him to the coveted post of Secretary of State, refused the use of the House chamber. Profiting from his Ghent experience, the Kentuckian used the diplomatic excuse that the floor of the room was not strong enough to support so great a crowd. Consequently, the last of our "Revolutionary" executives was sworn in by the black-robed Chief Justice Marshall on an elevated portico in front of the House of Representatives.[2]

Our fifth President, sixty-one years of age and six feet one inch tall, followed custom by making his inaugural address an outline of the course he intended to follow. Passing over in discreet silence the establishment of the second national bank, Monroe insisted that our recent phenomenal success against the world's greatest power was due to the fact that our "Government has been in the hands of the people." To the people, therefore, stated Monroe, and

---

[1]*National Intelligencer,* March 5, 1817.
[2]William P. Cresson, *James Monroe* (Chapel Hill: University of North Carolina Press, 1946), p. 282.

to their duly elected representatives, "is the credit due." These same liberty-loving people had seen to it that our Constitution had both created a national government with a "mild parental" control, as well as individual states with a "just proportion of the sovereignty."

This government, continued the President, will continue to protect "the great agricultural interest of the nation," but our manufactures, he was quick to add, "will likewise require . . . systematic and fostering care." The improvement of our country "by roads and canals" must go hand in hand with our great capacity to produce. Those engaged in commerce and navigation can rest assured that we will build an army and navy powerful enough to defend their rights. Henceforth our slogan will be: "National honor is national property of the highest value." Mindful of past secessionist threats, Monroe asserted that if war came again it might well be "the object of the adverse party . . . to break our union." Since war often breeds secession, the President urged military preparedness as our best guarantee against both calamities.

By way of conclusion, Monroe was gratified "to witness the increased harmony of opinion which pervades our union." It was his feeling that history would record that "never did a government commence under auspices so favorable." He would not fail to offer "fervent prayers to the Almighty that He will be graciously pleased to continue to us that protection which He has already so conspicuously displayed in our favor."[3]

A BUSINESS TRIP

Soon after his inauguration, Monroe, in imitation of Washington, made an extended tour northward. There were sound national and political reasons for making the trip. In the interest of national defense the President had announced shortly after his election that he intended to inspect all the forts along the coast from Baltimore to Portland, and from Portland to Detroit. These coastal fortifications were part of a new system then in process of construction under the capable direction of General Bernard, a French officer, who came highly recommended by Lafayette.

The President's political popularity was already nationwide.

---

[3]James D. Richardson, *A Compilation of the Messages and Papers of the Presidents,* Vol. II, pp. 573-579.

He was a hero in the West because of his agency in procuring a free Mississippi for the Union. The South was his very own. Even the Eastern Anglo-Federalists remembered him as the negotiator of the British Treaty of 1806 which Jefferson had rejected. "Blue Lights" and "Hartford Convention" were already words they would like to forget. As a result, Harrison Gray Otis and his friends offered to smoke the pipe of peace. They very much wished to be on good terms with the incoming administration. Speaking in their behalf, Daniel Webster, a representative from Federalist New England, saw Monroe, and urged a New England tour as a means of strengthening patriotism. Even though many members of his own party grumbled about the expense and time involved, Monroe decided to make the journey if only to placate the Federalists and restore political harmony.

The President left Washington May 31 on a trip of three and one half months. It took him through thirteen states in a triumphal tour such as had not been seen since the days of Washington. Baltimore, Philadelphia, New York, Hartford, Boston, Portsmouth, Portland, Detroit, and Pittsburgh—all gave him tremendous ovations. DeWitt Clinton and Rufus King in New York, and Harrison Gray Otis and Timothy Pickering in Boston, welcomed Monroe with cordial hospitality.[4]

Monroe returned to Washington in September, tired but consoled. His consolation was founded on the solid conviction that the old prejudices against him as a Southerner, a Virginian, and a president opposed to the interests of the North and East, had disappeared. By this time, the burned-out presidential mansion had been restored. A heavy coat of white paint having been applied to obliterate the marks of the fire, it was soon known as the "White House." Monroe, very apprehensive of the effects of the fresh painting and plastering, was in no mood to move in immediately. Besides, he was anxious to visit his family, and recuperate from his arduous journey. After spending two or three days in Washington, during which time he greeted his new Secretary of State, John Quincy Adams, he departed for Virginia.[5]

---

[4]James Schouler, *History of the United States of America* (New York: Dodd, Mead & Co., 1885), Vol. III, pp. 8-13.
[5]William P. Cresson, *James Monroe*, p. 290.

From nomination day, March 16, 1816, to inauguration day, March 4, 1817, James Monroe had given a great deal of thought to the selection of his Cabinet. It was his original intention to fill the four most important positions with men who were not only capable but whose appointments would preserve harmony among the sections of the country. This would mean that the various sections of the country would each furnish a statesman whose knowledge of local details would be of real value in cabinet discussions.

MONROE'S STAFF

For Secretary of State, a post generally held to be the likeliest route to the presidency, he did not hesitate to choose John Quincy Adams. Adams' experience and singular success in the foreign service, in addition to the fact that he represented a disgruntled North, made him, in Monroe's mind, the logical choice. The Chief Executive explained the motivation behind this appointment to Thomas Jefferson:

On full consideration of all circumstances, I have thought that it would produce a bad effect, to place anyone from this quarter of the union, in the dept. of State, or from the South or west. You know how much has been said to impress a belief, on the country, north and east of this, that the citizens from Virga., holding the Presidency, have made appointments to that dept. to secure the succession, from it, to the Presidency, of the person who happens to be from that state . . . It is, however, not sufficient that this allegation is unfounded . . . with this in view, I have thought it advisable to select a person for the dept. of State, from the Eastern States, in consequence of which my attention has been turned to Mr. Adams, who by his age, by experience in foreign affairs, and adoption into the republican party, seems to have superior pretensions to any there.[6]

Henry Clay, burning with presidential ambitions, was so furious at being passed over for Secretary of State that he coldly turned down Monroe's offer of the Department of War. The Georgian, William H. Crawford, Monroe's only serious rival for the presidency, was offered and accepted the Treasury Department. Looking for a Westerner for the War Department, the President approached both Isaac Shelby, Governor of Kentucky, and Andrew Jackson, in that order. When they refused, he abandoned the West for the South, and appointed John C. Calhoun, a rising young Congressman from South Carolina. To the Virginian, William Wirt, prosecutor for the

---
[6]Monroe to Jefferson, February 23, 1817, *Monroe MSS.*

government in the Burr trial, went the attorney generalship. Benjamin W. Crowninshield of Massachusetts, a holdover from the previous administration, continued on as Secretary of the Navy.

Thus, through no fault of his own, Monroe's original plan had not entirely succeeded. For the West had failed to secure representation, and the South had gained a definite preponderance of influence. The cabinet appointments out of the way, the President now focused his attention on the diplomatic corps. Richard Rush, the former Attorney General, replaced Adams at the Court of St. James, while Albert Gallatin remained on at Paris. George W. Campbell of Tennessee, a former Secretary of the Treasury, replaced William Pinkney at St. Petersburg. Pinkney, at one time Attorney General, had requested permission to retire to private life.[7]

AMERICA FACES INWARD

After almost twenty-two years (1793-1815) of continuous war, Europe slumped back into a peace of exhaustion. With Bonaparte safely confined to the island of St. Helena, some 5,000 miles away, deposed monarchs regained their battered thrones, and Europe pursued its old ways. The end of the Napoleonic nightmare meant an abrupt change in British foreign policy. In a secret dispatch, the British Foreign Secretary, Lord Castlereagh, advised his minister in Washington that the "avowed and true policy of Great Britain . . . in the existing state of the world . . . is to appease controversy, and to secure, if possible, for all states a long interval of repose."[8] International peace did indeed follow, and its long duration gave the American people a chance to work out their own destiny with a minimum of foreign meddling. Freed from the necessity of anxiously scanning the Atlantic horizon for every approaching sail, they turned their backs on the Old World, and faced resolutely toward the West. The undisturbed and steady tramp of American westward-moving pioneers would in some three decades round out the natural boundaries of the United States. Europe was forgotten. Interest in international affairs became so minimal that the disgusted Russian *chargé* in Washington remarked that they

---

[7]William P. Cresson, *James Monroe*, pp. 290-292.
[8]Castlereagh to Charles Bagot, British Minister at Washington, most private and secret, November 10, 1817, *Henry Adams Transcripts*.

"pay no more attention to us and our business than if we were so many Chinamen."[9] As early as September of 1815, the Washington *National Intelligencer* attributed its loss of subscriptions to the almost universal belief that European affairs no longer mattered.[10]

UNITED STATES VS. ALGERIA

If the general populace neglected their homework in foreign affairs from 1815 to 1820, the same cannot be said of the Department of State. Our diplomacy during these years was as direct as it was effective. Beginning with our North African policy, and ending with our transcontinental treaty with Spain, the Democratic party achieved a succession of triumphs.

The indignities that America suffered at the hands of Algiers during the War of 1812 were highlighted by the Dey's impertinent answer to our offer to pay ransom money for twelve American prisoners. Responding to our request from the quiet of his harem, the Algerian despot huffily declared: ". . . my policy and my views are to increase, not to diminish, the number of my American slaves; and that not for a million dollars would I release them."[11] Americans are ordinarily a patient people, but there are certain things they will not brook. This was one of them. Five days after Madison announced the treaty of peace with Britain, he asked for a declaration of war against Algeria. Congress complied with enthusiasm. Two squadrons were equipped for a Mediterranean cruise. After a fast trip, Commodore Decatur hunted down and smashed a good part of the Dey's fleet. The efficient Commodore then dictated a peace at the cannon's mouth. The terms of this treaty of 1815 provided for no more ransom and no more tribute by the United States. By way of reparation, the Dey was compelled to pay us $10,000. The Dey ever afterwards consistently resisted the

---

[9]William P. Cresson, *Diplomatic Portraits* (New York: Houghton Mifflin Co., 1923), p. 334.

[10]Thomas A. Bailey, *A Diplomatic History of the American People*, p. 163.

[11]Raynal Keen to M. M. Noah, May 22, 1814, in M. M. Noah, *Correspondence and Documents Relative to the Attempt to Negotiate for the Release of the American Captives at Algiers* (Washington: Government Printing Office, 1816), p. 25. Mordecai Manuel Noah was American Consul at Tunis in 1814. Keene, an American by birth, became a Spanish citizen and went to Algiers to attempt the release of the American prisoners.

temptation to insult Old Glory.[12] Direct measures had paid off well.

Diplomacy by the sword in Africa soon gave way to negotiation by verbal thrusts in London. Both England and America were somewhat anxious to renew commercial ties. As soon as the news of the Battle of Waterloo reached Downing Street, a commercial convention was signed between Great Britain and the United States. The negotiations were brief. Adams, Clay, and Gallatin faced two of their old Ghent acquaintances, Goulburn and William Adams. These two latter gentlemen were now assisted by Frederick John Robinson, Vice-President of the British Board of Trade. The convention, signed on July 3, 1815, provided for the reciprocal establishment of consuls and liberty of commerce, in British or American ships, between the United States and the territories of His Britannic Majesty in Europe. It called for equality of treatment of the products, ships, citizens, and subjects of each party in the ports of the other, with prohibition of discriminatory duties on exports and imports, or port charges. It also permitted American ships to trade directly between the United States and the British East Indies ports of Calcutta, Madras, Bombay, and Prince of Wales Island on most-favored-nation terms. In 1815, this seemed but a temporary arrangement; however, it was renewed in 1818 and thereafter. It is still in effect. Not long after its signing, the Convention of 1815 became a model for similar pacts between the United States and other countries.[13]

After 1816, the party of Thomas Jefferson had the field to itself. The Federalists had supported their last presidential candidate. Monroe, like Washington before him, preferred it this way. Both men felt that the two-party system hindered efficiency.[14] Monroe proceeded to offer as proof of this thesis, the accomplishment of a favorite ambition of American diplomacy ever since the peace

[12]Ray W. Irwin, *The Diplomatic Relations of the United States with the Barbary Powers, 1776-1816* (Chapel Hill: University of North Carolina Press, 1931), pp. 176-186.

[13]Samuel F. Bemis, *John Quincy Adams and the Foundations of American Foreign Policy*, pp. 224-225. It was called a convention rather than a treaty because of its limited scope. This was at Gallatin's insistence. See Raymond Walters, Jr., *Albert Gallatin; Jeffersonian Financier and Diplomat* (New York: Macmillan Co., 1957), pp. 291-294.

[14]Monroe to Andrew Jackson, December 14, 1816, as printed in the *Niles Weekly Register,* May 15, 1824.

of 1783: the demilitarization of the frontier. After months of conferences and correspondence, Monroe achieved his objective on April 29, 1817, in an exchange of notes between Richard Rush, Acting-Secretary of State, and Charles Bagot, British Minister in Washington. Monroe had been America's real negotiator in this famous Rush-Bagot agreement. Rush's only contribution was his signature. The pleasing personality of the able British Minister, Charles Bagot, had been no small factor in reaching an agreement. At a presidential reception he was heard to murmur, quite in contrast with Copenhagen Jackson, "Mrs. Madison looks every inch a Queen."[15] Needless to say, Bagot's tact and ability succeeded where less gentle methods had failed.

The substance of the Rush-Bagot executive agreement was that neither the United States nor Great Britain would maintain any armed naval forces on the Great Lakes except stipulated small revenue cutters. The nervousness of the British Ministry lest this executive agreement might not bind succeeding administrations was allayed when the Senate, on April 16, 1818, with no dissenting vote, approved the pact, thus giving it the status of a treaty.[16] The Rush-Bagot agreement, like the Convention of 1815, is still in force. The prohibition of naval armament on the Great Lakes gradually led both countries to permit their land fortifications to fall into decay. By 1871 the myth of the unguarded frontier had become a reality.[17]

FISHERIES, OREGON, AND SLAVES

Late in 1817, when John Quincy Adams took over as Secretary of State, he quickly addressed himself to other unfinished business that had been swept under the rug at Ghent. An almost immediate result of the new Secretary's diligence was the Convention of 1818 negotiated in London by Albert Gallatin and Richard Rush. In Article I of this treaty, signed on October 20, 1818, after six weeks of conferences, the British granted a permanent extension

---

[15]Thomas A. Bailey, *A Diplomatic History of the American People,* p. 158.
[16]James M. Callahan, "Agreement of 1817—Reduction of Naval Forces upon the American Lakes," *Annual Report of the American Historical Association,* 1895, pp. 369-392. This is the standard monograph on the subject.
[17]C. P. Stacey, "The Myth of the Unguarded Frontier, 1815-1871," *American Historical Review,* Vol. LVI, No. 1, October, 1950, pp. 1-18.

of fishing liberties on the following coasts: the southern coast of Newfoundland from Cape Ray to the Rameau Islands, and on the western and northern coasts from Cape Ray to the Quirpon Islands; also on the shores of the Magdalen Islands, and on the coast of Labrador from Mount Joly northward. In addition to all this, the citizens of the United States were also to enjoy the liberty forever to dry and cure fish on the unsettled shores of Labrador and southern Newfoundland.

Articles II and III of the Convention stated that the line of 49° north latitude should be the boundary of the United States and British North America westward from the Lake-of-the-Woods to the Rocky Mountains. Having thus adjusted the ill-defined northern boundary of the Louisiana Purchase, the negotiators reached an impasse on running the boundary on through the Oregon Territory. The deadlock was broken by settling for an arrangement popularly known as joint-occupation. For a period of ten years, subject to renewal, the Oregon country should be free and open to both the British and the Americans.

Article IV renewed the commercial treaty of 1815 for ten years. Article V dealt with slaves carried away by British forces. It was agreed that this question should be referred to the arbitration of some friendly sovereign. Finally, through the mediation of the Russian Czar, the United States in 1826 agreed to accept $1,204,960 in compensation for the loss of its slave property. The sixth and last article, besides stating that the treaty would become effective upon ratification by both governments, carried the signatures of Albert Gallatin and Richard Rush for the United States, and Frederick John Robinson and Henry Goulburn for Great Britain.[18]

SPAIN GIVES IN

During these postwar years, England was an accommodating negotiator. The same cannot be said for Spain. His Catholic Majesty tried in vain to recover both Louisiana and the Floridas at

---

[18]John H. Powell, *Richard Rush: Republican Diplomat, 1780-1859* (Philadelphia: University of Pennsylvania Press, 1942), pp. 109-117. Also Hunter Miller (ed.), *Treaties and Other International Acts of the United States of America* (Washington: Government Printing Office, 1931), Vol. II, pp. 658-662. Goulburn had been one of the British negotiators at Ghent.

the Congress of Vienna. No one would help him. Europe was tired. Great Britain sought repose. All this meant failure for Spain. European quiescence set the stage for American expansion. The Floridas, editorialized the *Niles Weekly Register* on May 29, 1819, ". . . will just as naturally come into our possession as the waters of the Mississippi seek the sea."[19]

A week after the declaration of war against England in 1812, the House secretly authorized the President to seize West Florida, but authorization was one thing and conquest quite another. The Anglo-American conflict ended in 1815 with Spain still in sovereign possession of her province. Among many other things, the Vienna peacemakers, while redrawing the European map, restored the Spanish monarchy under Ferdinand VII. Soon afterwards, regular diplomatic relations were re-established between the United States and Spain. The new Spanish Minister to the United States, Luis de Oñis, was barely accredited when John Quincy Adams entered into serious discussions with him on the East Florida question. These conversations were interrupted by General Andrew Jackson's invasion of the Floridas in 1818. Spain considered the General's action as an affront to her sovereignty. The hero of New Orleans had been commissioned to penetrate Spanish soil for the purpose of wiping out the bases of hostile Indian forays into American border territory. Jackson broke up the Indian strongholds, and caught and executed two British subjects, Alexander Arbuthnot and Robert Ambrister, who had been selling munitions to hostile tribes. For a brief moment, Spain thought she could rely on British indignation to help her preserve East Florida. She had good reason for this belief because Lord Castlereagh, British Foreign Secretary, was so incensed that he asserted that "war might have been produced by holding up a finger."[20] However, he regained his composure, and in the light of new evidence informed the British minister in Washington that the "unfortunate sufferers, Arbuthnot and Ambrister, had been engaged in unauthorized practices."[21] As a result of this instruction, Anglo-American relations resumed their peaceful ways. Spain despaired of any hope of British intervention.

---

[19]*Niles Weekly Register,* Baltimore, May 29, 1819.
[20]John H. Powell, *Richard Rush: Republican Diplomat, 1780-1859,* p. 129.
[21]Castlereagh to Bagot, January 2, 1819, *Henry Adams Transcripts.*

Although the President admitted that Jackson had been empowered to chase the redmen into Florida, he emphatically denied that the General had been instructed to seize Spanish property. Jackson had, in fact, captured every important post in Florida except St. Augustine.[22] The entire Cabinet, with the exception of John Quincy Adams, agreed with Monroe that General Jackson had committed an unauthorized and unwarranted act. Adams, in a notable state paper, warmly and thoroughly defended Jackson. The Secretary of State also pointed out for Ferdinand VII's benefit that it had been necessary to invade East Florida because of Spain's inability to restrain the hostile incursions of Indians. Since she was bound by Article V of Pinckney's Treaty to prevent these invasions, and since she palpably was unable to do so, she ought to cede East Florida to the United States. So spoke our Secretary of State. By this time Oñis saw the handwriting on the wall. Conversations were resumed. Both Adams and Oñis accepted the good offices of Hyde de Neuville, the French Minister in Washington, in suggesting compromises.

After protracted negotiations, the famous Adams-Oñis Treaty was signed in Washington on February 22, 1819. By its sixteen articles the United States acquired East Florida, a validation of its seizure of West Florida, and a definition of the western boundary of the Louisiana Purchase. This new line, originating at the mouth of the Sabine river, went northwesterly to the 42nd parallel. It then ran due west clear to the Pacific. In effect this meant that Spain yielded its claims to the Oregon country. In exchange, Adams surrendered America's claim to Texas, and assumed the claims of its own citizens against Spain to the amount of $5,000,000.[23]

Article II of the treaty seems to grant moral consolation to Ferdinand VII. It reads in part: "His Catholic Majesty cedes to the United States, in full property and sovereignty, all the territories

---

[22]The point is obscure. Jackson claimed his friend, Congressman John Rhea from Tennessee, transmitted to him by letter Monroe's approval of seizing Florida. Monroe denied this. This much is clear: the Administration understood Jackson's intentions toward Florida and did nothing to restrain him. Rhea testified that he had no recollection of having sent any such letter to Jackson. Marquis James, *The Life of Andrew Jackson* (New York: Bobbs-Merrill Co., 1938), pp. 285-286 and pp. 827-829.

[23]Philip C. Brooks, *Diplomacy and the Borderlands: The Adams-Oñis Treaty of 1819* (Berkeley: University of California Press, 1939), pp. 131-170.

which belong to him, situated to the eastward of the Mississippi, known by the name of East and West Florida."[24] The fact that the United States evacuated the Floridas and restored them to Spain two weeks before Adams and Oñis signed the treaty of 1819, seems to indicate that the "him" in the phrase "which belong to him," means Ferdinand VII. This interpretation would, of course, brand Jefferson's claim to and occupation of West Florida as highway-robbery. It is on the basis of Article II that partisans of the Iberian Peninsula proudly claim that the Adams-Oñis Treaty recognized the justice of Spain's claim to the two Floridas up to February 22, 1819. No doubt this balm did something to soothe the wounds of a once mighty empire.

The final article of the treaty stated that it should be ratified within six months from the date of signature. The Senate of the United States ratified it immediately and unanimously. Spain did not move so quickly. The full powers from the King of Spain, under which Oñis had signed the treaty, contained a solemn promise by His Most Catholic Majesty to ratify whatever might be signed by his plenipotentiary. In 1820, a revolt in Spain forced Ferdinand VII to accept the constitution of 1812 which required any cession of territory to be approved by the Cortes. Spain now adopted a policy of delay in an effort to coerce the United States into a promise not to assist the revolted South American colonies, nor to recognize their independence. A new Spanish Minister, General Vives, was sent to Washington to secure such a pledge.[25]

Spain's refusal to ratify disgusted Adams, and he counseled the President to recommend to Congress the forcible occupation of the Floridas. In his annual message, Monroe asked Congress for authority to do this. The House Committee on Foreign Affairs responded with a bill for the occupation of the Floridas. With sober second thoughts both Monroe and Adams agreed not to do any-

---

[24]Hunter Miller, ed., *Treaties and Other International Acts of the United States,* Vol. III, pp. 4-5. Bemis feels that the phrase "which belong to him" is obscure. He says that to make Article II out to be an unequivocal cession by Spain depends on whether the treaty contains commas to set off the phrase, "which belong to him." He states that the original manuscript copies of the treaty do not have commas. Samuel F. Bemis, *A Diplomatic History of the United States* (New York: Henry Holt & Co., 1957), p. 193.
[25]Arthur P. Whitaker, *The United States and the Independence of Latin America, 1800-1830* (Baltimore: Johns Hopkins Press, 1941), p. 272.

thing until the arrival of the new Spanish Minister, General Vives. When Vives finally arrived in April of 1820, he immediately revealed the new terms which Spain demanded as her price of ratification. They were: a strengthening of our neutrality laws, a formal guarantee of the integrity of Spain's American possessions, and a promise not to recognize any of the revolted provinces. Adams refused all these conditions. In refusing, our Secretary of State remarked that our neutrality laws were being enforced. He added that the policy of the United States towards the revolutions was one of neutrality. He insisted that it would be a violation of neutrality to agree never to recognize the independence of any of the South American colonies no matter what should happen. Adams was careful to intimate we "probably would not precipitately recognize the independence of the South Americans."[26]

When Vives informed his government that the United States would very probably occupy the Floridas and recognize the independence of the revolted colonies if the treaty was not ratified forthwith, the Cortes gave its secret approval, and the King signed the pact on October 24, 1820. Because the original term of six months stipulated for the exchange of ratifications had long since expired, Monroe once more submitted the treaty to the Senate. Once again that body approved it. This time there were four opposing votes. The President immediately ratified the treaty and the exchange of ratifications took place on February 22, 1812, precisely two years after Adams and Oñis initiated the pacts.[27]

FLORIDA BUT NOT TEXAS

A fierce and ominous Congressional debate over slavery was raging while Adams and Oñis played for high diplomatic stakes. Side by side with these two important events, the country was enduring its first major depression. These three desperate events, occurring as they did from 1819 to 1821, were not unconnected. For example, when Clay and Jefferson brought pressure to bear on Monroe not to yield Texas in the Adams-Oñis Treaty, the Presi-

---

[26]Diary of John Quincy Adams, May 1, 1820, *John Quincy Adams MSS.*
[27]Samuel F. Bemis, *The Latin-American Policy of the United States* (New York: Harcourt, Brace & Co., 1943), pp. 42-43.

dent wanted to oblige.[28] The quarrel over slavery made him hesitate. Monroe was quite aware that we could have compelled Spain to disgorge Texas as well as the Floridas. But the fight over whether Missouri should enter the Union as a slave or free state caused such a ruckus that Texas and secession became vital issues. The Chief Executive foresaw that if we took Texas it would immediately become another Missouri. The President wanted Texas, but he wanted peace between the North and South even more. Unburdening himself to Andrew Jackson, Monroe declared that the Missouri dispute

has excited feelings and raised difficulties . . . which did not exist before. Some parts of our union became less anxious for the acquisition of Florida, while others not content with that were desirous of taking possession of Texas . . . Having long known the repugnance with which the eastern portion of our Union has seen its aggrandizement to the West and South, I have been decidedly of the opinion that we ought to be content with Florida for the present.[29]

Monroe's apprehensiveness was more than borne out by the facts. Henry Clay wrote from Washington in January of 1820 that the words "civil war" and "disunion" were commonplace.[30] With prophetic insight, John Quincy Adams remarked on March 4, 1820, that if "the union must be dissolved, slavery is precisely the question upon which it ought to break."[31] The very next day the American Secretary of State received a report that Senator James Barbour of Virginia approached all the free-state members of the Senate "proposing to them to call a convention of the states to dissolve the union and agree on terms of separation."[32]

All things at the opportune time was one of Monroe's slogans. The time from 1819 to 1821 was inopportune for adding what was to become the Lone Star State to the Stars and Stripes. The political situation helped to create this inopportuneness. With the Federalists reduced to a corporal's guard in the House, and

---

[28]Charles C. Griffen, *The United States and the Disruption of the Spanish Empire, 1810-1822* (New York: Columbia University Press, 1937), p. 234.

[29]Monroe to Jackson, May 23, 1820, *Monroe MSS.*

[30]Glover Moore, *The Missouri Controversy, 1819-1821* (Kentucky: University of Kentucky Press, 1953), p. 92.

[31]Diary of John Quincy Adams, March 4, 1820, *John Quincy Adams MSS.*

[32]*Ibid.,* March 5, 1820.

with Massachusetts as the only state still adhering to Federalism, the Northern Democrats felt less and less need of collaboration with their Southern brethren. Fear of the Federalist party had been the cement that had united the Northern and Southern wings of the Democratic party. With this fear gone, disunity quickly set in. The fuse that blew unity to smithereens was lighted by James Tallmadge, Jr., a New York Democrat. It happened this way. On February 13, 1819, the House resolved itself into a Committee of the Whole to consider a bill to enable the people of Missouri to form a state government. During the ensuing discussion, Tallmadge moved to amend the bill in the following manner:

And provided also, that the further introduction of slavery . . . be prohibited . . . and that all children of slaves, born within the said state, after the admission thereof into the union, shall be free, but may be held to service until the age of twenty-five years.[33]

The debate on the Tallmadge amendment went on during February and March of 1819. Mightily as Tallmadge inveighed against the moral iniquity of slavery, he frankly stated that he also opposed its extension for political reasons. Southern slave representation was as anathema to him as it was to the New England Federalists. After their first presidential defeat, the Federalists found their scapegoat in the three-fifths compromise of the Constitution. They charged that at the

fourth Presidential Election, when Mr. Jefferson was first chosen President, he had 73 electoral votes, and Mr. Adams 64; making a majority of 9; and that, at that very time, the black representation from the Slave Country amounted to 15: so that the negroes turned the majority, and actually put in the President.[34]

As the House debate entered its second month, it became painfully apparent that the Democratic party was losing cohesion owing to a lack of political opposition. When the winds of oratory had finally subsided, the House voted separately on each clause of the Tallmadge amendment. The vote, even more than the debate, was to show that the disciples of Jefferson were not able to bind their

---

[33]*Annals of Congress, 15th Cong., 2nd Sess.* (Washington: Gales & Seaton, 1855), pp. 1166, 1170.
[34]Glover Moore, *The Missouri Controversey, 1819-1821,* p. 11.

northern and southern members together as effectively as in the past. The first clause provided that "the further introduction of slavery or involuntary servitude be prohibited, except for the punishment of crimes, whereof the party shall be duly convicted." It was passed by a vote of 82 to 78. On this vote southern unanimity attracted to itself but fourteen votes from free states.[35]

Many motives and issues were involved in this estrangement between northern and southern Democrats. Some northern Democrats voted against the admission of Missouri as a slave state for humanitarian reasons. Others were alienated by the southern monopoly of high government offices. From 1801 to 1819, the White House appeared to be the exclusive property of Virginia, and most of the Speakers of the House were southerners.

The Middle states might have contributed more to the cause of the South had these two sections not differed so much on the subject of the tariff and internal improvements. The panic of 1819, which began shortly before the Missouri debate, further accentuated this tariff disagreement. American industrialists, finding themselves hard-pressed by the depression, sought aid by demanding higher protective duties. To their disgust they watched the congressional delegation from the slave states take a stand in almost solid opposition to a higher tariff.

While Southern votes blocked higher protection for the Middle states, the vetoes of Virginia presidents thwarted them in the matter of internal improvements. In 1817 John C. Calhoun's bonus bill, which provided for the construction of roads and canals at federal expense, was vetoed by Madison on the ground that it was unconstitutional. President Monroe, following the lead of Madison, also declared federal internal improvements to be unconstitutional. Madison's and Monroe's rejection of the bonus bill hit New York and Pennsylvania the hardest. These two states cast half of the votes given in favor of the bill in the House of Representatives. While it is true that many southerners advocated federal internal improvements, nevertheless the Middle states were inclined to identify the views of Madison and Monroe with the South.

In the Senate the Tallmadge amendment was foredoomed to

---

[35]*Annals of Congress, 15th Cong., 2nd Sess.,* pp. 1214-1215.

failure. Besides having as many members as the free states in the Senate, the South could count on the support of Jesse B. Thomas and Ninian Edwards of Illinois. The people of Illinois at this time were mostly immigrants from the South. Thomas and Edwards, both Southerners by birth, were to be a tower of strength to the South throughout the Missouri controversy. The Senate struck out the first clause of the Tallmadge amendment by a vote of 22 to 16. The second clause was similarly treated but by a vote of 31 to 7.[36]

Obviously an impasse had been reached. It would be compromise or disunion. At this critical juncture, Mr. Henry Clay of Kentucky and Mr. Jesse B. Thomas of Illinois combined to produce the Compromise that saved the Union for forty years. Clay's opportunity came on December 30, 1820, just after Maine had applied for admission into the Union. On that day Clay gently reminded the northern Congressmen of the political facts of life. The Great Pacificator argued that if

you refuse to admit Missouri also free of condition, we see no reason why you should take to yourselves privileges which you deny to her—and until you grant them also to her, we will not admit you Maine.[37]

Events now moved quickly to a conclusion. In spite of Clay's warning, the House on January 3, 1820, passed a bill granting Maine's request to enter the Union. On February 16, 1820, in a Southern-controlled Senate, the Maine and Missouri bills were combined. Acting immediately, Senator Jesse B. Thomas of Illinois now offered the compromise amendment that brought concord out of chaos. The Thomas amendment proposed in substance to make Maine a free state, admit Missouri with slavery, leave Arkansas and Oklahoma open to future settlement by slaveholders, and prohibit slavery forever in the remainder of the Louisiana Purchase north of 36^0 30', the southern boundary of the state of Missouri. On February 18, 1820, the Maine-Missouri bill, including the Thomas amendment, was passed by the Senate 24 to 20.[38]

Clay now took over the seemingly impossible task of persuading a reluctant House to go along with the work of the Senate. By

---

[36]*Annals of Congress, 15th Cong., 2nd Sess.,* pp. 273 and 279.
[37]*Annals of Congress, 16th Cong., 1st Sess.,* p. 841.
[38]*Annals of Congress, 16th Cong., 1st Sess.,* p. 428-430.

a fusion of charm, persuasiveness, and parliamentary tricks, he finally succeeded. The decisive vote in the House came on March 2, 1820. By a vote of 90 to 87, the anti-slavery proviso in the House Missouri bill was stricken out. Four northern representatives were absent during this crucial vote, and twelve northerners voted with the south. Then by a vote of 134 to 42, the House passed the Thomas proviso excluding slavery from the remainder of the Louisiana Purchase north of 36° 30'. The deed was done, or so a tired Congress thought.

The anti-slavery forces headed by the Federalists, Clintonian Democrats, and the politicians of the Middle states did not die so easily. The compromise of 1820 admitted Maine to statehood on March 15, 1820, but did not specifically admit Missouri. Missourians were merely authorized to form a constitution and state government without requiring them to prohibit slavery. Missouri, if recent precedent were adhered to, could not actually enter the Union until its Constitution had been approved by both Houses of Congress. On Decemeber 12, 1820, the Senate passed a resolution by a vote of 26 to 18 for the final admission of Missouri. The very next day, the House rejected Missouri's admission by 93 to 79 on the ground that Article III, Section 26, Clause 4 of Missouri's constitution made it illegal for free Negroes and mulattoes to enter Missouri.[39] This clause was clearly unconstitutional since free Negroes and mulattoes were citizens in some of the states, and the federal Constitution provides that the "citizens of each state shall be entitled to all the privileges and immunities of citizens in the several states." Missouri tried in vain to justify herself by citing similar laws in a number of other states.

Three hours after the House rejected Missouri's Constitution, Representative Francis Jones of Tennessee wrote to a friend in his state that "I am sorry to tell you, that in my opinion, in fact the Union is now almost dissolved. I declare to you, that when the result of the vote was announced, my feelings were inexpressible."[40] Representative Benjamin Hardin of Kentucky struck a similar note in an address to the House. The Kentuckian declared that certain "Gentlemen think that if Missouri falls she will fall alone; but, sir,

---

[39]*Annals of Congress, 16th Cong., 2nd Sess.,* pp. 116, 440, 453-455, 669-670.
[40]*Nashville Clarion* and *Tennessee Gazette,* January 2, 1821.

I will go with her, and so will her sister states, who have blood and treasure." Several sections of the galleries promptly added ". . . and we'll go with you, Hardin."[41]

Once more Henry Clay assumed the role of Compromiser No. I. Using his great gifts of eloquence and dramatic ability, he begged, entreated, adjured, supplicated, and beseeched the northern representatives to have mercy on the people of Missouri. Tears welled up in the eyes of many in the galleries who were "lost in astonishment and wonder at the almighty powers of this most astonishing man."[42]

Nothing succeeds like success, and Clay, after weeks of oratory, parliamentary devices, and stacked committees, finally got the House on February 26, 1821, to admit Missouri into the Union. It was the second Missouri Compromise. In essence the House voted 87 to 81 to admit Missouri

upon the fundamental condition, that the fourth clause of the twenty-sixth section of the third article of the constitution submitted on the part of said state to Congress shall never be construed to authorize the passage of any law, and that no law shall be passed in conformity thereto, by which any citizen of either of the states in this Union shall be excluded from the enjoyment of any of the privileges and immunities to which such citizen is entitled under the Constitution of the United States.[43]

In June, 1812, the Missouri legislature made the promise which Congress desired. It was made in such sarcastic and defiant language that the anti-slavery press was aroused once more. Theodore Dwight's New York *Daily Advertiser* could "hardly imagine a more cutting satire" than Missouri's assent.[44] Robert Walsh in his Philadelphia *Gazette* asserted that Missouri's language merited a formal rebuke from at least one branch of the national government.[45] President Monroe, less squeamish than Dwight and Walsh, and happy to be rid of a vexatious problem, proclaimed the final admission of Missouri on August 10, 1821.

It is apparent that both fear of disunion and fear of Federal-

---

[41]*Georgetown* (D.C.) *Metropolitan,* February 3, 1821.
[42]Glover Moore, *Missouri Controversy, 1819-1821,* p. 148.
[43]*Annals of Congress, 16th Cong., 2nd Sess.,* p. 1228.
[44]New York *Daily Advertiser,* July 18, 1821.
[45]Philadelphia *National Gazette and Literary Register,* August 13 and September 6, 1821.

ism were vital elements in the South's corraling of eighteen northern votes in the House for the Compromise of 1821. These factors,
of course, were also not without their influence in making possible
the Compromise of 1820. On the day after the House passed the
second Missouri Compromise, the Philadelphia *Franklin Gazette*
remarked that everybody was happy "except the Hartford Convention men."[46] Nicholas Biddle, the Philadelphia banker, urged
the Democratic newspapers of Philadelphia to work for a peaceful settlement. As a patriotic American, Biddle was frightened
by the sectional animosities that could so easily lead to a breakup
of the Union. It was his desire that Pennsylvania should "interpose
between the conflicting parties and close a breach which rash and
violent spirits are daily evidencing."[47] Jefferson, Madison, and Monroe shared with Biddle the fear of disunion. They also insisted,
along with many northern Democrats, that the Missouri controversy was a plot on the part of the Federalists and Clintonian Democrats to regain political power.[48]

RECESSION

The Missouri debate was contemporaneous with the depression of 1819, and judging from the letters and newspapers of the
time, the people were much more interested in financial recovery
than they were in worrying over the expansion of slavery in distant
lands beyond the Mississippi. On February 8, 1820, Thomas G.
Percy, an Alabamian, wrote Senator John Walker that on his last
visit to town "the Spanish relations—the more momentous Missouri question and the defective revenue, were not thought of or
talked of by anyone; everyone had too much to occupy him in the
deficiency of his own revenue."[49] A New Jersey farmer, writing in
the spring of 1820, lamented that "go where you will your ears
are continually saluted with the cry of hard times! hard times!"[50]
The New York *Gazette* bemoaned the fact that "there never was

---

[46]Philadelphia *Franklin Gazette,* March 2, 1821.
[47]Nicholas Biddle to C. J. Ingersoll, February 18, 1821, *Biddle MSS.*
[48]Jefferson to Monroe, March 3, 1820, *Monroe MSS.* Madison to Monroe, February 10, 1820, *Monroe MSS.* Monroe to George Hay, January 5, 1820, *Monroe MSS.*
[49]Thomas C. Percy to John W. Walker, February 8, 1820, as cited in Glover
Moore, *Missouri Controversy, 1819-1821,* p. 572.
[50]Trenton *True American,* April 24, 1820, in Moore, *ibid.,* p. 172.

in the recollection of our oldest merchants, such a state of mercantile embarrassment." The Governor of Mississippi was informed by one of his constituents, that in parts of his state there was a "scarcity of money, or the want of it, among people generally."[51]

The people naturally turned to Congress for help in alleviating their suffering. Among the suggested remedies were: a national bankruptcy law, a tariff increase, and an extension of the time-limit for meeting payments on lands purchased from the government. But the 16th Congress was too occupied with the inflammatory Missouri question to give any lengthy consideration to methods for relieving the financial crisis. The Wilmington, Delaware *Watchman* begged Congress not to waste so much time on Missouri but to take up "other measures to which millions of sufferers are looking with the most agonizing solicitude for relief!"[52] The Philadelphia *Democratic Press* regretted that Congress's preoccupation with Missouri had resulted in the neglect of the "languishing interests of manufactures, of public lands, of the currency, of commerce."[53] A writer in the Baltimore *Federal Republican* urged the legislators to forget about slavery for awhile, and concern themselves with other matters of vital importance such as a bankrupt law.[54] But nothing would avail. The moral and political roots of slavery were so deep that Congress seemed impervious to any other issue.

ELECTION OF 1820

In any event, in spite of our first major depression, and the vicious sectional dispute over slavery, Monroe was not hurt politically. He incurred no opposition in the presidential election of 1820. In general the anti-Missourians did not try to defeat Monroe in 1820. Their hope was that there would be no more presidents from the slave states after the conclusion of his second term.

Monroe had tried desperately to blot out party differences. His efforts had resulted in the miracle of a partyless administration. It was his policy to accept Congressional and Cabinet solutions to perplexing problems. For example, he remained aloof during the

---

[51]George H. Nixon to David Holmes, October 8, 1819, in Moore, p. 173.
[52]Wilmington *American Watchman,* February 19, 1820, in Moore, p. 174.
[53]Philadelphia *Democratic Press,* February 22, 24, 1821, in Moore, p. 174.
[54]Baltimore *Federal Republican,* as quoted in Richmond *Enquirer,* November 28, 1820.

fight over slavery in Missouri. Before signing the "Enabling Act" for Missouri, he submitted the following two questions to his Cabinet. Was it constitutional to prohibit slavery in a territory? All the members, including Calhoun, answered in the affirmative to this question. The second question was: Did the word "forever" in the Missouri Compromise amendment extend to the time when the territory should be erected into a state?[55] The Cabinet could not agree on this. The form of the question was then changed, at Calhoun's suggestion, to an inquiry, if the proviso was constitutional. The Cabinet was unanimous in agreeing that it was. Monroe went along, and signed the Act on March 2, 1820.

There were no nominations prior to the presidential election of 1820. Five new states voted in this election. They were: Mississippi, Illinois, Alabama, Maine, and Missouri. A total of twenty-four states participated. The results were: Monroe, 231; John Quincy Adams, 1. For the vice-presidency, the final tabulation read: Daniel D. Tompkins of New York, 218; Richard Stockton of New Jersey, 8; Daniel Rodney of Delaware, 4; Robert G. Harper of Maryland, 1; and Richard Rush of Pennsylvania, 1.[56] It was only in Philadelphia that Monroe's re-election was seriously opposed. Here William Duane and his newspaper, the *Aurora,* sponsored an electoral ticket pledged to the support of DeWitt Clinton. Duane denounced Monroe as the candidate of slavery. In the city of Philadelphia, Monroe ran 1,233 votes as against Clinton's 793.[57]

The one vote that prevented Monroe from accomplishing what only George Washington had achieved, was cast by former Governor Plumer of New Hampshire. He voted for John Quincy Adams because he believed Monroe had shown "a want of foresight and economy."[58] When James Monroe, the last of the Virginia Dynasty, took the presidential oath on March 5, 1821— March 4 being a Sunday—the two party system was dead. However, this would not last long. American political life was too vigorous to endure this abnormality.

---

[55]The amendment read in part: ". . . and prohibit slavery forever in the remainder of the Louisiana Purchase north of 36° 30' . . ."
[56]Edward Stanwood, *A History of the Presidency,* pp. 118-121.
[57]Glover Moore, *Missouri Controversy, 1819-1821,* p. 340.
[58]William Plumer to William Plumer, Jr., January 8, 1821, *Plumer MSS.*

9

The Monroe Doctrine

THE MOST NOTABLE THING about Monroe's second inaugural was that it was postponed. The reason for the delay was fairly simple. For the first time since the establishment of the Constitution, March 4 fell on a Sunday. Uncertain as to protocol, the President consulted Chief Justice Marshall and his colleagues. After due deliberation, it was thought advisable to defer the inaugural until Monday.[1]

In spite of the fact that March 5, 1821, was a day of driving sleet, the House of Representatives was packed to overflowing. The large shivering crowd outside the Capitol so choked the passageway to the House that President Monroe literally had to force his way through. Caught in the same squeeze were the British Minister, Mr. Stratford Canning, and Mr. Antrobus, his Secretary of Legation. These distinguished gentlemen, clad in lace coats and silk stockings, were soaking wet and angry. "We were about ten paces from the door and utterly unable to get in until the arrival of the President, who, to our great concern and satisfaction, was squeezed as handsomely and detained as long as ourselves." His Majesty's representative concluded his vivid account by remarking that in "addition to the squeezing and shoving which the poor Prezzy experienced at the door, his speech, which was rather long, was occasionally interrupted by queer sounds from the gallery."[2]

With obvious relief, Monroe finally took his place on a platform graced by the presence of members of his Cabinet, members of the Supreme Court, the President of the Senate, and the Speaker of the House. The last of the Virginia Dynasty was dressed in a

---

[1]William P. Cresson, *James Monroe* (Chapel Hill: The University of North Carolina Press, 1946), p. 354.

[2]Canning to Joseph Planta, March 8, 1821, Stanley Lane-Poole, *The Life of the Right Honourable Stratford Canning* (London: Longmans, Green & Co., 1888), Vol. I, p. 318. Joseph Planta was Under Secretary of State for Foreign Affairs.

suit of black broadcloth, with shoe and knee buckles. His hair, still powdered in spite of the sleet, was tied in a queue at the back. Chief Justice Marshall administered the oath of office at the traditional hour of noon. The Chief Executive then stepped forward to address the huge throng.

Speaking in a grave and low voice, the President briefly dwelt on the ravages of the War of 1812. He then pointed out that the military buildup during his first administration was the "best expedient . . . to prevent war." Commenting on the economic progress made since the depression of 1819, Monroe pictured the current scene as one of "extraordinary prosperity." Needless to say, this was somewhat shy of reality, and may have accounted for some of those "queer sounds from the gallery." The President's optimism was not shared by either the hundreds of manufacturers and laborers working at half-capacity, or the same number of farmers still being cruelly dispossessed by foreclosures. The truth of the matter was that general prosperity was hardly just around the corner although conditions were on the upgrade.

On the foreign policy front, the acquisition of Florida by the recent Adams-Oñis treaty could not fail to serve "the highest interests of the Union." After briefly alluding to our improved relations with Great Britain, France, the Barbary States, and the Indians, our fifth President terminated his nine-page speech by expressing the deepest confidence in "the protection of Almighty God."[3] When the vigorous cheering had subsided, Mr. and Mrs. Monroe repaired to the White House where they received the congratulations of hundreds of friends. The day was concluded with the customary inaugural ball, held that year at Brown's Hotel.

THE SPANISH QUESTION

As soon as the festivities were over, Monroe was again confronted with the Spanish question. True, Spain had finally let go the Floridas, but she still hoped for European aid in preserving her remaining colonies. Napoleon's conquest of Spain in 1808 was followed by revolt in all of Spain's mainland colonies from the Rio Grande to Cape Horn. The restoration of Spanish monarchy

---

[3] James D. Richardson, *A Compilation of the Messages and Papers of the Presidents,* Vol. II, pp. 655-663.

in 1814 temporarily restored Spanish authority in the New World. Yet the flames of revolt again flared up in 1817, never to be extinguished until the last vestige of Spain's power in North and South America had disappeared in the Peruvian Battle of Ayachucho on December 9, 1824.

From 1818 to 1821, Argentina, Colombia, Venezuela, Chile, Mexico, and Central America sought diplomatic recognition as independent and sovereign nations.[4] American sympathies were fully echoed in Henry Clay's great speech of March 24, 1818, wherein he begged Congress to go on record in favor of the diplomatic recognition of the United Provinces of the Rio de la Plata.[5] For these heroic efforts in behalf of freedom, Clay's name would always be in benediction below the Rio Grande. Richard Rush, our minister to Great Britain, asserted that Clay "led the way to recognition."[6]

It so happened that during the years 1818 to 1821, while agents of the new republics were in Washington importuning for recognition, we were engaged in delicate negotiations with Spain over Florida. The Democratic administration, headed by Monroe, was forced to procrastinate on the question of recognition lest it antagonize Spain and thereby lose the Floridas for us.

The Neutrality Acts of 1818, passed by a Democratic Congress, were intended to placate Spain. However, Monroe was unwilling to bind the United States never to recognize the independence of the new Latin American States. Spain's final ratification in 1821 of the Treaty of 1819, by which we acquired the Floridas, freed our hands. With Florida safely under the Stars and Stripes, and with *de facto* independence already achieved, President Monroe signed an Act of Congress on May 4, 1822, appropriating $100,000 to set up United States embassies in the new republics of

---

[4] The precise names were: the United Provinces of Rio de la Plata (the Argentine), Greater Colombia (Colombia and Venezuela), Chile, Mexico, and the Central American Confederation. For the causes and development of the independence movement in Spanish America, see Charles K. Webster (ed.), *Britain and the Independence of Latin America* (London: The Oxford University Press, 1938), Vol. I, pp. 3-34.

[5] *Annals of Congress* (Washington, D.C.: Gales & Seaton, 1854), 15th Cong., 1st Sess., pp. 1465-1470.

[6] Rush to Clay, June 23, 1827, *Henry Clay MSS*. For South American praise of Clay, see Glyndon Van Deusen, *The Life of Henry Clay* (Boston: Little, Brown & Company, 1937), p. 131.

Spanish America. The initiative in this matter was entirely Monroe's. On March 8, 1822, he had sent a message to Congress to the effect that "the Provinces which have declared their independence and are in enjoyment of it ought to be recognized." In response to this presidential message, the Committee on Foreign Affairs of the House of Representatives reported on March 19, 1822, "that it is just and expedient to acknowledge the independence of the several nations of Spanish America." We were the first outside government to give diplomatic recognition to these fellow-American countries.[7] As our own revolution of 1776 pushed Europe out of a goodly section of America, so the revolution beginning in 1808 drove Europe out of another great part of North America and out of practically all of South America. On the mainland, only Russian Alaska and British North America were left to European control.

AN INHARMONIOUS CONCERT

Europe was not happy with the United States policy of giving diplomatic recognition to the independent states of Latin America. After the defeat of Napoleon, Czar Alexander I of Russia had united the Continental allies, England, and the restored Bourbon monarchy of France into a concert of Europe. By 1818 this union was known as the Quintuple Alliance of Austria, Prussia, Russia, Great Britain, and France. The purpose of the Alliance was to protect the peace of Europe. In a series of summit conferences, at Aix-la-Chapelle in 1818, at Troppau in 1820, at Laibach in 1821, and at Verona in 1822, the allies dealt with threats to peace. At Troppau in 1820, Russia and Prussia formally agreed with Austria to act jointly against revolutionary disturbances anywhere in Europe. Great Britain refused to be a party to this decision, and thereafter, the concert was practically a continental affair. Needless to say, if England had stayed with the Congress System, it seems very

---

[7]Charles C. Tansill, "War Powers of the President," *Political Science Quarterly,* Vol. XLV, No. 1, March 1930, pp. 18-19. Dexter Perkins, "John Quincy Adams" in *American Secretaries of State and Their Diplomacy,* ed. by Samuel F. Bemis (New York: Pageant Book Co., 1958), pp. 36-55. The United States formally received the diplomatic representatives of Colombia on June 19, 1822; of Mexico on December 12, 1822; of the Empire of Brazil on May 28, 1824; of the Central American Federation on August 4, 1824. We appointed formal diplomatic agents to the United Provinces of Rio de La Plata on January 27, 1823; to Chile on January 27, 1823; and to Peru on May 2, 1826. The independence of Brazil was proclaimed on October 12, 1822.

probable that the *status quo* of 1820 would have been preserved not only in Europe, but in Latin America as well. With regard to Spanish America, the years 1815 to 1817 were crucial ones, for during that time, Madrid unsuccessfully begged London for aid in crushing the Spanish colonial rebellions. It is interesting to recall, especially in the light of the Monroe Doctrine of 1823, that in 1818 and 1819 both James Monroe and John Quincy Adams made vigorous but unsuccessful attempts to draw England into a joint demonstration with the United States on behalf of Spanish-American independence.

Bereft of British help, and in a sort of "go-it-alone" policy, the Holy Allies promptly crushed liberal insurrections in Naples and Piedmont. This was accomplished in 1821 by Austrian armies under a mandate from the Congress System. Armed with similar authority, French troops invaded Spain in 1823, and defeated the insurrectionary Spanish liberals who had held captive the Spanish King Ferdinand VII. Thoroughly grateful, Ferdinand pleaded with the Holy Alliance to go further. He begged them to send armies and navies to the New World to put down his rebellious subjects and give him back his rich provinces. The concert of Europe was sympathetic. Preparations were made to meet at another summit to discuss this subject.[8]

Great Britain was worried. She feared that if the Holy Alliance intervened in Spain's colonial affairs it would mean French predominance in Latin America. These British anxieties were justified. It was the ambition of French diplomacy in 1823 to set up in Spanish America a host of monarchies under Bourbon princes. France saw in this plan a program of recovery from her economic prostration of 1815. France, in nominal partnership with Spain, would acquire for herself political and commercial privileges in Central and South America.[9]

European archives reveal that there was not very much pros-

---

[8]Samuel F. Bemis, *John Quincy Adams and the Foundations of American Foreign Policy* (New York: Alfred A. Knopf, 1949), pp. 369-372. Charles K. Webster, ed., *Britain and the Independence of Latin America, 1812-1830* (London: Oxford University Press, 1938), Vol. I, p. 14. Arthur P. Whitaker, *The United States and the Independence of Latin America, 1800-1830* (Baltimore: The Johns Hopkins Press, 1941), p. 255.

[9]William S. Robertson, *France and Latin-American Independence* (Baltimore: The Johns Hopkins Press, 1939), 253-295.

pect of the Old World interfering in the New. Prussia, Russia, and Austria, as much as they frowned on the independence of the Spanish colonies, were powerless to prevent it. The danger was that they might allow France to work out some settlement with Spain. But France would certainly be impotent before the formidable British fleet. And Britain was determined to use her naval power, if this proved necessary, to thwart French designs in Spanish America.[10]

The policies of Great Britain and the United States toward Spain's former colonies were not dissimilar. Both nations were intent on continuing their new and profitable commerce with the liberated Latins. The difference was that whereas Britain had refused diplomatic recognition, we had granted it. However, Lord Castlereagh, British Foreign Secretary, was moving rapidly in the direction of Monroe's policy of recognition. His Majesty's government actually favored reconciliation between Madrid and her transatlantic wards. Should England's peaceful mediation help to effect this result, she would insist that trade should remain open to the outside world. At no time did Great Britain contemplate the use of force to help her Spanish ally regain the lost provinces. When finally Castlereagh realized the futility of his conciliatory attempts, he began preparing to recognize the independence of Latin America. His death on August 12, 1822, postponed recognition until 1824. Had he lived, the Court of St. James might have recognized the new republics and the Monroe Doctrine might never have been born.[11]

George Canning, Castlereagh's successor, more out of deference to Spain than to the Holy Alliance, insisted on more positive signs of independence before imitating the United States in her policy of recognition. In order to be more fully informed he sent commissioners to Mexico and Colombia. They were to report to him on the exact status of independence in those countries. In the

---

[10]Dexter Perkins, *The Monroe Doctrine, 1823-1826* (Boston: Harvard University Press, 1932), pp. 141-142. In October, 1818, at the Congress of Aix-la-Chapelle, France and Russia favored intervention in Latin America and asked Great Britain to go along with this plan. Castlereagh, British Foreign Secretary, refused. See Charles K. Webster, ed., *Britain and the Independence of Latin America, 1812-1830*, Vol. I, p. 15.

[11]Charles K. Webster, ed., *Britain and the Independence of Latin America, 1812-1830* (London: Oxford University Press, 1938), I, 12-17.

meantime, Stratford Canning, Minister to the United States, and cousin to George Canning, reported on the vast stores of good will towards England in Washington. He insisted that the European diplomacy of his cousin "had the effect of making the English almost popular in the United States." He was sure that the time was opportune for bringing "the two countries nearer together."[12]

George Canning thought so too. Painfully aware of Spain's appeal to the Holy Alliance, he turned to the United States seeking their cooperation. On August 16, 1823, in a famous *tête-à-tête* with the American Minister Richard Rush, Canning made a direct plea for an Anglo-American alliance. The Foreign Secretary confided to Rush that although England felt that Spanish America was permanently lost to Madrid, yet His Majesty's government would not impede any arrangement between Spain and her colonies by friendly negotiations. Canning stated that the question of recognition was one of time and circumstances. Rush was told that even though England had no territorial ambitions in Spanish America, she could not with indifference see any portion of Spain's former provinces transferred to any other power. Finally, Canning suggested that the United States and Great Britain jointly declare these principles to the world. This joint declaration would, said Canning, contain a self-denying ordinance by which Great Britain and the United States would pledge themselves not to acquire any Spanish territory in the Western Hemisphere.

Rush was willing to accept the proposal provided Canning would alter it to include immediate recognition of the new states. If Canning refused this amendment, Rush would have to refer the proposition home for advice. Canning was crestfallen. He would not agree to recognition, and it was his feeling that he could not wait for some two months for what might turn out to be an American rebuff. Actually, Canning was on the verge of recognizing the colonies when he was confronted with the French invasion of Spain in the spring of 1823. This attack, an expression of the will of the Congress System, so angered him that he devoted all his efforts to destroying the European Alliance. Latin America could wait.[13]

---

[12]Stratford Canning to George Canning, May 8, 1823 in Dexter Perkins, *The Monroe Doctrine, 1823-1826,* p. 60.

[13]Rush to John Quincy Adams, August 19, 1823, *Dispatches, Department of State.* Cf. W. W. Kaufmann, *British Policy and the Independence of Latin America,* 147ff.

The Rush-Canning conversations continued through August and September. Each had hopes that the other might concede on the vital point of recognition. Almost immediately after his last interview with Rush on September 26, 1823, Canning reached an understanding with France. This entente was reached in a series of conferences between the French Minister to London, Prince Polignac, and George Canning. The talks were held in September and early October. The nub of the settlement is contained in the Polignac Memorandum of October 9, 1823. In this document, Polignac declares, among other things, that France "abjured in any case any design of acting against the colonies by force of arms."[14] After extracting this written promise from France, Canning promptly lost all interest in the joint declaration he had proposed to the United States. By this time, Rush suspected that Canning was making some other arrangement. In a letter to Monroe, he voiced these suspicions by remarking that "the Spanish-American topic has been dropped by Mr. Canning in a most extraordinary manner."[15]

At this juncture, it seems apparent that Canning had given up on his project of Anglo-American amity. When Castlereagh had the Foreign Office, the British minister to the United States was instructed "to smooth all asperities between the two nations, and to unite them in sentiments of good will as of substantial interest."[16] It would seem that if Canning was sincerely interested in forging this understanding with the United States, he would have let Rush know of the Polignac Memorandum. He did not do so until the end of November. By that time, the substance of the memorandum was known in European diplomatic circles, and James Monroe was on the point of issuing what would eventually be called the Monroe Doctrine. It is the opinion of at least one competent specialist that the responsibility for the failure of this brief but earnest effort at Anglo-American cooperation rests on the shoulders of George Canning.[17]

[14]William S. Robertson, *France and Latin-American Independence*, pp. 269-274.

[15]Rush to Monroe, October 22, 1823, *Monroe MSS.*

[16]Charles C. Tansill, *The European Background of the Monroe Doctrine in Modern Hispanic-America*, ed. by A. Curtis Wilgus (Washington, D.C.: George Washington University Press, 1933), p. 507.

[17]Arthur P. Whitaker, *The United States and the Independence of Latin America, 1800-1830* (Baltimore: The Johns Hopkins Press, 1941), pp. 446-447.

Rush, who had the complete confidence of Monroe, was willing to go along if Great Britain would recognize Spain's former colonies. If Canning had accepted this condition, Great Britain and the United States might well have marched down the nineteenth century hand-in-hand instead of being at sword's point. United States' relations with Spanish America would certainly have been improved since much of the antagonism between North and South America was a by-product of Anglo-American rivalry.[18]

Before Rush's dispatches containing Canning's proposals reached Washington, Russo-American relations were to go through a difficult phase. St. Petersburg's desire to foster friendship with Washington proved to be the solvent for the friction that occurred on the Pacific Northwest in 1821. Czar Alexander I's desire for an alliance with the United States commenced in 1819. On May 24 of that year, Pierre de Poletica, the Russian Minister to the United States, informed Secretary of State John Quincy Adams that he was "charged only with the most cordial and earnest assurances of the Emperor's regard and friendship for the United States; that the Emperor was extremely solicitous to be on the best terms with us."[19]

About a month later, June 17, 1819, Poletica called at the State Department for the express purpose of informing Mr. Adams that the Emperor was earnestly desirous that the United States "should accede to the Holy Alliance." By way of explanation, he added that the Holy Alliance was nothing more than a "league of peace." Poletica assured Adams that Alexander was especially anxious for the United States to join the league because if the American government had "any little points of difference with European powers, Great Britain, for instance, he could interpose his influence in their favor." Adams replied that it would be "advisable to ascertain what were the dispositions of the members of the Senate."[20]

The matter was thus postponed but on August 3, and on November 17, 1819, Poletica again brought up the subject of the

[18]J. Fred Rippy, *Rivalry of the United States and Great Britain over Latin America, 1808-1830* (Baltimore: The Johns Hopkins Press, 1929), pp. 112-120.
[19]*Memoirs of John Quincy Adams,* ed., by Charles F. Adams (Philadelphia: J. B. Lippincott & Co., 1876), Vol. IV, pp. 370-371.
[20]*Memoirs of John Quincy Adams, ibid.,* Vol. IV, pp. 394-395.

United States adherence to the Holy Alliance. When the Russian minister received no encouragement from Adams, it was finally decided on January 25, 1820 "to postpone indefinitely the question as to whether the United States would join the Holy Alliance."[21]

On September 16, 1821, in the midst of this friendly atmosphere, the Russian-American Company inhabiting certain islands off Russian Alaska, secured from the Imperial government a ukase barring all trade with the coast down to 51°. In addition, the same decree prohibited navigation by all foreign vessels between the Gehring Straits and this same line of latitude, within one hundred Italian miles of the shore, on pain of confiscation. These claims of territorial and maritime jurisdiction were to be immediately challenged by both Great Britain and the United States.

The ukase was communicated to Adams by the Russian Minister, Poletica, on February 11, 1822. Two weeks later, on February 25, Adams replied contesting the decree. Since Poletica had no powers to settle the matter, and since he was just about to depart on leave-of-absence, Adams sent instructions to Henry Middleton, American Minister at St. Petersburg, to file a protest there.

Fortunately, relations between the United States and Russia were much too cordial to make it necessary to adopt a very belligerent tone. Besides, the decree of September 16 had been secured, if not by fraud, at least without much deliberation by Czar Alexander I. When Middleton prepared to address a strong note of protest to Count Nesselrode, the Russian Minister for Foreign Affairs, he was urged by Count Capodistrias, Nesselrode's colleague, to drop the matter. "The Emperor has already had the good sense to see that this affair should not be pushed too far,"[22] he was told. Middleton was also informed that Russian warships on the Northwest coast had been instructed merely to prevent contraband trade with the existing Russian settlements. These assurances actually ended all danger of serious friction between Russia and the United States.

It was now necessary to arrange a permanent settlement of the dispute. After a good deal of delay, it was agreed that a treaty

---

[21]Charles C. Tansill, *The European Background of the Monroe Doctrine*, p. 511.
[22]*Proceedings of the Alaskan Boundary Tribunal*, United States Senate Document No. 162, 58th Cong., 2nd Sess. (Washington, D.C.: Government Printing Office, 1904), Vol. I, pp. 42-45.

should be worked out in St. Petersburg. Therefore, on July 22, 1823, Adams drew up new instructions for Middleton. At about the same time, he informed Baron de Tuyll, the newly arrived Russian Minister, of the contents of these instructions. The United States "would contest the right of Russia to any territorial establishment on the American continent, and that they would distinctly assume the principle that the American continents were no longer subjects for any new European colonial establishments."[23] Here is the non-colonization principle, which some four months later would be incorporated almost verbatim in President Monroe's famous message of December 2, 1823.

After prolonged but friendly conversations at St. Petersburg, the Russo-American Treaty of April 17, 1824, was concluded. By its terms, the United States secured recognition of its trading rights on the Northwest coast for a period of ten years. The boundary line north of which no American establishments were to be founded was put at 54° 40′. A provision was inserted in the treaty forbidding the trade in arms, ammunition, and spirituous liquors. Middleton had done his work well. The exchange of ratifications took place on January 13, 1825.[24]

In the midst of these negotiations with Russia, Adams fled steaming Washington for the cooler climes of his native Massachusetts. He was assured by the dispatches from St. Petersburg that all would come out well with Russia concerning our Pacific Northwest. Apparently interventionistic tendencies in Latin America on the part of the Holy Alliance did not disturb the tranquility of the American Secretary of State. Adams spent a large part of the late summer and early autumn of the critical year of 1823 some five hundred miles away from his office. It would require more than a week for a letter to reach him.

When, therefore, Rush's reports of Canning's proposals reached Washington on October 9, 1823, Adams was still out of town. Monroe, after reading the dispatches, was genuinely alarmed. Rush had been in his post for five years. He was our most experienced diplomat in Europe. The President had a great deal of respect

---

[23]Dexter Perkins, *John Quincy Adams*, p. 95.
[24]Benjamin B. Thomas, *Russo-American Relations, 1815-1867* (Baltimore: The Johns Hopkins Press, 1930), pp. 40-45.

for him. Rush's comments revealed that the British government was truly concerned by the threat from Continental Europe to Spanish America. If England, better informed and more powerful than the United States, perceived danger, it is small wonder that Monroe was upset.

SAGE ADVICE FROM THE SAGE OF MONTICELLO

Monroe's first move was to consult his two immediate predecessors in the Presidency, Jefferson and Madison. He wrote Jefferson on October 17, 1823, enclosing the Rush dispatches. Monroe felt that the present case might justify a departure from the maxim of "no foreign entanglements." So much so, continued the President, that it was his own impression that we "ought to meet the proposal of the British government." The Chief Executive further declared that the joint declaration ought to be directed against any interference with Spanish America, especially against an attack on it by the Holy Alliance. Finally, it should be understood that such interference or attack would be regarded as a danger to the United States. Monroe asserted that it must be presumed that if the European powers were successful in Spanish America, they would attempt to subjugate the United States.[25]

In the main Jefferson agreed with Monroe: Canning's proposal should be accepted. The founder of the Democratic party admitted to Monroe that "our first and fundamental maxim should be, never to entangle ourselves in the broils of Europe." But, continued Jefferson, the object of the proposed Anglo-American alliance is "to introduce and establish the American system, of keeping out of our land all foreign powers." Canning's proposals, wrote Jefferson, protect the idea of an American system. Succinctly stated, this system means that "America, North and South, has a set of interests distinct from those of Europe, and peculiarly her own. She should, therefore, have a system of her own, separate and apart from that of Europe."

To maintain this American system, concluded Jefferson, we should accept Canning's offer. We should do this even though it might lead to war; for "Great Britain is the nation which can do

---

[25]Monroe to Jefferson, October 17, 1823, *Jefferson MSS.*

us the most harm of anyone, of all on earth; and with her on our side, we need not fear the whole world."[26]

Thus did the philosopher of the Democratic party reconcile cooperation with England with the notion of America for the Americans. This was no sudden switch for Jefferson. In his inaugural speech of 1801, he had advised against "entangling alliances." Now in 1823, he repeated that we ought "never to entangle ourselves in the broils of Europe." In 1802, in a letter to Du Pont de Nemours, he pledged that if France reoccupied New Orleans, the United States would marry itself to the British fleet and nation. Now in 1823, he advocated that if Europe, meaning France, attacked Spanish-America, the United States ought to fight "side-by-side" with Great Britain.[27] In 1808, he stated that it was the policy of the United States and Spanish America to exclude all European influence from this hemisphere. In 1823, he maintained that North and South America had an American system, wholly different from that of Europe, in which Europe should never be allowed to interfere. Needless to say, this letter from Jefferson to Monroe played an important part in the formulation of the Monroe Doctrine.

On October 24, 1823, Jefferson wrote to Madison enclosing the Rush documents and Monroe's letter. Soon afterwards, Madison sent his advice to Monroe. He too concurred "in the policy of meeting the advances of the British government." Yet the architect of our Constitution added the suggestion that Monroe have "an eye to the forms of our Constitution in every step of the road to war."[28] Like Jefferson, Madison believed that "with the British power and navy combined with our own we have nothing to fear from the rest of the nations."[29] Madison then proceeded to diverge from Jefferson's vision of two worlds by advocating a one-world

---

[26]Jefferson to Monroe, October 24, 1823, *Monroe MSS.*

[27]Jefferson to Monroe, October 24, 1823, *Monroe MSS.* To obtain British help against the Holy Alliance, Jefferson was willing to make a pledge of self-denial with regard to Cuba. However, this would not necessarily prevent the annexation of a free and independent Cuba some day to the United States. See Jefferson to Monroe, June 11, 1823, *Monroe MSS.*

[28]Madison to Monroe, October 30, 1823, *Monroe MSS.* A copy of this letter is also in the Madison collection.

[29]Madison to Jefferson, November 1, 1823, *Jefferson MSS.* Neither Jefferson nor Madison insisted on prior recognition by Great Britain of the new republics.

policy. This Madison did by suggesting that the United States invite Great Britain to join in aiding the cause of liberty in Spain and Greece. By his advocacy of United States interference in the affairs of Europe, Madison was at odds with the basic principle of the American system as proposed by Jefferson.

When Adams finally returned to Washington on October 11, 1823, the replies of Jefferson and Madison had not as yet reached Monroe. No sooner had the American Secretary of State read the Rush dispatches, than he was the recipient of two communications from the Russian Court which increased the gravity of the situation. The first was an oral statement from the Russian Minister, Baron de Tuyll. On the same day, October 16, 1823, he reinforced his verbal presentation by an official note. Both the verbal and written communiqués were identical. In each, Alexander I bestowed tongue-in-cheek praise on the United States for its declared neutrality in the Spanish-American conflict. The Russian Emperor went on to say that "faithful to the political principles which he follows in concert with his allies," he could not "under any circumstances receive any agent whatsoever" from any of the new states of Latin America.[30]

This bit of Russian diplomacy coming on the heels of the French victory in Spain, and of Canning's warning about European intervention, caused no little disturbance in the Monroe Administration. In effect, it asserted the solidarity of the Holy Alliance, of which France and Russia were members. The anxieties of the American President and his Cabinet were not minimized by the arrival a month later of a note from Russia in which Alexander I expressed intense satisfaction with the success of French intervention in Spain.[31]

Although the military threat from Europe was alarming, yet Monroe and his advisors did not deem it imminent. Therefore, they conducted their deliberations without undue haste. Rush's initial report of the British proposal for a rapprochement had been in America for nearly two months before the Democratic administra-

---

[30]Worthington C. Ford, "John Quincy Adams and the Monroe Doctrine," *American Historical Review*, Vol. VIII, No. 1, October 1902, pp. 30-32.
[31]*Writings of John Quincy Adams,* ed. by Worthington C. Ford (New York: Macmillan Co., 1917), Vol. VIII, pp. 29-32.

tion decided what to do about it. When the British *chargé* in Washington, Henry U. Addington, pressed John Quincy Adams for a quick decision, the American Secretary of State stated the reasons for the delay. Adams told Addington that the question "was of such magnitude . . . that the President was anxious to give it the most deliberate consideration." According to Adams, Monroe considered it ". . . the most . . . important incident of his whole administration."[32]

When once the Cabinet had completed its tedious homework on the complex issues, the tempo was stepped up considerably. In the famous eleven days from November 15 to November 26, 1823, Monroe and his associates hammered out an answer. That answer, subsequently to be called the Monroe Doctrine, and drawn up without the knowledge of the Polignac Memorandum, was communicated to Congress only a week later, December 2, 1823.

THE BIRTH OF A DOCTRINE

The now-famous Monroe Doctrine, consisting of two distinct parts, was included in the President's Annual Message to Congress of December 2, 1823. It comprised about two printed pages out of a total of thirteen. After an introductory page, Monroe, alluding to the negotiations with Russia over the Northwest coast, asserted the non-colonization principle:

In the discussions . . . the occasion has been judged proper of asserting . . . that the American Continents, by the free and independent condition which they have assumed and maintain, are henceforth not to be considered as subjects for future colonization by any European powers.

The principal author of this, the first part of the Monroe Doctrine, was unquestionably John Quincy Adams.[33]

After a seven-page intermission, devoted primarily to domestic affairs, the President inserted the second part containing the doctrine of the two spheres and the warning to Europe to keep within its own sphere:

The political system of the allied powers is essentially different . . . from that of America . . . We owe it therefore to candor and to the amicable relations

[32]Arthur P. Whitaker, *The United States and the Independence of Latin America, 1800-1830,* p. 462.
[33]Dexter Perkins, *The Monroe Doctrine, 1823-1826,* p. 8.

existing between the United States and those powers to declare that we should consider any attempt on their part to extend their system to any portion of this hemisphere as dangerous to our peace and safety.

It was obvious that Monroe had the rumored intervention of the Holy Alliance in mind. He continued:

With the existing colonies or dependencies of any European power we have not interfered and shall not interfere. But with the governments who have declared their independence . . . we could not view an interposition for the purpose of oppressing them, or controlling in any other manner their destiny, by any European power in any other light than as the manifestation of an unfriendly disposition towards the United States.

At the conclusion of his development of the doctrine of the two spheres, Monroe stated: "Our policy in regard to Europe, which was adopted at an early stage of the wars which have so long agitated that quarter of the globe, nevertheless remains the same, which is not to interfere in the internal concerns of any of its powers." This meant that Crawford and Adams had been successful in persuading the President to drop Madison's suggestion about intervening in the Greek war for independence.[34] In return for this act of self-denial, Europe would be expected to keep her hands off Spanish America.[35]

The Monroe Doctrine is one of the greatest bequests of the Democratic party to the United States. Although no one questions the predominant role of Adams in shaping the non-colonization part of the message, the authorship of the doctrine of the two spheres is somewhat more complex. It was really the work of several hands. The dispatches of Richard Rush provided the Cabinet with excellent material pointing towards an American system. Adams's insistence that the Administration should "make an American cause, and adhere inflexibly to that," established a clear line between the Old World and the New. If the ideas of Jefferson, Madison, and Monroe had been followed, this distinction would have been less clear. However, if it had been left entirely to Adams, the presidential message would have contained only the first part, the

---

[34]Margaret L. Coit, *John C. Calhoun* (Boston: Houghton Mifflin & Co., 1950), p. 127.
[35]James D. Richardson, *A Compilation of the Messages and Papers of the Presidents,* Vol. II, pp. 776-789. These pages contain the text of the Monroe Doctrine.

principle of non-colonization. As a matter of fact, it was Adams's thinking that this exposition of American foreign policy known as the Monroe Doctrine should have been expressed only in diplomatic correspondence. It was Monroe who determined on a significant statement to Congress and to the world. In fine, the second part of the message, which contains the doctrine of the two spheres with its warning to Europe and its notion of an American system, has for its chief architects, Jefferson and Monroe.[36]

The fact that the Monroe Doctrine is a unilateral declaration is due primarily to George Canning. The knowledge that the British Foreign Secretary had abandoned his proposals for a bilateral declaration was contained in Rush's dispatch of October 10, 1823. This dispatch was received in Washington on November 16, 1823, at the beginning of the all-important series of Cabinet meetings which resulted in the formulation of the Monroe Doctrine. Upon its reception, the only alternative open to the American government was to make a unilateral declaration or none at all. Although Monroe was prone to go along with England had she persisted in her offer, yet he did realize that a joint declaration might well lose for the United States the important friendship of France and Russia.[37]

Even though Monroe is cited as having said that his message was aimed at France, yet he by no means excluded Great Britain.[38] Rush's dispatch of October 10, 1823, by which Monroe learned that Canning had changed his mind, also contained a clear warning about England's intentions. Rush reminded the President and his Cabinet that "the governing portion of the British nation . . . rejoice . . . in the downfall of the Constitutional System in Spain." Great Britain, continued Rush, "in its collective, corporate capacity has no more sympathy with popular rights and freedom now,

---

[36]Arthur P. Whitaker, *The United States and the Independence of Latin America, 1800-1830*, pp. 489-491. In a Fourth of July speech in 1821, Adams advocated a policy of non-intervention in European and Latin American affairs. He was replying to an article in the *Edinburgh Review* of May, 1820, which appealed for American cooperation in supporting the principles of liberty and reform throughout the world. See Samuel F. Bemis, *John Quincy Adams and the Foundation of American Foreign Policy*, pp. 355-359.

[37]Edward H. Tatum, Jr., *The United States and Europe, 1815-1823* (Berkeley: University of California Press, 1936), p. 270.

[38]Arthur P. Whitaker, *The United States and the Independence of Latin America, 1800-1830*, p. 502.

than it had on the plains of Lexington in America." Furthermore, Rush was disturbed about British activities in Spanish America. His Majesty's government was sending consuls to some of the Spanish-American countries. To Mexico, she was sending three commissioners. Canning himself had asserted that one of them might remain there as minister. Rush thought that England's interest in Mexico might be based on its proximity to the United States and on the fact that it possessed rich mines.[39]

In summary, Rush proved that Britain was essentially part of the European system. This sharp reminder at such a crucial moment in our history was of incalculable importance. Monroe's hearty approbation of Rush's work in London was expressed in writing and was greatly appreciated.[40]

President Monroe was faced with an agonizing decision in less than twenty-four hours after he delivered his memorable message. European newspapers were replete with rumors that an army of 12,000 Spaniards was on its way to Spanish America with the full backing of the Holy Alliance. The Monroe Doctrine was apparently receiving its first challenge. Monroe acted decisively. He was willing to unite with Great Britain to prevent the interference of the Holy Alliance in Spanish America. The President immediately ordered Adams to send fresh instructions to Rush. Our Minister to the Court of St. James was to tell Canning that the United States "will unite with the British government, in measures, to prevent the interference of the allied powers, in the affairs of South America, and particularly, in sending troops there."[41] It is interesting to note that in these instructions, Monroe was not holding Canning to immediate recognition of the new Latin republics. A mere promise would suffice.

Fortunately, Rush did not read these instructions to Canning. He did not have to. When they reached him in London, Rush had already been informed by Canning of the Polignac Memorandum. Since this precluded any attack on Spain's former colonies in the

---

[39]Rush to Adams, October 10, 1823, *Dispatches, Department of State.*

[40]Rush to Monroe, January 28, 1824, *Monroe MSS.*

[41]Monroe to John Quincy Adams, December 3, 1823, *Adams MSS.* It is worthwhile noting that in all questions of foreign policy, Mr. Adams took direction and orders from Mr. Monroe. See *Memoirs of John Quincy Adams,* Vol. VI, p. 171 and p. 211.

New World, Rush saved his government the embarrassment of appealing for British help. Although these rumors of European intervention are now known to be fanciful, they were nevertheless real for Monroe and his Cabinet.

The Monroe Doctrine was, generally speaking, received enthusiastically by the people of the United States. The British *chargé* in Washington wrote Canning that the message "seems to have been received with acclamation throughout the United States." The "manly tone . . . with which the President has treated the subject of European interference in the affairs of this hemisphere . . . has evidently found in every bosom a chord which vibrates in strict union with the sentiments so conveyed." The *chargé* finished his dispatch by remarking that in his opinion "a closer union between this Republic and Great Britain with a view to the preservation of the liberties of this hemisphere" would be more than welcomed by the United States.[42]

In London, the *Times* applauded the "resolute policy" of the United States.[43] The press in England at first welcomed Monroe's message but abruptly changed its tone when George Canning gave the cue. Canning was not pleased. His government would by no means subscribe to the dictum that the American continents were no longer to be regarded as proper places for European colonization. Besides, the British Foreign Secretary was angered to see Monroe gain prestige in Spanish America by posing as its protector. Canning hastened to have copies of the Polignac Memorandum passed around among the diplomatic corps. From then on, the Monroe Doctrine and the Polignac Memorandum were in competition for the political and commercial favor of the new republics.[44]

All over South America, liberal statesmen were deeply grateful for the presidential pronouncement. Both Brazil and Colombia officially endorsed it. However, the conservative heads of the new governments realized full well that it was the British Navy rather than the ideals of the American President that afforded them real

---

[42]Henry U. Addington to George Canning, January 5, 1824, in Charles K. Webster, *Britain and the Independence of Latin America, 1812-1830,* Vol. II, p. 508.

[43]London *Times,* January 6, 1824.

[44]With regard to the commercial aspects of the question, Jefferson put it somewhat crudely when he wrote: "Great Britain and the United States prepare for milking the cow." Jefferson to William Short, March 28, 1823, *Jefferson MSS.*

protection. The principles contained in the message undoubtedly appeared somewhat theoretical to Chile and Colombia in 1824, and Brazil in 1825, when those nations were rebuffed in their petition for an alliance with the United States in support of the Monroe Doctrine. The advances of Mexico in 1825, and of the Argentine in 1826 for provisional assistance were declined by the United States in language that must have seemed evasive compared with the strong tones of the Monroe Doctrine.[45]

Europe had nothing but contempt for the message. Metternich, the Austrian Chancellor, decried the "indecent declarations" of Monroe. The Russian Emperor informed his minister in Washington that "the document in question . . . merits only the most profound contempt." The French Foreign Minister remarked jeeringly of the gulf between American pretensions and naval power. European statesmen regarded the Polignac Memorandum as the decisive document rather than the unilateral declaration of Monroe.[46]

Message or no message, the Holy Alliance was still bent on calling a congress to deal with Spain's colonial problems. Both France and Austria hoped to use the Monroe Doctrine to persuade Great Britain to attend the conference. Metternich stated to the British minister to Austria that if England should refuse, "it would be imputed to her that she meant to follow the line taken by the United States."[47] Chateaubriand, French Foreign Minister, told Polignac that Canning "can have no more desire than I to favor military insurrections, the sovereignty of the people, and all the beautiful things which Mr. Monroe tells us about *de facto* governments. Please point out to him," concluded Chateaubriand, "that it would be a very good thing for him to accept mediation with us and the allies."[48]

George Canning's note of January 30, 1824, in which he definitely declined to be associated with the Holy Alliance in any program of intervention, gave definite pause to European diplomats. If Great Britain had gone along with the allies, Spain, in all prob-

---

[45]George Dangerfield, *The Era of Good Feeling*, p. 304.

[46]Thomas A. Bailey, *A Diplomatic History of the American People*, p. 189 and George Dangerfield, *The Era of Good Feeling*, p. 304.

[47]Dexter Perkins, "Europe, Spanish America, and the Monroe Doctrine," *American Historical Review*, Vol. XXVII, No. 2, January 1922, p. 215.

[48]*Ibid.*, p. 215.

ability would have regained her lost provinces. Monroe, owing to Rush's admirable dispatches, was able to sense the British decision, and concluded correctly that the Holy Alliance "would make no attempt in favor of Spain for their subjugation of the new governments."[49] Actually, therefore, it was Canning's note of January 30, 1824, rather than Monroe's message of December 2, 1823, that spelled security for the new states of Spanish America.

THE VERDICT OF HISTORY

Richard Rush was one of the few statesmen who presciently wrote that the message "will mark an epoch in our history."[50] Not everyone had the perceptiveness of Rush. For it must be recalled that when the Doctrine was first announced in 1823, it had no real force behind it. Nevertheless, the words and the philosophy behind them not only helped the United States at the time, but raised the standard of independence and sovereignty for the entire hemisphere. A generation would pass before the United States would be powerful enough to make effective the principles of non-colonization and non-intervention. These principles so bravely proclaimed by a Democratic president in 1823 have stood the test of time.

---

[49]Monroe to Madison, January 26, 1824, *Madison MSS.*
[50]Rush to Monroe, February 19, 1924, *Monroe MSS.*

10

The Death of a Dynasty

As MONROE PREPARED TO JOIN Madison and Jefferson in leisurely
retirement, he could look back with no little satisfaction on his
eight years in the White House. His presidential years, 1817-1825,
had witnessed our acquisition of the Floridas, the settlement of
the Missouri question, the conquest of our first major depression,
and finally, the Monroe Doctrine. However, running concurrently
with these major achievements, and consuming vastly more energy,
was the persistent struggle for the right of succeeding Monroe in
the presidential office.

The campaign of 1824 actually began as early as 1816.[1] No
sooner had Monroe been inaugurated in 1817 when John Quincy
Adams observed that the deals then being made were not in preparation for the election of 1820 "but for the one after."[2] At about
the same time, the New Englander recorded the fact that "all public
business in Congress now connects itself with intrigues, and there
is a great danger that the whole Government will degenerate into
a struggle of cabals."[3] By 1820, this Congressional friction had
fanned out to the country at large as friends of the rival candidates
engaged in bitter factional fights. Two years later, in 1822, there
were some sixteen aspirants all "preening themselves more or less
conspicuously in the public view."[4]

Indeed the woods were full of presidential timber. But by

---

[1] *Memoirs of John Quincy Adams,* Vol. V, p. 89.
[2] *Ibid.* Vol. IV, p. 193.
[3] *Ibid.,* Vol. IV, p. 212.
[4] Meade Minnigerode, *Presidential Years, 1787-1860* (New York: G. P. Putnam's
Sons, 1928), p. 128. At this time DeWitt Clinton, the Father of the Erie Canal,
was seriously thought of as a candidate. However, the anti-Clinton Albany Regency under Van Buren had the upper hand in New York. Because of this control, it seemed unlikely that Clinton would get any electoral votes from his home
state. He therefore dropped out of the race.

1823, the ranks had been considerably thinned. Adams, Crawford, Calhoun, Clay, and Jackson now remained as serious candidates. In no presidential contest before or since have so many distinguished and nationally known figures been active candidates. Personalities much more than issues were to signalize the campaign of 1824. For the struggle over slavery had hardly begun to manifest itself, and Clay's American System of banks, tariff, and internal improvements had not as yet reached the stage of acute controversy. Finally, the perplexing question of States' rights versus national control was still in a mild and incipient stage.[5]

But the old order was definitely passing, and a movement toward a more complete democracy was clearly discernible. Growing hostility to party dictation by Washington politicians was in the air. This animosity had for its object the wresting of party control from the politicians and the placing of it in the hands of the people acting through popular nominating conventions.[6]

NORTHERN STANDARD BEARER

The contest for the presidential prize turned out to be a sectional one but one without any clearly defined sectional issues. The five contestants lived on the arc of a circle from Calhoun in South Carolina to Crawford in Georgia, Jackson in Tennessee, Clay in Kentucky, and Adams in New England.

John Quincy Adams, the only Northern candidate, besides being the son of our second President, and the pride of New England, was the Secretary of State in Monroe's cabinet. He had not been regarded as a presidential possibility when he took over the State Department in 1817. Yet by precedent, Mr. Adams could assert his rights to the highest office. After all, he was Secretary of State, and for twenty-three years, the Secretary of State had automatically walked right into the White House after locking up his office at the State Department. He was also aided by sectional jealousy of Virginia's monopoly of the presidency. His wide learning and successful diplomacy were offset by a cold, austere personality which denied him widespread popularity. Adams's anti-

---

[5]Thomas R. Hay, "John C. Calhoun and the Presidential Campaign of 1824," *North Carolina Historical Review,* Vol. XII, No. 1, January 1935, p. 22.
[6]C. H. Ramelkamp, "The Campaign of 1824 in New York," *Annual Report of American Historical Association,* 1904, p. 177.

slavery principles, shown during the Missouri Compromise debates, while helping him somewhat in the North, East, and West, did not seem to hurt him overmuch in the southland. For States' rights men in Virginia, and even farther south, tended to favor him as a second choice to Crawford. His sympathy towards the West on internal improvements and the tariff was challenged by Clay. The New Englander refused to allow his private papers on these matters to be made public on the ground that he was opposed to electioneering. This answer apparently hurt him in Ohio, but in the long view, it may well have been good politics.[7]

VOICES OF THE SOUTH

Two nominees were placed in opposition to the choice of the North. They were Calhoun and Crawford, both members of Monroe's Cabinet. William Harris Crawford, Secretary of the Treasury, had developed into an ardent States' rights advocate who insisted on a return to strict constructionist principles. Born in Virginia, he had migrated to South Carolina and eventually to Georgia where he became the leader of the slave-holding forces against the Democrats in the interior. He was blessed both with an engaging affability, and an imposing presence. Six feet two in height and well-proportioned, his fine features, fair complexion and blue eyes made him one of the really handsome men in Washington. His conversion to strict construction had been gradual, for as a Senator from Georgia he had in 1811 argued for a rechartering of the Bank on the basis of the doctrine of implied powers. Needless to say, his enemies cast this up at him in 1824. Nevertheless, his very real ability made him a formidable foe, whether on the dueling field where he had killed his man, or in the great arena of politics.

Former Secretary of War and Minister to France, Crawford had in effect withdrawn from the Congressional caucus of 1816 rather than oppose Monroe. Even without trying, he had come within 11 votes of the nomination. Now, in 1824, he felt that he had earned the right to succeed Monroe. The Georgian's strength lay with the old-line Democrats of the South. He was generally considered the "heir apparent," especially if the Virginia Dynasty was to continue. The patronage of the Treasury Department helped

[7]Eugene H. Roseboom, *A History of Presidential Elections,* p. 80.

him build up a powerful political machine. John Quincy Adams considered Crawford to be a selfish and scheming politician, and characterized him as "a worm preying upon the vitals of the Administration in its own body."[8]

John C. Calhoun of South Carolina, the other Southern candidate, served Monroe as Secretary of War. A friend of Clay's, he was an ardent young Democrat. Besides championing the needs of the nationalistic West, he was considered along with Crawford as one of the important leaders of the South. A former War Hawk, he was opposed by Thomas Ritchie, the editor of the Richmond *Enquirer,* and one of the leaders of the States' rights school. Ritchie and company thought Calhoun far too radical in his approval of internal improvements, banks and the tariff.[9] This criticism is interesting in the light of Calhoun's subsequent career.

SONS OF THE WEST

Out of the West as favorite sons, came Henry Clay of Kentucky, the gamey and gallant "Harry of the West," and Andrew Jackson of Tennessee, the tall, white-maned, hollow-cheeked "Old Hero" of New Orleans. Clay was looked upon as the epitome of all that Kentucky represented: honor, sporting blood, whiskey, and poker. Adams referred to him as one who was "in politics, as in private life, essentially a gamester."[10] Speaker of the House, author of the American System, his magnetic personality did much to insure him the loyal support of thousands of Americans.

While Clay made his appeal to the business and property interests, Andrew Jackson was the hero of the rough and rampant West. Often pictured as a coonskin-capped frontiersman, this gaunt, lantern-jawed, choleric soldier was comparatively unknown outside his native Tennessee until his heroic and opportune defeat of the British in 1815. This image of Jackson as a backwoods Democrat was erroneous. He was a frontier conservative with experience as a cotton planter, slave-owner, judge, land speculator, and merchant. He became the great surprise of the campaign, at least to the professional politicians. Poorly educated, inexperienced in

[8]William P. Cresson, *James Monroe,* p. 454.
[9]Charles H. Ambler, *Sectionalism in Virginia from 1776-1861* (Chicago: The University of Chicago Press, 1910), p. 128.
[10]*Memoirs of John Quincy Adams,* Vol. V, p. 59.

political affairs, quick-tempered, and with a dueling record, Washington Democrats did not at first take him seriously. But when the groundswell from the back country finally hit the Capital, the experts were quick to accord the Old Hero the respect due him.

This popularity, while no doubt deserved, was carefully nurtured by a shrewd Nashville group, led by Major William B. Lewis, Senator John H. Eaton, and John Overton. When the presidency was first proposed to him in 1821, Jackson commented in his usual decisive manner: "Do they think I am a damned fool! No sir; I know what I am fit for. I can command a body of men in a rough way, but I am not fit to be President."[11] When this Nashville, Tennessee, Junto started to work on Jackson, they realized that his choice was Adams, but that if Calhoun's name was brought forward, he would support the South Carolinian.[12] As for Clay, Jackson, no doubt remembering his hostility in the Florida affairs, remarked prophetically: "Whatever may be thought of the pretensions of Mr. Clay to the presidency by the Kentuckians, he has not the prospect of being elected."[13] With regard to Crawford, Old Hickory "would support the Devil first."[14]

Finally Lewis and company secured Jackson's election as Senator from Tennessee against his wishes. Old Hickory appeared in Washington for the session of 1823-1824. He spoke little, but did vote for the protective tariff and internal improvement bills, thereby proving his fidelity to the West. Somehow this vote did not seem to hurt him in the South. The Jackson managers were so adroit as to make it appear almost unpatriotic to criticize the Old Hero, who had saved his country at New Orleans. It was the man, not the issues, that really counted.

In 1821, the first year of Monroe's second administration, it

---

[11]James Parton, *Life of Andrew Jackson* (New York: Mason Brothers, 1860), Vol. II, p. 354. Lewis was Jackson's army quartermaster. Eaton was a Senator from Tennessee. Overton was Old Hickory's second when Jackson fought a duel with Dickinson, the best shot in all Tennessee.

[12]Jackson to James Gadsten, December 6, 1821, *Jackson MSS*. Gadsten, loyal supporter of Jackson, is Colonel James Gadsten of Florida. Jackson was grateful to Adams for his support in 1818 when he was in danger of being censured for his Florida invasion. At this time, Jackson was unaware that Calhoun had voted to censure him. Clay and Crawford had both worked to have the Old Hero offically rebuked.

[13]Jackson to Andrew J. Donelson, May 2, 1822, *Donelson MSS*. Donelson was an adopted son of Jackson's.

[14]Jackson to James Gadsten, December 6, 1821, *Jackson MSS*.

was generally acknowledged among Democrats in Congress that Crawford would be the next president. Old-fashioned Jeffersonians took it for granted. Nathaniel Macon, member of the House from North Carolina, wrote to his friend Bartlett Yancey that although Crawford did not stand as high in Washington as formerly, he still stood highest.[15]

Indeed, if the traditional Jefferson-hallowed party caucus had been adhered to by the Democrats, Crawford would have been the sole nominee, Realizing that if a caucus was held it would favor Crawford, the adherents of the other candidates opposed it. Besides this formidable opposition, the caucus suffered from exclusiveness and remoteness from popular control. Used in the elections of 1808, 1812, 1816, and 1820, "King Caucus" was dethroned in 1824. Recommendations of presidential candidates by state legislatures or meetings of citizens replaced the caucus, and gradually led to our national convention type of nomination.

The attack on the caucus began on December 8, 1821, when the South Carolina legislature nominated her able and popular William Lowndes for the presidency. Calhoun, although he thought the movement was "rash and foolish,"[16] yet remained good friends with Lowndes. After the latter's death on October 27, 1822, the Palmetto State chose Calhoun as its standard bearer. Tennessee, like South Carolina, had a favorite son, and on July 20, 1822, its legislature nominated Andrew Jackson. Shortly afterwards, at a mass meeting in Blount County, Tennessee, the selection of Jackson was heartily seconded. The Kentucky legislature put the name of Henry Clay in nomination on November 18, 1822. The Blue Grass State based its choice on the right of the West to a fair participation in the executive branch of the government. By early 1824, New England had declared for John Quincy Adams, and Pennsylvania came out for Jackson. As the collective voice of the North, South, East, and West roared its challenge, the Virginia Dynasty of Washington, Jefferson, Madison, and Monroe trembled.

---

[15]Curtis W. Garrison, "The National Election of 1824," Dissertation, Johns Hopkins University, 1928, p. 42. Yancey was an outstanding North Carolinian Democrat.

[16]Calhoun to Virgil Maxcy, December 3, 1821, *Maxcy MSS.* Maxcy was a Maryland attorney, and a Democratic politician.

THE OLD GUARD

If the caucus had enemies, it also had friends. For example, Nathaniel Macon, the Nestor of Congress, was convinced that the number of candidates represented a lack of belief in Jeffersonian principles, and a want of confidence in the Democratic party.[17] Senator Martin Van Buren was shocked by the refusal of his fellow Democrats to honor the national caucus. The Little Magician blamed the President for deliberately wrecking the party. Monroe "pursued a course," he wrote, "well designed to weaken the influence of the caucus system, and to cause its abandonment."[18] Thomas Ritchie felt the same way as Van Buren. He did not think that a national convention was feasible until faster and better transportation was established. The Richmond editor looked upon the caucus as the only available means of choosing a suitable candidate. In a long editorial defending King Caucus, he stated that anyone "who would deprive the people of this country of the adoption of some means of concert in their elections, cannot mean them well."[19] Mordecai M. Noah, editor of the New York *Advocate,* pleaded with Monroe to "advocate regular nominations as the only means to concentrate the will of the party and keep us united."[20] George W. Erving, former United States Minister to Madrid, asserted that Monroe's actions had done much to "demoralize the Republican party . . . there would have been no contest . . . had Monroe pursued the course of those who raised him to power."[21] The Washington *Gazette* reminded its readers that Jefferson, Madison, and Monroe were caucus candidates. Furthermore, a convention of delegates might be elected by a cabal motivated by partisan interests.[22] William L. Marcy, a leader in Van Buren's Albany Regency, reported that Congress is "fully aware of the dangers of changing the mode of election at this time when the Democratic party is dis-

---

[17]Macon to Van Buren, May 9, 1823, *Van Buren MSS.*

[18]Martin Van Buren, *Inquiry into the Origin and Course of Political Parties in the United States* (New York: Hurd & Houghton, 1867), pp. 4-5. In 1824 Van Buren was a Senator from New York, and leader of the Albany Regency. He was a Crawford supporter, and tried desperately to deliver the electoral vote of the Empire State to the Georgian. He failed. Adams won it.

[19]Richmond *Enquirer,* January 1, 1824.

[20]Curtis W. Garrison, "The National Election of 1824," p. 48.

[21]Erving T. Crawford, April 20, 1824, *Crawford MSS.*

[22]Washington *Gazette,* December 3 and 4, 1823.

tracted in its choice among the various candidates."[23] Governor
Lewis Cass of Michigan regretted all the "excitement in the presidential question. Either of the distinguished gentlemen, whose
names are before the public, would administer the national affairs
with ability."[24] Caucus or no caucus, there would still be an election, and it was coming on apace.

By 1822 Crawford seemed to be far out in front, but in early
September, 1823, a stroke prostrated the strapping Georgian. He
was paralyzed in every limb. The first words that he murmured
on regaining consciousness indicated that he intended to fight on.
Months later he even dragged himself to Cabinet meetings, led
down the corridors like a child.[25]

The Crawford adherents, like their leader, refused to quit.
They saw to it that the presidential caucus, the last one ever held,
convened on February 14, 1824. In spite of the opposition of
Adams, Calhoun, Clay, Jackson, and sundry others, sixty-six Demo-
crats attended. One hundred and fifty-two remained away. The hall
of the House rang with the jeers of the anti-Crawford Democrats.
Someone in the jammed gallery moved to adjourn. Van Buren, the
Little Magician, needing all the magic he could muster was on his
feet in an instant and forced down the motion. The Senator from
New York then immediately called for a vote, and Crawford was
quickly nominated, receiving sixty-four votes. The distinguished
Pennsylvanian, Albert Gallatin, a close friend of Crawford, was
named for the vice-presidency. Hardly a quarter of the combined
total of both Houses had attended. The plans of Van Buren and
Ritchie to use the caucus to build a union of Virginia, New York,
and Pennsylvania came to nothing. The Pennsylvanians stayed
away, and half of the New York and Virginia members did the
same.[26]

The Adams, Clay, Calhoun, and Jackson factions of the Democratic party, now eagerly presented the caucus as proof that Crawford was an intriguer who was attempting to maneuver himself into

---

[23]Marcy to Van Buren, December 14, 1823, *Van Buren MSS.*
[24]Cass to Van Buren, March 17, 1824, *Van Buren MSS.*
[25]J. E. D. Shipp, *Giant Days or the Life and Times of William H. Crawford* (Americus, Ga.: Southern Printers, 1909), p. 174.
[26]Curtis W. Garrison, "The National Election of 1824," p. 56. The combined votes of Virginia, New York, and Pennsylvania totaled half of the entire electoral vote.

the White House through the machinations of Congressional politicians. Jackson probably was the chief gainer since the Tennessee legislature had been the first to oppose the holding of a caucus. The West, regarding party machinery as a means of perverting the popular will, drew even closer to Old Hickory.[27] Daniel Webster observed that the caucus "is more likely to hurt than to help Mr. Crawford."[28] John Quincy Adams went much further than Webster when he asserted that the caucus "destroyed" Crawford.[29]

THE VICE-PRESIDENCY

Adams, Jackson, and Crawford, foreseeing that the election would go to the House unless the field could be narrowed, attempted to use the vice-presidency as a means of eliminating an opponent, and absorbing his strength. Adams had the audacity to express approval of Jackson as his running mate, remarking that the second office would afford "an easy and dignified retirement to his old age."[30] Jackson's immense popularity soon caused the New Englander to drop his plan. The Jackson and Calhoun forces finally arranged a joint ticket with the South Carolinian as the vice-presidential nominee. Eventually the Adams electors voted for Calhoun too, thus granting him an easy victory. The Crawfordites, seeing that Gallatin's name brought no strength to their ticket, prevailed upon him to withdraw in favor of Clay. Van Buren then intimated to the Kentuckian that Crawford might not live out his term if elected, but Clay, Speaker of the House, thought too much of his own chances in the probable event of a House election. He therefore refused.[31]

As the year 1823 began, no one of the candidates enjoyed such wide popularity as Calhoun. From Maine to Louisiana, the Secretary of War was, in all but a few states, still second choice at

[27]Eugene H. Roseboom, *A History of Presidential Elections,* p. 82.

[28]Daniel Webster to Jeremiah Mason, February 15, 1824, *Memoirs of Jeremiah Mason,* ed., by G. J. Clark (Boston: Boston Law Book Co., 1917), p. 275.

[29]William Plumer, Jr. to William Plumer, December 9, 1824. Everett S. Brown, ed., *The Missouri Compromises and Presidential Politics, 1820-1825* (St. Louis: Missouri Historical Society, 1926), p. 121.

[30]*Memoirs of John Quincy Adams,* Vol. VI, p. 333.

[31]*The Autobiography of Martin Van Buren.* ed. by John C. Fitzpatrick, *Annual Report of the American Historical Association for the Year 1918* (Washington: Government Printing Office, 1920), Vol. II, p. 665.

least. Jackson himself viewed with favor Calhoun's prospects in the West.[32] When on January 20, 1823, Calhoun advised Jackson that "I am the only man from the slave-holding states that can be elected,"[33] he had good grounds for his convictions. New England-born Justice Joseph Story thought him "superior to most, if not all of the candidates."[34] Daniel Webster was quoted as saying that "at heart Massachusetts preferred Calhoun to Adams, and that Calhoun alone could challenge Crawford's strength.[35] Van Buren looked upon the South Carolinian as the "undoubted favorite of the President."[36]

That Crawford considered Calhoun dangerous is evidenced by the fact that all through the 16th Congress, the War Department came under heavy fire from the supporters of the Secretary of the Treasury. When the military program proved sound, they indulged in personal abuse of the Secretary of War. The strain on Calhoun was apparent. When the session ended on March 3, 1821, the Army had been reduced to four regiments of artillery and seven regiments of infantry. The inadequate $800,000 of the previous year allotted for fortifications was cut to $202,000. Adams himself blamed Crawford for these attacks, and wrote in his diary that "all attacks against the War Department during this Congress have been stimulated by him and promoted by his partisans." The Secretary of State believed that Crawford's motive was based on the knowledge that "Calhoun is not prepared to support him for the next presidency." With regard to himself, Adams added: "It has been the policy of all the parties to keep hostilities in reserve against me this session."[37]

The Calhounites were not slow in retaliating. The Congressional session of 1822-1823 was marked by a counter-offensive in which the partisans of the Secretary of War carried the fight to Crawford. This time it was the record of the Secretary of the Treasury that was scrutinized as minutely as Calhoun's had been.

---

[32]Calhoun to Virgil Maxcy, December 31, 1821, *Maxcy MSS.*
[33]Calhoun to Jackson, January 20, 1823, *Maxcy MSS.*
[34]Story to Mason, February 21, 1822, *Memoirs of Jeremiah Mason,* pp. 264-265.
[35]Henry Shaw to Henry Clay, February 11, 1823, *Clay MSS,* and Webster to Mason, March 23, 1822, *Memoirs of Jeremiah Mason,* pp. 265-266.
[36]*The Autobiography of Martin Van Buren,* p. 116. Monroe claimed to be neutral. See William P. Cresson, *James Monroe,* pp. 455-456.
[37]*Memoirs of John Quincy Adams,* Vol. V, pp. 314-316.

From January 20 to March 3, 1823, the Washington *Republican,* a Calhoun paper, carried a series of letters over the signature A.B., which, in effect, accused Crawford of wilfully mismanaging the public funds. After two Congressional investigations, the Secretary of the Treasury came out with a clean bill of health. However, the publicity was widespread and damaging. By the spring of 1823, Calhoun was confident that "the Radicals are much broken; . . . their Chief is also much distressed."[38] Samuel D. Ingham, congressman from Pennsylvania, wrote Senator Ninian Edwards of Illinois that Crawford's popularity was definitely on the wane. He dated the Georgian's decline in public favor from the appearance of the A.B. letters.[39]

Daniel Webster's comments on King Caucus proved prophetic with regard to Calhoun's candidacy. The caucus, observed the godlike Daniel, "has hurt nobody but its friends . . . Mr. Adams and General Jackson are likely to be the real competitors at last."[40]

Four days after the caucus, Calhoun retired from the contest. His decision came with astonishing suddenness. Powerful Pennsylvania with its 28 electoral votes was to hold a state convention on March 4, 1824. The Secretary of War ardently hoped for the nomination in the Keystone State. His capable manager in Philadelphia, George M. Dallas, predicted victory. As late as January 25, 1824, Calhoun had written: "Pennsylvania is as firm as a rock."[41] The voice of Pennsylvania, speaking for the South Carolinian, would sweep hesitant North Carolina and New Jersey into the Calhoun fold. A triumph in the Quaker State would also be a signal for a drive on New England, Maryland, and New York.

Yet the eyes of Jackson were also intently fixed on Pennsylvania. After correctly predicting that "Mr. Van Buren cannot

[38]Calhoun to John Ewing Calhoun, April 14, 1823, *Calhoun MSS.* Crawford's followers were called Radicals because their opponents claimed that they cut the budget at the expense of the military, and thus left the country with weak defenses. John Ewing was the cousin and brother-in-law of John C. Calhoun.

[39]Ingham to Edwards, August 20, 1823, Ninian Edwards, *History of Illinois from 1778-1833* (Springfield: Illinois State Journal Company, 1870), p. 497. Senator Edwards of Illinois was the author of the A.B. letters.

[40]Daniel Webster to Ezekiel Webster, February 22, 1824, *The Writings and Speeches of Daniel Webster,* ed., by Fletcher Webster (Boston: Little, Brown & Company, 1903), Vol. I, p. 346. Ezekiel was Daniel's brother.

[41]Calhoun to Joseph G. Swift, January 25, 1824. Thomas R. Hay, "John C. Calhoun and the Presidential Campaign of 1824," p. 39. Swift was Chief of Army Engineers. Dallas was a Senator from Pennsylvania.

manage New York," Old Hickory remarked that his managers had carefully calculated that "if Pennsylvania declares for me, North Carolina is certain. South Carolina, Alabama, Mississippi, Louisiana, Tennessee, Kentucky, Ohio, and Maryland will all come out in my favor."[42]

The town and county mass meetings to honor General Jackson in the Keystone State, so carefully arranged by the Nashville Junto, were whipping up tremendous enthusiasm for the Old Hero of New Orleans. The final blow that felled Calhoun was struck on the evening of February 18, 1824, when Dallas addressed a meeting of ward leaders of Philadelphia. After reminding them of his partiality for Calhoun, he grimly announced that the time had come when "predilections must be sacrificed: the cause of the nation . . . is at stake." Calhoun's manager then electrified the audience by introducing a resolution urging "all sound Democrats" to unite in favor of "a single illustrious individual . . . Andrew Jackson."[43] On March 4, 1824, the Pennsylvania state legislature did the expected by taking Dallas' advice and nominating Jackson.

The Secretary of War, though bitterly disappointed, took the blow in stride. Writing to his close friend, Virgil Maxcy, he asserted the "movement at Philadelphia was as unexpected to me as . . . to any of my friends. Had Pennsylvania decided favorably, the prospect would have been most fair. Taking the U.S. together, I never had a fairer prospect than on the day we lost the state."[44] However, Calhoun wasted no more words on what might have been. The remaining five pages of this six-page letter to Maxcy carefully laid out plans for clinching the vice-presidency.

JACKSON'S STAR CONTINUES TO RISE

After the Pennsylvania nomination of Jackson, the Calhoun organization in North and South Carolina, in Maryland and New Jersey, went over to Old Hickory. In exchange, Calhoun received second place on the Jackson ticket. The Jackson lieutenants worked hard against Clay in Kentucky, Ohio, Illinois, and Missouri. In

[42]Jackson to Andrew J. Donelson, January 18, 1824, *Jackson MSS.* Donelson was an adopted son of Jackson.
[43]William M. Meigs, *The Life of John C. Calhoun* (New York: G. E. Stechert & Company, 1917), Vol. I, pp. 305-306.
[44]John C. Calhoun to Virgil Maxcy, February 25, 1824, *Maxcy MSS.*

New York, they took satisfaction at observing the Little Magician's difficulties in controlling the legislature for Crawford. Even New England felt the stir for the Old Hero of New Orleans. "I have no doubt," Jackson wrote his manager, "if I was to travel to Boston where I have been invited that would insure my election—But this I cannot do—I would feel degraded the balance of my life."[45]

Calhoun's elimination and Pennsylvania's choice of Jackson, were indeed pleasant birthday presents for Old Hickory who was fifty-eight years old on March 15, 1824. At this time, Jackson's appeal did not rest on erudite disquisitions on the tariff or internal improvements. All his followers had to do, quipped John Quincy Adams, was to shout "8th of January and battle of New Orleans." Yet Adams felt that Jackson would be better than Clay, Calhoun, or Crawford. The New Englander harbored a special resentment against Calhoun for what he termed his "underhand course." Among Clay, Calhoun, and Crawford, Adams preferred Clay.[46]

The gentlemanly manners exhibited by General Jackson during his senatorial term of 1823-1824 helped his candidacy no end. Nor was the General unaware of the effects of his conduct. When, for example, he effected a reconciliation with Winfield Scott instead of pressing for a duel, he was justly proud of himself. Conveying the good news to a fellow Tennessean, Jackson wrote: "This has destroyed . . . the stronghold of those who minds were prepared to see me with a tomahawk in one hand and a scalping knife in the other."[47]

Representative Daniel Webster, campaigning for Adams, but preferring Calhoun, was one of the many duly impressed. He informed his brother that "General Jackson's manners are more presidential than those of any of the candidates. He is grave, mild, and

---

[45]Jackson to William B. Lewis, March 31, 1824, *Lewis MSS*. In those days it was not considered good taste for candidates to campaign personally. Their friends did this for them. Jackson went even further and wrote: "I have never been a candidate for any office. I never will . . . But when the people call, the Citizen is bound to render the service required." Jackson to James C. Bronaugh, July 18, 1822, *Jackson MSS*. Bronaugh had been Jackson's military physician.

[46]*Memoirs of John Quincy Adams*, Vol. VI, pp. 273 and 340. Adams was angered because in New England where he did not need Calhoun's support, the South Carolinian hitched his vice-presidential ambitions to Adams' candidacy; and in the West, where he did need it, Calhoun ran under Jackson's standard.

[47]Jackson to Major George W. Martin, January 2, 1824, *Correspondence of Andrew Jackson*, ed., by John S. Bassett (Washington: Carnegie Institute of Washington, 1928), Vol. III, p. 222.

reserved. My wife is decidedly for him."[48] Both Clay and Adams were among those who remained somewhat unconvinced. The Great Pacificator could not "believe that killing 2500 Englishmen at New Orleans qualifies for the various, difficult, and complicated duties of the Chief Magistracy."[49] When Adams was dangling the bait of the vice-presidency before Jackson, he privately observed that the position was one "in which the General could hang no one."[50] The New York *Evening Post,* with no little sarcasm, remarked that if the country were under martial law, General Jackson would be the best man for president.[51]

It is undoubtedly true that the newly developed courtesies of the General aided him considerably with the staid segments of the electorate. The masses of the people, however, were more impressed with his frontier fighting qualities. Since these latter voters were the majority by far, they were given much more attention by the Jacksonian strategists. When little flurries of disapproval over Jackson's internal improvements and tariff votes blew through the West, they were effectively dissipated when Old Hickory's supporters referred to their Hero as the man who "has slain the Indians and flogged the British."[52] When Jacksonians concluded that these vigorous actions make the General "the wisest and greatest man in the nation,"[53] the ordinary citizen was inclined to agree. The common man might be perplexed over the intricacies of the tariff, but he had no difficulty appreciating heroism.

Bank, tariff, and internal improvement orators experienced great difficulty in holding their own with Jackson campaigners who toasted their candidate as "the last of the Revolutionary patriots whose history is the record of his country's glory."[54] At one Jackson dinner, the toastmaster suggested a novel approach: "May the skins of the enemies of Jackson be converted into a carpeting for

---

[48]Daniel Webster to Ezekiel Webster, February 2, 1824, *The Writings and Speeches of Daniel Webster,* Vol. I, p. 346.

[49]Henry Clay to Francis P. Blair, January 29, 1825, *Clay MSS.* Blair, at this time a Clayite, later became a Jacksonian Democrat and founded the Washington *Globe* in 1830.

[50]*Memoirs of John Quincy Adams,* Vol. VI, p. 333.

[51]New York *Evening Post,* August 22, 1822.

[52]Marquis James, *The Portrait of a President,* p. 404.

[53]*Ibid.,* p. 404.

[54]*Ibid.,* p. 404.

his friends to dance on."[55] How could Adams, Crawford, or Clay cope with such publicity as "Under Washington our independence was achieved; under Jackson our independence was preserved. Washington, Lafayette, and Jackson, Brandywine, Yorktown, and New Orleans."[56] There was no question but that Jackson, the war hero, had the strongest personal appeal.

All four rivals, Jackson, Adams, Crawford, and Clay, were outstanding figures as well as strong nationalists. Generally speaking, they were all presumed to have identical views on such issues as the bank, internal improvements, and the tariff. Long before the voting began, it was apparent that there would be no choice of a president by the electors. The choice would be made, for a second time, by the House of Representatives.

As in 1820, twenty-four states took part in the election. By Act of Congress, they had from October 27 until December 1 to choose presidential electors. In Vermont, New York, Delaware, South Carolina, Georgia, and Louisiana, the electors were appointed by the legislatures, but in the other eighteen states, they were chosen by the people.

Pennsylvania and Ohio acted first, casting their ballots on October 29. South Carolina and Louisiana concluded the voting on November 22. The results were carried to Washington by stagecoach, pony express, river steamers and ocean vessels. Not until mid-December was the final result known.

The election in New York, which began on November 10, was crucial. A clean sweep here would give the candidate 36 electoral votes, insure him at least second place in the national total, and add to his chances in the House election. The Albany Regency stood stoutly for the caucus candidate. But Van Buren's organization lost great popular support by removing DeWitt Clinton from his office as Canal Commissioner, and by refusing to meet the demand that the electors be chosen by the people. When the legislature met to select the presidential electors, a People's Party, formed by the supporters of Clay and Adams, had already started a campaign that eventually defeated the Regency, and elevated Clinton

[55] Alexandria *Herald,* June 30, 1824, quoted in Curtis W. Garrison, "The National Election of 1824," p. 72.
[56] Curtis W. Garrison, "The National Election of 1824," p. 74.

to the governorship.[57] Crawford's chances of capturing the Empire State's votes began to fade.

As early as September 2, 1824, Clay had consented to cooperate with Adams in New York.[58] Peter B. Porter, Clay's campaign manager, advised his candidate that if a compromise were made it would probably be with the friends of Adams.[59] Thurlow Weed, the "Wizard of the Lobby," now became a principal figure in the negotiations between the Clay and Adams leaders. Weed, a Rochester editor, and a fervent Adams man, lived up to his sobriquet. Clay estimated correctly that he must receive seven electoral votes in New York to keep him in the running. These were guaranteed by Weed representing Adams, and a split ticket was arranged. The device succeeded, and 25 Adams, 7 Clay, and 4 Crawford electors were chosen.

Had the Weed-Adams group kept its word, Clay would have tied Craword for third place in the electoral college. But in an atmosphere charged with duplicity and intrigue, Clay lost three of his votes when the electors met in December. The Weed-Adams contingent had violated its pledge.[60]

The New York vote was almost equally fatal to Crawford. Had the Georgian received the entire 36 votes of New York, as Van Buren anticipated, he would have finished well ahead of Adams. He would then have been in a strong position to bargain for the support in the House necessary to make him president.

The final results of the noisy presidential campaign of 1824 were interesting but confusing. In the Electoral College, Jackson received 99 votes, Adams 84, Crawford 41, and Clay, 37. The popular vote read: Jackson, 153,544; Adams, 108,740; Crawford, 46,618; and Clay, 47,136.[61] Old Hickory had polled almost as many popular votes as his next two rivals combined, but he had

---

[57]Dorothie D. Bobbe, *DeWitt Clinton* (New York: Minton, Balch & Company, 1933), p. 267.

[58]Clay to Porter, September 2, 1824, quoted in Glyndon G. Van Deusen, *The Life of Henry Clay*, p. 176.

[59]Porter to Clay, October 6, 1824, *Clay MSS*. Porter was a Representative from Buffalo, New York.

[60]Glyndon G. Van Deusen, *Thurlow Weed, Wizard of the Lobby* (Boston: Little, Brown & Company, 1947), p. 30.

[61]Eugene H. Roseboom, *A History of Presidential Elections*, p. 84. This is the first record of the popular vote in any presidential election. It was but a rough approximation.

failed to win a majority of the electoral vote. In such a deadlock, the House of Representatives, as directed by the Twelfth Amendment, was obliged to choose among the first three candidates. This eliminated Clay, but his powerful position as Speaker of the House placed him in a position to help throw the election to the man of his choice.

Both the New York *Statesman* and the New England *Galaxy* were sure that the House would choose Jackson. The *Galaxy* was so confident that it was already choosing the General's cabinet.[62] The *Statesman* reasoned that Old Hickory, having carried eleven states to Adams' seven, needed only two more to win in the House. It was obvious to this New York newspaper that Jackson would get the votes of Missouri, Ohio, and Kentucky on the first ballot. The logic behind this conclusion was that in these states the General's vote had been more than double that of the New Englander.[63]

The importance of Clay as a president-maker was apparent. John Adams had admonished his son John Quincy not to betray any doubts of Clay's sincerity, and to be careful to cultivate the talented Speaker of the House.[64] The veteran New Hampshire statesman, William Plumer, sagely warned his congressman son that "it will be well for your members and for your country if no improper motives should have an influence in the final result."[65] William, Jr., replied solemnly and seriously that: "It is in fact very much in Mr. Clay's power to make the President."[66] No one was more aware of his importance than the Great Pacificator himself: "I am sometimes touched on the shoulder by a friend of General Jackson . . . 'My dear sir, all our dependence is on you . . . we want a Western President.' " "Immediately afterwards," continued Clay, "a friend of Mr. Crawford will accost me: 'The hopes of the Republican party are concentrated on you.' Next a friend of Mr. Adams . . . 'Sir, Mr. Adams has always had the greatest . . . admiration of your talents.' . . I sometimes wish it was in my power to accommodate each of them."[67]

James Buchanan, representative from Pennsylvania and future

[62]The New England *Galaxy*, December 24, 1824.
[63]New York *Statesman*, December 17, 1824.
[64]John Adams to John Quincy Adams, March 6, 1823, *John Adams MSS.*
[65]William Plumer to William Plumer, Jr., December 13, 1824, *Plumer MSS.*
[66]William Plumer, Jr. to William Plumer, December 16, 1824, *Plumer MSS.*
[67]Henry Clay to Frank P. Blair, January 8, 1825, *Clay MSS.*

President of the United States, was apparently anxious to aid Clay in making his choice. Finding the Speaker in the home of Robert P. Letcher, congressman from Kentucky, Buchanan steered the conversation towards the next cabinet. Letcher asked where he would find the equal of the men who served under Jefferson. Buchanan, who had had a confidential talk with Jackson a few days before, replied reassuringly that Old Hickory "would not go outside of this room for a Secretary of State." Clay laughingly retorted that the only cabinet timber he observed in the room was the gentleman from Pennsylvania.[68]

A few days before this delightful conversation, Buchanan had engaged in an equally delightful one with Jackson. The Pennsylvanian had asked Old Hickory "whether he had ever declared he would appoint Mr. Adams Secretary of State in case he were elected President."[69] Jackson's answer was in the negative. Two years later, the General declared that he had been aware that Buchanan had offered him a bribe. Futhermore, he had instructed Buchanan to "say to Mr. Clay and his friends that before I would reach the presidential chair by such means . . . I would see the earth open and swallow both Mr. Clay and his friends and myself with them."[70] Buchanan disagreed vigorously with the Old Hero's interpretation of his visit, and was "at a loss to determine how General Jackson could have believed I came to him as an emissary from Mr. Clay or his friends to make a corrupt bargain."[71]

These quiet, political conferences continued. On January 9, 1825, exactly one month before the House picked a president, Clay and Adams had a long private talk. According to the New Englander, the Kentuckian desired satisfaction "with regard to some principles of great public importance, but without personal considerations for himself."[72] The arrangements that finally brought about this meeting commenced on December 15, 1824. On that

---

[68]*The Works of Henry Clay,* ed., by Calvin Colton (New York: G. P. Putnam's, 1904), Vol. I, p. 440.

[69]*Ibid.,* pp. 441-443.

[70]Jackson to Carter Beverly, June 5, 1827, *Jackson MSS.* Beverly, a Tennessee friend of Jackson was anxious to document what he felt had been a corrupt bargain.

[71]Buchanan to Ingham, July 12, 1827, quoted in George W. Curtis, *Life of James Buchanan* (New York: Harper & Bros., 1883), Vol. I, p. 52.

[72]*Memoirs of John Quincy Adams,* Vol. VI, pp. 464-465.

day, Edward Wyer, a political journalist friend of Adams, called on the Secretary of State to say that the Speaker's support was available if by that means Clay "could be useful to himself."[73] Two days later, Robert P. Letcher called on Adams and asked him point-blank what he thought of Henry Clay. The New Englander replied that "he harbored no animosity." Letcher assured Adams that Clay's sentiments were similar. From such exchanges, Adams concluded that "Clay would willingly support me if he could serve himself thereby." He desires "a prominent place in the Administration."[74]

A little over a week before the House began balloting, the *Columbian Observer* of Philadelphia printed a letter accusing Clay and Adams of plotting a corrupt bargain. Since the editor of the newspaper was a close friend of Senator John Henry Eaton of Tennessee, the Senator was accused of being the author. The article purporting to be from a Pennsylvania congressman stated that for

some time past the friends of Clay have hinted that they, like the Swiss, would fight for those who pay best. Overtures were said to have been made by the friends of Adams to the friends of Clay, offering him the appointment of Secretary of State for his aid to elect Adams. And the friends of Clay gave this information to the friends of Jackson, and hinted that if the friends of Jackson would offer the same price, they would close with them. The friends of Jackson refused.[75]

Clay's reaction was one of indignation, and he immediately asserted that he believed the letter was a forgery. However, he declared that "if it be genuine, I pronounce the member, whoever he may be, a base and infamous calumniator, a dastard, and a liar."[76] George Kremer, Representative from Pennsylvania, then came forward, and admitted that he was the author of the letter. He claimed he had proof for his assertions. A Congressional committee was formed before which Kremer refused, on constitutional grounds, to appear. The committee then composed a milk-and-water report which was promptly forgotten in the excitement of the House election.

As the day of decision dawned, a heavy snow began to fall. It was February 9, 1825, and the House would begin voting just a

[73]*Ibid.*, p. 444.
[74]*Ibid.*, p. 447.
[75]*Columbian Observer,* January 28, 1825.
[76]Edward Stanwood, *A History of the Presidency,* p. 138.

few minutes after twelve noon. Van Buren, who had failed to deliver New York for Crawford, was back in Washington looking "like a wilted cabbage."[77] The Little Magician reasoned that Adams would probably have 12 states on the first ballot, or only one short of a majority. On the same ballot, Jackson was expected to receive the votes of seven states. Van Buren was determined that New York's vote should not go to Adams. If Adams did not make it on the first ballot, Jackson's second-line strength would have an opportunity to show itself. Old Hickory's chances would be much better if the voting continued beyond the first ballot.[78]

The New York delegation was tied, 17 votes in the hands of Van Buren, and 17 for Adams. This meant that until the deadlock was broken, the vote of the Empire State would count for no one. General Stephen Van Rensselaer, the Albany patroon and largest landowner in the Eastern states, was an important member of the House from New York. Somewhat henpecked, this pious old gentleman suffered somewhat from the malady of indecision. Once asked if he had read Baron Von Humboldt's latest work, the General pondered and hesitatingly answered: "I—I—really am not sure." Glancing helplessly at his wife, he importuned: "Have I read Humboldt's work, my dear?" Margaret Schuyler Van Rensselaer looked vexed and hastily replied: "Certainly, you know you have read it."[79]

The Clay men were after the old land baron, but he had promised Van Buren that he would under no circumstances vote for Adams. In fact, his last expressed preference was for Jackson.[80] At breakfast on the morning of the House election, Van Rensselaer reassured the Little Magician. Van Buren would have done well to have stayed with his protegée for when the old patroon arrived at the Capitol, Clay and Webster guided him into the Speaker's

[77]Thomas R. Hay, "John C. Calhoun and the Presidential Campaign of 1824," p. 42.

[78]There are various opinions on the candidate Van Buren intended to support. Some historians feel he would have swung to Adams after the first ballot, and thereby receive the credit of being king-maker. Others feel he would have remained with Crawford. Still others argue that he would have gone for Jackson. For a convenient summary see Marquis James, *The Portrait of a President*, p. 849.

[79]Gaillard Hunt, ed., *The First Forty Years of Washington Society* (New York: Scribners Sons, 1906), p. 185. This book is based on the family papers of Margaret Bayard Smith. Her husband, William Harrison Smith, came to Washington in 1800 and founded the *National Intelligencer*. He was a very close friend of Jefferson.

[80]Marquis James, *The Portrait of a President*, p. 438.

room. The Kentuckian and the New Englander, two of the greatest orators in American history, frightened the old man with a black picture of national disaster that would certainly follow if there was not an immediate, orderly choice of a president. Visibly shaken, Van Rensselaer would not retreat from his promise.[81] As he left the Speaker's office, he encountered Louis McLane of Delaware, a friend of Van Buren. "The election turns on my vote," stammered the General. "One vote will give Adams the majority—this is a responsibility I cannot bear. What shall I do?" McLane, the sole representative from Delaware, replied, "Do what honor, what principles direct . . . You have no motive but duty to sway you . . . my vote, like yours, would turn the scale. But, General, the greater the responsibility, the greater the honor . . . Let us march boldly in and do our duty." Apparently McLane served as a good antidote to Clay and Webster, for Van Rensselaer declared: "I am resolved. Here is my hand on it."[82]

By this time, most of the members of the House were in their seats. Van Rensselaer sat at his desk taut, head bowed, visibly perspiring. No doubt what he needed most of all—was his wife. But on that snow-swept election day of 1825, she passed him no note of instructions.

Three times in the course of the last hour, Van Rensselaer had given his word of honor not to vote for Mr. Adams. It was now five minutes to twelve. Henry Clay, Speaker of the House, rose. Smiling and confident, he strolled down the aisle. He paused before the General's seat, bent down, and whispered something in his ear. A minute later, he occupied the Speaker's chair as the vote-counting began. Van Rensselaer sat immobile, with eyes closed. He prayed for help. Opening his eyes, he saw a discarded ballot on the floor directly in front of him with the name of John Quincy Adams written on it. Accepting this as an answer to prayer, the old man picked up the ticket, and quickly stuffed it into the ballot box.[83]

---

[81]*The Autobiography of Martin Van Buren*, Vol. II, p. 152. This is Van Rensselaer's account of the interview as reported by Van Buren.

[82]Gaillard Hunt, ed., *The First Forty Years of Washington Society*, p. 191.

[83]*The Autobiography of Martin Van Buren*, Vol. II, p. 152. Nathan Sargent in his *Public Men and Events* (Philadelphia: J. B. Lippincott & Co., 1875), p. 76, claims Van Rensselaer was antagonistic to Van Buren and wished to thwart the Little Magician's plan to elect Crawford. The trouble with this argument is that Van Buren and Van Rensselaer were good friends.

It was all over. New York had cast her vote for Adams. The New Englander received the votes of 13 states, Jackson 7, and Crawford 4. The Virginia Dynasty was dead.

Overwhelmed by the enormity of his action, Van Rensselaer, with "tears running down his cheeks," cried out: "Forgive me." "Ask your own conscience, General, not me," snapped McLane of Delaware. Crawford injected a note of sympathy by remarking that "I do pity him, for it was weakness and only weakness that betrayed him." The sallow face of Randolph of Roanoke hardened: "It was impossible to win the game, gentlemen. The cards were stacked." Cobb of Georgia was boiling mad: "It is enough to make a saint swear," he declared. "Treachery, treachery! Damnable falsehood!" Van Rensselaer was the target of his anger: "The poor miserable wretch."[84]

When Adams was formally informed of his election by a special House committee, he presented an unusual spectacle. "Sweat rolled down his face. He shook from head to foot and was so agitated that he could hardly stand to speak." One member of the committee thought he was going to decline the honor. Adams told the gentlemen that he would avail himself of the precedent set by Jefferson and give them his answer in writing.[85]

Margaret Bayard Smith could hardly control her temper that evening at the sight of Clay "walking about with exultation and a smiling face . . . as if he had done a noble action." Occasionally someone would flash a look at Adams, and remark: "There is our Clay President."[86]

The anti-Adams segment of the press reiterated again and again that the people had been defrauded of their choice. The Washington *Gazette* in a typical editorial, insisted that the "Warrior, the Hero, the Statesman, and Republican were discarded for the cold-blooded calculator, the heavy diplomatist, the reviler of Jefferson . . . the haughty, unrelenting aristocrat."[87]

When it was known that the first place in Adams' cabinet had been offered to Clay, and that he would undoubtedly accept, Jack-

---

[84]Gaillard Hunt, ed., *The First Forty Years of Washington Society*, pp. 181, 184, 192.

[85]*Ibid.*, p. 186.

[86]*Ibid.*, p. 183.

[87]Washington *Gazette*, November 29, 1825.

son's anger blazed forth. In a letter to his campaign manager, Old Hickory commented sharply: "So you see the Judas of the West has closed the contract and will receive the thirty pieces of silver. His end will be the same. Was there ever witnessed such bare-faced corruption?"[88]

John C. Calhoun, who had been elected vice-president by more than two-thirds of the electoral votes, tried to warn Adams. He cautioned the President-elect that if "Mr. Clay should be appointed Secretary of State, a determined opposition to the Administration would be organized from the outset; the opposition would use the name of General Jackson." Adams appreciated the frankness of his Vice-President, but was determined to stand by Clay.[89] Calhoun, not unconcerned about his own future presidential possibilities, recalled to a crowded Senate Chamber on Inauguration Day that he had been "called to the vice-presidency by the voice of my fellow-citizens."[90] It sounded to some like a stab at Adams.

As John Quincy Adams took his oath of office at twelve noon on March 5, 1825, as our sixth president, no one could say that he had not been forewarned. Clay's acceptance of Adams' offer of the post of Secretary of State with its time-hallowed right of succession attached, gave the Jacksonians their issue. They made the most of it.

---

[88]Jackson to William B. Lewis, February 14, 1825, *Jackson MSS.*
[89]*Memoirs of John Quincy Adams,* Vol. VI, pp. 506-507.
[90]*National Intelligencer,* March 5, 1825.

11

The Old Hero Captures the White House

OLD MAN ELOQUENT, as the second Adams was affectionately called, was our first minority president. His enemies never allowed him to forget that fewer than one-third of the voters had cast their ballots for him. The manner of his triumph rankled deeply within him. His diary gloomily mentions his elevation to the "summit . . . not however in a manner satisfactory to pride . . . with perhaps two-thirds of the whole people adverse to the actual result."[1]

John Quincy Adams was so depressed with the results of the campaign that in his formal response to the official notification of his election, he seriously thought of refusing to serve. The New Englander stated that if by declining the office, he would be assured that an immediate re-election would be held, then he would gladly thrust aside the honor of the presidency. However, the President-elect observed that the Constitution itself was not prepared to cope with "the contingency which would arise in the event of any refusal." He therefore dutifully accepted "the post assigned him by the call of my country, signified through her constitutional organs."[2]

Appalled at the splintering of the Democratic party during the contest of 1824, Adams faced the task of Cabinet making with the notion of unity uppermost in mind. Like his predecessor, he desired to abolish party lines. With Calhoun, a recent opponent, already Vice-President, he continued two of Monroe's Cabinet, Wirt and Southard, in the Justice and Navy Departments. He then offered reappointment to Crawford, who declined. His selection of his former rival Clay for the State Department was to ruin the political aspirations of both. The Adams Cabinet was completed with the

---

[1] Bennett C. Clark, *John Quincy Adams* (Boston: Little, Brown & Company, 1932), p. 228.
[2] James D. Richardson, *A Compilation of the Messages and Papers of the Presidents*, Vol. II, p. 859.

choosing of Richard Rush for the Treasury and James Barbour for the War Department. Both men had supported Crawford for the presidency. Barbour was really a second choice since Adams wanted Jackson. He was restrained from making the offer to Old Hickory by the information that the Old Hero would by no means accept it.[3] It was indicative of the new President's magnanimity that not a single member of the new Cabinet had openly supported him in the recent presidential election.

This conciliatory atmosphere was further fostered when on the evening of Adams' election, General Jackson greeted his successful rival with warm cordiality. When the new President delivered his inaugural address, the first to grasp his hand was Senator Jackson, who, as the oldest member of the Senate present, had just sworn in Vice-President Calhoun. This was the last act of friendship between the Old Hero and Old Man Eloquent, for with the sending of Clay's nomination to the Senate, Jackson turned bitterly against Adams. The General immediately made a determined fight in the Senate against Clay's confirmation. Many Crawford and Calhoun followers joined him in this attempt to keep the Great Pacificator out of the State Department. That they failed, mustering but fourteen opposition votes, did not extinguish their zeal. The incident was really the beginning of a powerful Jacksonian offensive to achieve the presidency in 1828. In fact, the campaign of 1828 was almost an uninterrupted extension of that of 1824. By 1825, the well-organized Jacksonian machine became a veritable powerhouse by enlisting the services of Crawford, Calhoun, and Van Buren. The Adams-Clay faction, having unsuccessfully tried appeasement, dug in for the struggle. Soon the press would be calling them National Republicans, and the Jacksonians, Democratic Republicans. Both sides would claim to be true Jeffersonians.

As early as his inaugural address, Adams emphasized the national aspect of his new party by coming out strongly for internal improvements at federal expense. Along with the tariff, this would be the main issue in the next presidential election. However, Old Man Eloquent realized that "bargain," "corruption," and "usurpa-

---

[3]Henry Minor, *The Story of the Democratic Party*, p. 123. William Wirt of Maryland, and Samuel L. Southard of New Jersey were both close friends of Monroe. James Barbour, Senator from Virginia, had taken the side of the slave interests in the Missouri Compromise debate.

tion" would be the principal vote-getters. He therefore pleaded for "one effort of magnanimity . . . by the individuals . . . who have hitherto followed the standards of political party . . . that of discarding every remnant of rancor."[4] He pleaded in vain as vitriolic volumes of personal abuse all but obscured the only two issues before the country—the tariff and internal improvement. As a matter of fact, there was not a great deal to choose between Adams and Jackson on these two important issues. Both supported Clay's American System. Yet the Jacksonians were better politicians. It was their object to portray Old Hickory in the East as a friend of protection, in the West as a federal road and canal advocate, and in the South as a very mild tariff and improvements man. To a very great extent, they were successful. For example, with regard to taxing imports, Jackson had voted for the Tariff of 1824. His explanation of this vote shows his political sagacity, He was, he wrote, "in favor of a judicious examination and revision of the tariff." His vote, he continued, was based on the need for fostering the means of national defense and independence. He also regarded the tariff as useful in paying off the national debt, and for providing markets for breadstuffs.[5]

This was good politics in that it was calculated to win the votes of all sections. Northern manufacturers looked upon their goods as necessary for defense, while Southern planters made the point that a judicious tariff was the only kind favored by Jackson. On this, as on internal improvements, he was not as forthright as Adams. In 1826, the Tennesseean wrote James K. Polk that the general government had no right to make improvements without first obtaining the permission of the state involved.[6] The Old Hero's papers contain a memorandum of points to be considered in the administration of the general government. Point number six of this interesting account reads: "no power usurped over internal improvements."[7] His opinion on the tariff and internal improvements, un-

---

[4]James D. Richardson, *A Compilation of the Messages and Papers of the Presidents*, Vol. II, pp. 862-863.
[5]Jackson to Dr. Littleton H. Coleman, April 26, 1824, *Jackson MSS*. Coleman, from North Carolina, was a physician and friend of Jackson's.
[6]Florence Weston, *The Presidential Election of 1828* (Washington: Catholic University Press, 1938), p. 24.
[7]*Ibid.*, p. 25.

like his opponent's, was open to doubt. What was not open to doubt was that the middle and lower classes saw in Jackson one of their own. To them he was the embodiment of democracy. On the other hand, they tended to identify Adams with aristocracy. The fact is that by 1828, they had the power to put a common man in the White House. They used it.

JACKSON'S TEAM

Between Adams' inaugural and his first annual message, Jackson resigned his seat in the Senate, and set out for Tennessee. His leisurely progress home was one continuous ovation. Never mealy-mouthed about expressing his feelings, the General let it be known that Clay had deliberately traded his vote for a Cabinet post. The Tennessee legislature forthwith presented Jackson to the country as a candidate in 1828, in resolutions which vividly denounced the bargain by which he had been deprived of his merited success in 1824. The Old Hero then retired to a life of dignified ease at "The Hermitage," while his campaign was taken in hand by a group of dedicated and astute politicians. Van Buren, the key figure among the Jackson managers, was determined to leave nothing undone to insure Old Hickory's success at the next election. The Red Fox of Kinderhook viewed the break in the party as a throwback to the old division between Hamilton and Jefferson. It was the Little Magician who united the followers of Calhoun and Crawford with the Jacksonians. And it was also Van Buren who renewed the alliance between the North and South.[8]

ADAMS' PHILOSOPHY

John Quincy Adams' first annual message seemed to bear out the Van Buren analysis of the split in the Democratic party, for with typical Federalist broad interpretation of the Constitution, the President boldly asked for federal aid for an adequate system of

---

[8]Robert V. Remini, *Martin Van Buren and the Making of the Democratic Party*, pp. 124-125. Other prominent Jackson managers were: John H. Eaton, Hugh Lawson White, William B. Lewis, Francis Preston Blair, James Buchanan, Thomas Ritchie, Isaac Hill, Amos Kendall, and Thomas Hart Benton. Kendall, Blair, and Hill were important newspaper men. Kendall was the editor of the *Western Argus of America* (Kentucky), and Blair wrote for this paper. Hill was the editor of the New Hampshire *Patriot*. White was a Senator from Tennessee. Van Buren was from Kinderhook, N.Y.

highways and canals, the building of all necessary lighthouses, and the improvement of commerce by the deepening of our rivers and harbors. This in itself was enough to shock the strict constructionists who had been Crawfordites in the election of 1824. But Adams did not stop there. He advocated the establishment and maintenance by government aid of a great national university as well as several astronomical observatories. All this was obnoxious enough to the raw New Democracy, but when Old Man Eloquent urged the members of Congress not to be palsied by the will of their constituents[9] he "gave evidence," in the words of Old Hickory, "of a want of discretion."[10]

Crawford, who was much closer to Adams than to Jackson in the election of 1824, could no longer restrain his followers. They were pure Jeffersonians, and when they learned of the President's latitudinarian views, they flocked in a solid body to the banner of Jackson.

No sooner had the controversy over the President's annual message subsided when Adams found himself engaged in a bitter four-month debate over foreign policy. For in 1825, the United States was invited to send delegates to the Panama Congress to discuss problems common to the American republics. The call for this Congress was issued by Simon Bolivar, the Liberator. Although Bolivar failed to invite the United States, this failure was rectified by the governments of Colombia and Mexico, who through their ministers extended formal invitations to the United States. Clay, ever an enthusiast for Latin American cooperation, persuaded Adams to accept. It is important to note that Great Britain was the only non-American country invited by Bolivar.[11]

The President now sought Senatorial approval for his two Panama delegates and an appropriation from the House for their expenses. The Jacksonians, sensing that they had a good issue, mustered their strength for an attack on the Administration. Enjoying a majority in the Senate, they wisely chose to make their initial stand there. Senator John Randolph of Roanoke, probably the

---

[9]James D. Richardson, *A Compilation of the Messages and Papers of the Presidents*, Vol. II, p. 882.

[10]Jackson to Richard K. Call, March 9, 1829, *Jackson MSS.*

[11]Joseph B. Lockey, *Pan Americanism, Its Beginnings* (New York: The Macmillan Company, 1920), p. 312.

greatest master of invective that American public life has ever known, led the onslaught. Being well fortified with strong porter, continually supplied to him in the course of his speech by the Assistant Sergeant-at-Arms of the Senate, Randolph charged Clay with having forged the invitation to the Panama Congress. Calling upon his rich vocabulary, he abused the President and his Secretary of State again and again. He referred to Clay as "this being, so brilliant yet so corrupt, which, like a rotten mackerel by moonlight, shines and stinks and stinks and shines." In the midst of a wealth of Latin quotations, the Virginian exclaimed: "Let Judas have his thirty pieces of silver." They might "go to buy a potter's field, in which to inter this miserable Constitution of ours, crucified between two gentlemen, suffering for conscience's sake, under the burden of the first two offices of this Government." Randolph climaxed his efforts by a vicious attack upon Adams followed by a mock confession: "I was defeated, horse, foot, and dragoons—cut up—and clean broke down—by the coalition of Blifil and Black George— by the combination, unheard of till then, of the Puritan with the black-leg."[12]

Vice-President Calhoun, by now a confirmed Jacksonian, sat complacently in the chair while the President and his Secretary of State were subjected to these abusive and insulting epithets. Adams and Clay immediately went into action. Old Man Eloquent, using the pseudonym of Patrick Henry, made a vicious attack on Calhoun as being equally guilty with Randolph by not restraining him. Old Harry of the West immediately challenged Randolph to a duel. The Senator from Virginia accepted the challenge after formally protesting against "the right of any minister of the Executive Government of the United States to hold him responsible for words spoken in debate."[13]

It was arranged that the meeting should take place just across the Potomac from Georgetown, on the afternoon of Saturday, April 8, at half-past four. The weapons were pistols at ten paces. Firing was to begin upon the word "fire," and end as soon as the words

---

[12]*Register of the Debates in Congress* (Washington: Gales & Seaton, 1826), Vol. II, 19th Cong., 1st Sess., March 30, 1826, pp. 390-404. Blifil, a hypocritical rogue, and Black George, a candid rogue, are characters in Henry Fielding's novel *Tom Jones.*
[13]Bennett C. Clark, *John Quincy Adams,* p. 244.

"one, two, three, stop" had been rapidly uttered. This was agree-able to Randolph who was an excellent pistol shot. Clay was so unfamiliar with the use of firearms that he feared that he would not be able to fire at all within the limited time of a rapid count. The Kentuckian therefore proposed that the count be given very deliberately so that at least he might be able to fire once. When Randolph heard of Clay's proposal, he construed it to mean that the Great Pacificator intended to kill him. The Virginian, who had already confided to Thomas Hart Benton that he did not intend to fire at Clay, now let it be known that he might change his mind. A lot would depend, he remarked to one of his seconds, whether or not "I see the devil in Clay's eye."[14]

Just as the sun was setting behind the Virginia hills, the con-testants and their seconds assembled at the dueling ground. Clay seemed in deadly earnest. Randolph was chagrined by the accidental discharge of his pistol while he and Clay were receiving instructions. Clay promptly called out that it was an accident; another pistol was furnished, and the duelists finally took their places.

At the agreed signal, each man fired and missed. Randolph's shot hit a stump almost directly behind Clay, and the latter's bullet after passing through the Virginian's clothes, kicked up the gravel behind him. Mediation was offered by Benton, but Clay waved it aside saying, "This is child's play." Randolph also petitioned for another fire. Again, the Senator calmly received the Secretary of State's bullet, which passed so close to his hip as to pierce his coat. The Virginian then discharged his gun in the air exclaiming, "I do not fire at you, Mr. Clay." When Randolph extended his hand, Clay grasped it, and in a voice choked with emotion said: "I trust in God, my dear sir, you are untouched; after what has occurred, I would not have harmed you for a thousand worlds." Randolph replied: "You owe me a coat, Mr. Clay." The Kentuckian, with a smile of relief, retorted: "I am glad the debt is no greater." The whole party then returned to Washington in high spirits.[15]

PRESIDENT VS. VICE-PRESIDENT

The other duel which was a by-product of Randolph's famous

[14]Glyndon G. Van Deusen, *The Life of Henry Clay*, p. 221.

[15]My account is based upon that in the *National Intelligencer*, April 10, 1826. A sign indicates the site today, within fifty yards of the old Chain Bridge.

speech was fought on the newspaper front. We have mentioned that the President, angered at the failure of his Vice-President to preserve the decorum of the Senate, had penned a bitter denunciation of Calhoun, writing under the name of "Patrick Henry." The South Carolinian promptly replied in an article under the name of Onslow, in which he not only defended himself, but pilloried Adams and his Administration. The debate continued for several weeks. Adams contended that Calhoun's office gave him the authority to restrict debate within proper limits. Calhoun insisted that, although he was the Presiding Officer of the Senate, he had no power to call a Senator to order unless such authority were conferred upon him by the rules of that body. As a result of this newspaper controversy, the Senate amended its rules so as to grant the Vice-President this additional power. It was now Calhoun's duty, if it had not been before, to confine the members of the Senate to the amenities of debate. As is usual in such contests, both Adams and Calhoun claimed the victory.

The danger of duels notwithstanding, John Randolph continued his verbal thrusts at the Adams Administration. The very picturesqueness of his phrases gave them the widest currency. Jacksonians eagerly repeated his sarcastic taunts. "Meanness," Randolph once stated, "is the key word that deciphers everything in Mr. Adams' character." Whenever he mentioned the Adams family, he always referred to them as the "American House of Stuart." He struck the President in a tender spot when he remarked: "I have borne some humble part in putting down the dynasty of John the First, and by the Grace of God, I hope to aid in putting down the dynasty of John the Second." On another occasion, he acidly remarked: "This is the last four years of the Administration of the father renewed in the person of the son." With regard to the Panama Mission, the fiery Virginian was sure that there was enough gunpowder in it "to blow not the first of the Stuarts, but the last of another dynasty sky-high."[16]

After the Jacksonian Democrats had lambasted the Panama Mission for a good month in the Senate, their confrères in the House took up the struggle. After a four-month debate there, the Adams

---

[16]Bennett C. Clark, *John Quincy Adams*, pp. 247-248. The five quotes of Randolph's words are given on these two pages.

Democrats finally won out, and Congress gave its grudging consent; however, one of the delegates died enroute, and the other started so late that he finally abandoned his efforts to reach Panama. The Adams-Clay wing of the party, after having engaged in a prolonged partisan conflict, had nothing to show for its efforts. Jacksonians everywhere rejoiced.

Meanwhile, on June 22, 1826, the Panama Congress convened. It turned out to be a failure in that none of its recommendations was ever adopted and none of its proposed meetings was ever held; however, in all fairness, it must be said that the germs of the Pan-American ideal, so important today, were definitely planted at this initial Congress.[17]

Nothing seemed to go well for John Quincy Adams. His title tarnished by charges of corruption, the presidency brought him only burdens and sleepless nights. Badgered by his own Cabinet to make generous use of the patronage to strengthen the party, he resolutely refused. His diary records his position clearly: "I see yet no reason sufficient to justify a departure from the principle with which I entered upon the administration, of removing no public officer for merely preferring another candidate for the presidency."[18] When John Binns, editor of the Philadelphia *Democratic Press,* learned to his dismay that he was not to receive the public printing concession, and that Adams did not intend to make any removals, he averred: "I have no doubt, Mr. President, that the consequence will be you yourself will be removed as soon as your term expires."[19] Edward Everett, Congressman from Massachusetts, summed up what he considered to be a formula for defeat: "For an Administration to bestow its patronage, without distinction of party, is to court its own destruction."[20] Both Clay and Webster agreed with him. The Secretary of State, in giving his own position, wrote: "The principle ought to be adhered to of appointing only friends to office. Such, I believe, is the general conviction of the Cabinet."[21] Webster felt the same way as Clay, and asserted that "all patronage, which

---

[17]Joseph B. Lockey, *Pan Americanism, Its Beginnings* (New York: The Macmillan Company, 1920), pp. 312-354.
[18]Edward Stanwood, *A History of the Presidency,* p. 142.
[19]James Parton, *Life of Andrew Jackson,* Vol. III, p. 92.
[20]Everett to McLean, August 1, 1828, *McLean MSS.*
[21]Clay to Webster, April 14, 1827, *Webster MSS.*

can be justly afforded by the Executive Government, must be given to friends."[22] The philosophy of the majority of the men who had worked to elect Adams was concisely phrased by one of Clay's supporters: "I like the Jeffersonian System: Take care of my friends and let my enemies take care of themselves."[23]

In spite of pressure, Adams remained adamant. His associates knew a stone wall when they struck one. The President not only refused to find places for his supporters by removing his opponents, but he would not even dismiss public officials who were openly working to elect Jackson in 1828. A case in point is Postmaster-General John McLean, who all during Adams' administration did not hesitate to use the patronage to further Jackson's cause. He was left undisturbed by the President in spite of the pleas of Clay, Webster and of every other important member of the Adams team.

The President undoubtedly lost a considerable following because of his idealism in the matter of appointments. The editor of the *Federal Republican* informed Clay that hundreds of former Adams men in Maryland would not "turn on their heel to promote his re-election."[24] Bitterly disappointed in the Administration, they turned towards the Jacksonians who promised political preferment in return for hard work.[25]

As fantastic as it may seem, Adams was actually accused of using the patronage to entrench himself in office, and thus defeat the will of the people. Congressman George McDuffie of South Carolina asserted at a public dinner in July, 1826, that Adams was using the spoils system to keep himself in power.[26] Virgil Maxcy, Jacksonian leader in Maryland, wrote that all those who craved political promotions and favors in his State were for Adams.[27] Calhoun referred to the attempts on the part of Adams to mold public opinion by "an artful management of the patronage of government."[28] Jackson was indignant to find that "the patronage of the government for the last three years has been wielded to corrupt

[22]Webster to Clay, March 25, 1827, *Clay MSS.*
[23]J. D. Learned to Clay, September 27, 1827, *Clay MSS.* Learned was the editor of the *Federal Republican.*
[24]J. D. Learned to Clay, September 27, 1827, *Clay MSS.*
[25]R. Warfield to Clay, July 25, 1826, *Clay MSS.*
[26]*Niles Weekly Register,* September 2, 1826, Vol. XXXI, p. 13.
[27]Florence Weston, *The Presidential Election of 1828,* p. 58.
[28]Calhoun to Jackson, June 4, 1826, *Jackson MSS.*

everything that comes within its influence."[29] Even in New York, a state not unused to the spoils system, a vigorous protest was made against the attempt to secure the vote of that state for Adams by the use of patronage.[30] Hugh L. White, Senator from Tennessee, declared that under Adams, appointments were being made not for the public good but to increase the number of people friendly to the President.[31]

Yet the established fact is that during his four years as president, Adams removed only twelve men from office, all for official misconduct.[32] A clue to the apparent contradiction is found in McLean's remark that the policy of those surrounding the president is usually quite vital in forming of reputation of the entire administration.[33] Clay, for example, was not deterred by any scruples as was his chief. For though Adams himself followed the merit system, he could not control the appointments of his subordinates.[34]

If John Quincy Adams was losing votes and destroying his party because of naïvete in the give-and-take of politics, his brilliant diplomatic record presaged success in foreign affairs. However, after fumbling the Panama affair, he proceeded to bungle the West Indian trade issue. The problem of reopening the lucrative trade with the British West Indies, closed to Americans since our successful war for independence, became a burning question in 1826. In that year, George Canning agreed to reopen the West Indian trade to Americans under certain restrictions. Instead of accepting this half loaf, Adams sent the veteran Albert Gallatin to London in the hope of obtaining more favorable terms. The President felt that access to West Indian ports should be demanded by Gallatin as an American right, and not requested as a privilege. Canning, no doubt remembering Adams' role in the Monroe Doctrine, bristled when he heard Adams' bold viewpoint. In blistering terms he told Gallatin that what Great Britain did with the trade of her colonies was her

---

[29]Jackson to General John Coffee, May 12, 1828, *Jackson MSS*. Coffee, an Alabama planter, was one of Jackson's advisers.

[30]Michael Hoffman to William L. Marcy, August 14, 1826, *Marcy MSS*. Both Hoffman and Marcy were members of Van Buren's Albany Regency.

[31]White to Crawford, June 19, 1827, *Jackson MSS*.

[32]Frederick Jackson Turner, *Rise of the New West, 1819-1829* (New York: Harper & Bros., 1906), p. 273.

[33]McLean to Edward Everett, August 27, 1828, *McLean MSS*.

[34]Florence Weston, *The Presidential Election of 1828*, pp. 59-60.

own business. The British Foreign Secretary then promptly withdrew the offer completely.[35]

The Jacksonians were quick to denounce Adams for having lost an opportunity to resume the West Indian trade. Thomas Ritchie's Richmond *Enquirer* was sharply critical as it described "the clumsy and mischievous manner, in which the benefits of the Colonial Trade" have "been lost by the Administration."[36] This diplomatic failure of Adams became one of the most vulnerable spots in his armor during the presidential campaign of 1828.

ORDEAL BY SLANDER

No sooner had the Panamanian and West Indian episodes passed into oblivion when the Congressional elections of 1826 returned a majority in each House adverse to the Administration. The second half of Adams' term was, therefore, a period of marking time in so far as any important legislation was concerned. Practically all the action in both Houses had to do with the presidential campaign then in progress. It is a fair statement that Adams' four years as First Magistrate were almost completely devoid of important incidents other than those pertaining to the coming election of 1828.

Both in and outside of Congress, the struggle for the presidency went on incessantly. During the year immediately preceding the election, the contest increased in fury until it reached an unparallelled pitch of vilification. Both President Adams and General Jackson had rendered conspicuous public service, and their characters were beyond reproach; yet neither qualification spared them from the stream of merciless slander that was poured upon them.

The assaults on Adams by the Jacksonians began with the unjust charge that he had misappropriated public funds, and had padded his accounts as a diplomat abroad. Even more preposterous was the canard that as minister to St. Petersburg he had acted as procurer for the Czar and had been party to the seduction of a beautiful American girl by Alexander I. The Russian minister in Washington sought redress for this slur on his master, but no apol-

---

[35]Frank Lee Benns, *The American Struggle for the British West Indian Carrying Trade* (Indianapolis: University of Indianapolis Press, 1923), pp. 121-162.
[36]*Richmond Enquirer*, March 13, 27, 30, 1827.

ogy could be obtained.[37] The Chief Executive seethed with indignation at these baseless tales, but he thought it best to take no public notice of them.

Meanwhile his own partisans were by no means outdone in the trade of calumny. Old Hickory was denounced as a murderer, a ruffian, a traitor, an adulterer, and a speculator in Florida lands while he was governor of that territory. The adultery accusation was the meanest one of them all. This was the work of Charles Hammond, editor of the Cincinnati *Gazette*. The circumstances of Jackson's marriage are now known. He had married Mrs. Robards on the frontier when communications were exceedingly slow. At the time of the ceremony, they both honestly believed that her renegade first husband had obtained a divorce by Act of the Virginia legislature. Jackson had lived with his bride for some time before discovering that the Legislative Act was merely a preliminary decree. To their mutual dismay, the Jacksons found out that Robards had only recently obtained his divorce. The Old Hero and his wife were immediately remarried and lived happily until her death. These facts were tortured to form the basis of a nasty attack on Rachel Jackson as an adulteress. Hammond followed his newspaper account with a pamphlet which read in part: "Ought a convicted adulteress and her paramour husband be placed in the highest offices of this free and Christian land?"[38]

The General fought hard for self-command. With a quill quivering with almost uncontrollable rage, he wrote: "How hard it is to keep the cowhide from these villians. I have made many sacrifices for my country—but being . . . unable to punish those slanders of Mrs. J. is a sacrifice too great to be well endured."[39] Jackson's love of his wife was the great passion of his life. He had killed, in a duel, Charles Dickinson, reputed the best shot in Tennessee, for defaming her fair name. If he could now fix definite responsibility for those campaign attacks on Rachel, not even the prize of the White House would have prevented him from obtaining adequate revenge.

---

[37] Isabel Thompson Kelsay, "The Presidential Campaign of 1828," *The East Tennessee Historical Society's Publications*, No. 5, January, 1933, p. 79.

[38] Marquis James, *The Life of Andrew Jackson*, p. 467. For the entire account, see the Cincinnati *Gazette*, March 23, 1828.

[39] Marquis James, *The Life of Andrew Jackson*, pp. 465-466.

When the story was carried in the *National Journal,* the official organ of the Adams party, Jackson included the President in his rage. It was his judgment that the New Englander could have prevented its publication. Ever afterwards, Old Hickory refused to accord Adams the ordinary civilities of life. It is to Jackson's honor that when Duff Green, editor of the Washington *Telegraph,* proposed to retaliate in kind, the General replied: "I never war against females." The Old Hero went on to urge his friends to avoid all such action.[40]

The Adams press now switched to garbled accounts of all the military executions that ever took place under Jackson's command. The tale of the six mutinous militiamen, who were executed after sentence by a Jackson-appointed court-martial board, received the most publicity. Binns of the Philadelphia *Democratic Press* devised a circular which speedily became known as the "coffin handbill." On it were depicted the victims of these executions standing by the side of their coffins. They were pictured as innocent patriots sacrificed to appease the savage lust of Jackson.

This criticism of Old Hickory's military record proved ill-advised. The Jackson press joyously accepted the challenge. The following paragraph is a typical retort:

Cool and Deliberate Murder
Jackson coolly and deliberately put to death upward of twenty-five hundred British troops on the 8th of January, 1815, on the plains below New Orleans, for no other offense than that they wished to sup in the city that night.[41]

The main political result of this ordeal by slander was to embitter the candidates against each other. Jackson and Adams blamed one another. Each felt that the other could have prevented the vituperation by a word to subordinates. The enmity between two old friends was made permanent from that time on.

THE MASONS AND THE ELECTION

Lord Arthur Ponsonby, a distinguished British Parliamentarian, once remarked that in time of war, truth is the first casualty. This

---

[40] Duff Green to Jackson, July 8, 1828 and Jackson to Green, August 13, 1828, *Jackson MSS.* Duff Green was the Jacksonian editor of the *United States Telegraph.*

[41] Bennett C. Clark, *John Quincy Adams,* p. 273.

adage might well be applied to political campaigns as well. In any event, the formation of an Anti-Masonic Party in Western New York in 1826 provided the major parties with an opportunity for further mendacity.

This Anti-Masonic movement, destined to become nationwide before the presidential election of 1832, was non-political in its origin. William Morgan, a Freemason living in Batavia, New York, let it be known that he intended to write a book revealing the secrets of Freemasonry. The master of the Canandaigua lodge, learning of this intention, had him arrested for a small debt he owed. During the night, Morgan was removed from the jail by a band of Masons and taken to Fort Niagara. On the night of September 29, 1826, he vanished, leaving no traces. Since the Masons were eager to get rid of him a rumor started that they had killed him.[42] John Quincy Adams claimed to "know something about the Masonic murder of Morgan," but he never told what he knew.[43] Thurlow Weed, at this time a prominent anti-Mason, testified that John Whitney told him he had been in a boat when Morgan was bound with weighted ropes and thrown into the Niagara River;[44] however, Weed's evidence, like that of Adams, was not substantiated, and the fate of Morgan remains a mystery.

The affair created tremendous excitement in western New York. Committees were appointed to help in the detection of the criminals. Meetings in Batavia and nearby towns resolved to withhold all political support from Masons. When a committee of investigation in Canandaigua appealed to the Jacksonian-controlled state legislature, it was told that the courts possessed all the necessary power. Taking this as a rebuff, the disaffected anti-Masonic elements now began to turn towards Adams and his followers. Before the Morgan incident, the Adams party was notoriously weak in the Empire State. Anti-Masonry injected new life into it. Important Jacksonian Democrats grew fearful. Thomas Ritchie of the *Richmond Enquirer* expressed his alarm lest the anti-Masonic element

---

[42]Charles McCarthy, *The Anti-Masonic Party: A Study of Political Anti-Masonry in the United States, 1827-1840* (Washington: Annual Report of the American Historical Association for the Year 1902), Vol. I, pp. 371-383.

[43]John Quincy Adams to Alexander H. Everett, August 12, 1832, *Adams MSS.*

[44]*Autobiography of Thurlow Weed*, ed. by Harriet A. Weed (Boston: Houghton, Mifflin & Company, 1884), Vol. I, p. 333.

combine with the Administration men in New York, Ohio, and Kentucky, and carry those states in the forthcoming presidential election.[45] Van Buren wrote that he was "heartsick" at Mordecai M. Noah's indiscretion in ridiculing the new party in the *New York Enquirer*.[46] The state elections of 1827 justified these anxieties. For the anti-Masonic party carried five counties, electing fifteen members to the Assembly.

The major parties immediately sat up and took notice. The President gave assurance that he was not, never had been, and never would be, a Mason.[47] Since it was common knowledge that Jackson was a Mason, he did what he could by asserting that he had not attended lodge sessions for several years. Furthermore, Old Hickory denounced as "a stain on our history" any attempt to use the Morgan episode in the interests of the Adams party.[48] Both parties did their best, without scrupulous adherence to the truth, to turn the movement to their own advantage. The influence of the anti-Masonic movement in the presidential election of 1828 is patent. All the Western counties, without exception, voted for Adams. The vote of the Empire State was thus divided, Adams receiving 16, and Jackson 20 votes.

THE TARIFF AND THE ELECTION

As soon as the Adams wing of the Democratic party surged forward in the New York State elections of 1827, the Jackson wing of the same party contrived a plan by which they hoped to recoup their losses. It was probably the work of the Little Magician. In any event, one of the Jacksonian strategists rigged up a tariff bill in 1828 that was more concerned with manufacturing a president than with protecting manufacturers. John Randolph put it well when he said: "The bill referred to manufacturers of no sort or kind, except the manufacture of a president of the United States."[49]

Under President Monroe in 1824, Congress had increased the

---

[45]Charles H. Ambler, *Thomas Ritchie*, p. 116.

[46]Van Buren to Churchill C. Cambreling, October 23, 1827, *Van Buren MSS.* Cambreling was a New York Congressman and a close friend of Van Buren.

[47]*Albany Argus*, August 22, 1828.

[48]Jackson to James A. Hamilton, April 29, 1828, *Jackson MSS*. Hamilton was the son of Alexander Hamilton and a Van Buren supporter.

[49]Frank W. Taussig, *The Tariff History of the United States*, pp. 101-102. Clay stated that Van Buren was the brains behind the bill. See Taussig, pp. 95-96.

protective tariff of 1816 from 25 percent on the value of dutiable goods to 37 percent, but the woolen manufacturers agitated for still higher rates. The Jacksonians, whose main object was to unseat Adams, now presented the "Tariff of Abominations." Their scheme pushed the duties as high as 45 percent on the value of certain manufactured goods. At the same time, a heavy tariff was placed on certain raw materials, principally wool. One theory has it that such items were so urgently needed for manufacturing in New England that the Jackson forces felt confident that this industrial section would reject the entire bill.

However, the New Englanders spoiled the plot. Sixteen of them choked down the new duties on raw materials, and desirous of continuing the principle of protection, voted for the bill. These 16 votes forced its passage in the House by a 105 to 94 decision.[50] Daniel Webster was one of the sixteen that voted for the tariff. He was undoubtedly influenced by the advice of Mr. Abbott Lawrence, a founder of a leading commercial firm in Massachusetts. Lawrence carefully examined the bill, and informed Webster that it was "good enough," and, "if adopted as amended will keep the South and West in debt to New England the next hundred years."[51]

The commonly accepted opinion of Van Buren's chagrin after the passage of the bill is upset by Professor Remini. For after marshalling a good bit of evidence, Remini remarks: "At no time did Van Buren intend to defeat the tariff." Rather the Little Magician considered New England as unalterably attached to Adams; and therefore he raised the duties on the principal commodities of Kentucky, Missouri, Illinois, Pennsylvania, Ohio, New York, and Indiana in the hope of getting their votes for Jackson. Finally in order to have New England vote for the tariff, so Remini argues, Van Buren arranged to have the rates on woolen manufactures raised.[52]

While there still exists a dispute as to Van Buren's intentions, nevertheless the rage of the South over the tariff of 1828 is universally accepted. This anger caused no little apprehension in both

---

[50]*Ibid.*, pp. 89-98.
[51]Abbott Lawrence to Daniel Webster, May 7, 1828, as quoted in Raynor G. Wellington, *The Political and Sectional Influence of the Public Lands, 1828-1842* (Cambridge & Riverside Press, 1914), p. 27.
[52]Robert V. Remini, "Martin Van Buren and the Tariff of Abominations." *American Historical Review,* Vol. LXIII, No. 4, July 1958, pp. 913-916.

parties. Something had to be done. It was, but not until two weeks after Andrew Jackson had been elected President. Then, Vice-President John C. Calhoun secretly wrote the "South Carolina Exposition." The South Carolina Legislature immediately published it. The "Exposition" denounced the tricky tariff as unconstitutional. Taking a leaf from the Virginia and Kentucky resolutions of 1798, it proposed that the states should declare the Tariff of 1828 null and void within their borders. Fortunately for the Union, no other state joined South Carolina in her anti-tariff protest. Yet with the Carolina-born Jackson in the White House, the South felt more secure.[53]

Desperate as the campaign had been, the electoral vote was not even close. Outside of New England's 50 votes, Adams received only New Jersey's 8, Delaware's 3, 6 of Maryland's 11, and 16 of New York's 36. Jackson obtained 1 vote in Maine, 20 in New York, 5 in Maryland, and the solid votes of the rest of the states. To Clay's embarrassment, Kentucky joined with her neighbors in voting for Old Hickory. The final vote was: Jackson, 178; Adams, 83. The popular vote read: Jackson 647,276; Adams, 508,064. Calhoun was re-elected Vice-President 171 votes to Richard Rush's 83. Calhoun fell shy of Jackson's total because 7 of Georgia's 9 electors voted for William Smith of South Carolina in a Crawford gesture of dislike for Calhoun.

It is clear that Jackson's sweeping victory in the electoral college was due to the predominance of the general ticket system now universally adopted. Although the Old Hero gained more than twice as many electoral votes as the New Englander, his popular majority was only 139, 212, or 56 percent of the total vote cast.[54] General Jackson was "filled with gratitude."[55] Few realized it, but the Age of Jackson had begun.

----

[53]Charles M. Wiltse, *John C. Calhoun: Nationalist, 1782-1828*, pp. 390-397. At the time no one knew that the Vice-President was the author of the "Exposition." The main objection of the South to high tariffs was an economic one. Without the tariff many British articles were cheaper than Yankee ones.

[54]Florence Weston, *The Presidential Election of 1828*, p. 182.

[55]Jackson to John Coffee, November 24, 1828, *Jackson MSS*. Professor McCormick destroys the assumption that the common man suddenly rushed to the polls in 1828. Actually the election of 1828 did not bring the polls "the proportion of the electorate that had voted on occasion in previous elections." Richard P. McCormick, "New Perspectives on Jacksonian Politics," *American Historical Review*, January, 1960, vol. LXV, No. 2, p. 295.

12

Philosophy and Politics

THE TRIUMPH OF ANDREW JACKSON in 1828 was heralded by the Jeffersonian Democrats as but the climax of their movement. This movement, with its roots deep in American Colonial history, was crystallized in the form of a political party by 1792-1793. Our Founding Fathers, with all their wisdom, had not anticipated the formation of political parties. It was their view that intelligent voters in each presidential election would select the members of an Electoral College. This learned group would then convene, scan the nation carefully, and select the most capable man for President. But political parties soon gained possession of the machinery for selecting the Chief Executive, and the Electoral College became in effect a rubber stamp. One unfortunate by-product of this system is that parties have tended to choose not necessarily the best man but the best vote-getter.

American political parties sprang into being as a result of the clashes between Hamilton and Jefferson, especially over foreign policy and monetary programs. By 1792-1793 two well-defined parties were in the field: the Hamiltonian Federalists and the Jeffersonian Republicans soon to be called Democrats. The two-party system has existed in the United States since that day. It has proved indispensable in the functioning of democratic self-government. The party of the "outs" has traditionally played the important role of both admonitor and brake.

Those who had been federalists in the pre-Constitution period of 1787-1789 became, with some few exceptions, Federalists during the presidential years of George Washington. Under the organizational leadership of Alexander Hamilton, Secretary of the Treasury under President Washington, they were welded into an effective party by 1793. Casting suspicious eyes on the notion of state sover-

228

eignty, they advocated a powerful central government which would not only protect lives and property, but which would also quickly crush any disobedience against the national government. In addition, their partiality to the mercantile and investing classes was evident. In a way, this was only natural since the Hamiltonian Federalists were composed in the main of merchants, manufacturers, and shippers. Through Hamilton's device of funding the national debt, through his national bank, and other policies, those who invested in public securities, commerce and manufactures were in effect subsidized by the government. Unfortunately as much of the tax burden as possible was thrown on the broad shoulders of the planters and farmers. These husbandmen, "the chosen people of God,"[1] as Jefferson called them, happened to be in the majority, and it was not long before they formed their own political party to defend their interests.

In the field of foreign policy the Federalists were basically pro-British. This is not surprising since the bulk of our trade in the early days of the Republic was with Great Britian. Then too, most of the Loyalists of Revolution days, who remained in the United States, became Federalists. Fundamentally conservative in outlook, and retaining some sentimental attachment to England, they rejoiced in the bias of the Federalist party towards the Mother Country.

The Whiskey Rebellion, which occurred in southwestern Pennsylvania in 1794, acted as a catalyst in uniting the Jeffersonian Democrats. The Federalist Excise was a distinct hardship on the frontiersmen of the Keystone State. After all, they argued, John Barleycorn was not a luxury for them but rather an economic necessity. It was actually used as a medium of exchange, and even contributions for the upkeep of the clergy were made in: "Old Monongahela rye." Raising the cry: "Liberty and No Excise," the defiant distillers tarred and feathered certain revenue officers. The collecting arm of the federal government was thus temporarily paralyzed.

President Washington, with the enthusiastic encouragement of Hamilton, swung into action by summoning the militia of several states. An army of about 13,000 men rallied to the colors, and accompanied by both the President and his Secretary of the Treasury,

---

[1]Richard Hofstadter, *The American Political Tradition and the Men Who Made It,* p. 27.

marched towards the troubled area. When they reached the hills of western Pennsylvania they found no difficulty in dispersing the rebellious "Whiskey Boys." Washington magnanimously pardoned all and sundry much to the dismay of Hamilton.[2]

In a military sense it was a small rebellion, only three rebels were killed, but it had deep political significance. For one thing, the federal government commanded a new respect. On the other hand the numerous anti-Federalists condemned the administration for its heavy-handed solution to what they considered to be an unjust system of taxation. These back-country men, referred to by their beloved Jefferson as: "Those who labor in the earth,"[3] now saw the wisdom of using the ballot box to adjust their grievances.

Thomas Jefferson now emerged as the Moses of these home-spun pioneer people. Eventually to be known as Democrats, they demanded a weak central regime, for they believed that the best government was the one that governed least. Like Jefferson, their leader, they held that the bulk of the power should be retained by the states. Regarding the national debt as a burden rather than a blessing, the Jeffersonians vowed to pay it off when they won control of the government. Primarily agrarians, they insisted that there be no special privileges for manufacturers. Utopia, for Jefferson, meant a nation of farmers. He exhorted his huge constituency of husbandmen that: "While we have land to labor . . . let us never wish to see our citizens occupied at a work-bench, or twirling a distaff." Far better, he reasoned, to: "let our workshops remain in Europe." Indeed the founder of the Democratic party regarded farming as essentially ennobling. He felt it wiser to send our materials to Europe for manufacture, than to bring workingmen to our virgin shores: "and with them their manners and principles." He warned about "the mobs of great cities," who "add just so much to the support of pure government, as sores do to the strength of the human body."[4] Needless to say, the agricultural South and Southwest produced the vast majority of Jeffersonians.

---

[2]Thomas A. Bailey, *The American Pageant: A History of the Republic* (Boston: D. C. Heath and Co., 1956) p. 160. Washington accompanied the troops only part of the way, Hamilton all the way.

[3]Hofstadter, *The American Political Tradition*, p. 27.

[4]Arthur M. Schlesinger, Jr., *The Age of Jackson* (Boston: Little Brown and Co., 1945), p. 8.

The Democrats, unlike the Federalists, were basically pro-French. They warmly supported the liberal ideas of the French Revolution while detesting what they termed the reactionary notions of the Tory King, George III.

Above all, Jefferson was an advocate of the rule of the people. This did not mean that he believed in giving the vote to every adult, white male. The ignorant, he contended, were incapable of self-government. The Sage of Monticello believed in government for the people, but not by all the people. Universal education was an imperative antecedent to universal suffrage, according to the learned Virginian. He had a profound belief in the ability of the average man, when educated, to elect rulers who would conduct the government according to the best interests of society.

Jefferson fought for a maximum of safeguards for the great mass of the people. He had constant fear of tyranny by privileged groups. Shays' Rebellion in western Massachusetts in 1786 was the occasion for his oft-quoted statement that: "A little rebellion now and then is a good thing."[5] The fear of revolt, he claimed, would compel the governing class to abide by the Constitution.

No one espoused the cause of free speech more than Thomas Jefferson. The open-minded Virginian was convinced that without free speech the corrupt deeds of the office-holders could not be exposed. He once remarked that, if compelled to choose between a government without newspapers, and newspapers without a government, he would choose the latter provided that every man received the papers and was capable of understanding them.[6] Like Washington, Jefferson suffered foul abuse from editorial pens. Admitting his sensitivity to criticism, he wrote Francis Hopkinson in 1789 that: "I find the pain of a little censure, even when it is unfounded . . . more acute than the pleasure of much praise." Yet in spite of this, he asserted in 1801 that: "Error of opinion may be tolerated where reason is left free to combat it."[7]

When Jefferson was elected president in 1800, many Federalists were sure that the end of the world had come. Was not this

---

[5]Hofstadter, *The American Political Tradition*, p. 24.
[6]Charles E. Merriam, *A History of American Political Theories* (New York: Macmillan Co., 1936), p. 159.
[7]Bailey, *op. cit.*, p. 164.

the man who had said that the tree of liberty must be watered periodically with the blood of tyrants! It was Jefferson who had proclaimed that a rebellion every twenty years was an excellent thing, and who insisted that constitutions should be entirely rewritten every twenty-five or thirty years. Was not Charles Carroll of Carrollton correct when he called Jefferson: "a theoretical and fanciful man"? No less a distinguished Federalist than Fisher Ames anticipated that now that Jefferson was President-elect the people would soon scent: "the loathsome steam of human victims offered in sacrifice."[8]

However, among those who really knew Jefferson there were no such fears. Alexander Hamilton in a shrewd estimate of Jefferson's character admitted that his old enemy's views were: "tinctured with fanaticism, that he is too much in earnest with his democracy." Yet it is untrue, continued Hamilton, in an analysis that is at once penetrating in substance as it is unfair in phraseology,

that Jefferson is zealot enough to do anything in pursuance of his principles which will contravene his popularity or his interest. He is as likely as any man I know to temporize—to calculate what will be likely to promote his own reputation and advantage; and the probable result of such a temper is the preservation of systems, though originally opposed, which, once being established, could not be overturned without danger to the person who did it. To my mind a true estimate of Mr. Jefferson's character warrants the expectation of a temporizing rather than a violent system. Add to this that there is no fair reason to suppose him capable of being corrupted, which is a security that he will not go beyond certain limits.[9]

How well Hamilton had taken the measure of the man was almost immediately demonstrated. For when Jefferson assumed command he faced a Hamiltonian system that had been in operation for twelve years. The country was prosperous. To smash Hamilton's plan of banks, revenues, and funding might well bring on a depression. It might even split the Union.

Jefferson did not hesitate. His first Inaugural Address was in the nature of a conciliatory document. He would heal the wounds of the bitter period from 1798 to 1800, and win over to his party as many moderate Federalists as possible. "We are all republicans—

---

[8]Hofstadter, *The American Political Tradition*, p. 32.
[9]Hamilton to Bayard, January 16, 1801, *Hamilton MSS.*

we are all federalists,"[10] he declared. Soon after the new President was confiding in his friend Du Pont de Nemours in words that describe his adaptability:

When the government was first established, it was possible to have kept it going on true principles, but the contracted, English, half-lettered ideas of Hamilton destroyed that hope in the bud. We can pay off his debts in 15 years: but we can never get rid of his financial system. It mortifies me to be strengthening principles which I deem radically vicious, but this vice is entailed on us by the first error. In other parts of our government I hope we shall be able by degrees to introduce sound principles and make them habitual. What is practical must often control what is pure theory.[11]

Throughout his presidency, Jefferson led his party in the process of accommodation. When, for example, the Bank of Baltimore applied for assistance, he wrote to Secretary of the Treasury Albert Gallatin that:

I am decidedly in favor of making all the banks Republican by sharing deposits among them in proportion to the disposition they show . . . It is material to the safety of Republicanism to detach the mercantile interest from its enemies and incorporate them into the body of its friends. A merchant is naturally a Republican, and can be otherwise only from a vitiated state of things.[12]

It was obvious that Jefferson was beginning a process, which when completed, would make it unnecessary for the Federalists to exist. The economic changes of the early 1800's blasted his dream of an agricultural America. The first Democratic president always remained a man in whom intense desire for his country's welfare always overcame loyalty to "pure theory." By 1805 he reversed himself by exclaiming that: "As yet our manufacturers are as much at their ease, as independent and moral as our agricultural inhabitants." By the spring of 1809 he set John Jay's mind at rest by conceding that a proper balance of commerce, agriculture, and manufacturing had now become imperative if the United States would remain prosperous and free. By 1816 Jefferson was courageous enough to go on record that: "Experience has taught me that manufactures are now as necessary to our independence as to our com-

[10]*National Intelligencer,* March 4, 1801.
[11]*The Works of Thomas Jefferson,* ed. by Paul L. Ford (New York: G. P. Putnam's Sons, 1904-1905), Vol. VIII, p. 125.
[12]*Ibid.,* p. 252.

fort."[13] Two terms in the White House had resulted in the victory of the statesman over the theorizer.

Madison and Monroe, the two Democratic presidents who followed Jefferson, occupied the executive mansion from 1809 to 1825. During that time they continued what they considered to be a compromise with necessity. The approval of the second Bank of the United States in 1816 by President Madison, who twenty-five years before had been the staunchest opponent of the first Bank, is indicative of this trend. Madison went along with the tariff of 1816, and although he refused to concede the constitutionality of internal improvements, he stressed their importance. And, like Jefferson, he advocated amending the Constitution in order to make them an actuality. Monroe shocked many Jeffersonians by not only signing a bill for internal improvements but also by permitting the tariff duties to be increased in 1824.

With the Federalist party largely destroyed by its resistance to the War of 1812, the two-party system disappeared during the period from 1812 to 1828. By the end of 1816 the Democrats had taken over the whole apparatus of Federalist policies: banks, tariffs, army, navy, and manufactures. Josiah Quincy complained bitterly that the Jeffersonians had: "out-federalized Federalism." Nathaniel Macon, one of the last of the intransigent Jeffersonians, bewailed the fact that: "the opinions of Jefferson and those who were with him are forgotten."[14] Federalism, as Jefferson himself told Albert Gallatin in 1823, has: "changed its name and hidden among us . . . as strong as it has ever been since 1800 . . . The judges as before are at their head and are the entering wedge."[15]

The extremely close election of 1824 resulted in the election of John Quincy Adams. Although a professed Jeffersonian, Adams was suspected of being a Federalist in sheep's clothing. Besides, he appointed Henry Clay, the most outspoken champion of the American System, with its bank, tariff, and internal improvements, as his Secretary of State. More often than not this post led to the presidency.

With Andrew Jackson's election in 1828, the two-party sys-

[13]Arthur M. Schlesinger, Jr., *The Age of Jackson,* p. 18.
[14]Richard Hofstadter, *The American Political Tradition,* p. 41.
[15]Arthur M. Schlesinger, Jr., *The Age of Jackson,* p. 26.

tem returned to American politics. For in this election the loser, John Quincy Adams, was the standard bearer of a new political party: the National Republicans. Moving into the vacuum created by the demise of the Federalists, they adopted Clay's American System as their political *credo*. Jackson's victory cheered the hearts of the old-time Jeffersonians, for Old Hickory sounded very much like Jefferson. He had recently declared that: "I am one of those who do not believe that a national debt is a national blessing, but rather a curse to a republic; inasmuch as it is calculated to raise around the administration a moneyed aristocracy dangerous to the liberties of the country."[16] Jefferson was dead by 1826 but in Jackson, so his followers announced, the country had a man who would carry on the traditions of the Democratic party.

---

[16]Jackson to Dr. Colman, April 26, 1824, *Jackson MSS.*

INDEX

Abercrombie, Rev. Dr., 29

Adair, Senator, 83

Adams, John, and political parties, 4; candidate for president, 12; last Federalist president, 14; and the Supreme Court, 44; letters to his son, 78, 203; and the election of Monroe, 141

Adams, John Quincy, minister to St. Petersburg, 108, 120; peace with Great Britain, 127-131; as Monroe's Secretary of State, 147, 151, 174, 176; and the Florida question, 153-156; candidate for president, 188-189; elected president, 207-209; administration, 210-227

Adams, Oñis Treaty, 154-155, 167

Adams, Dr. William, 124, 150

Adet, Pierre, 13

Advocate (New York), 193

Alexander I, Czar, 108, 120-121, 169, 175, 179, 221

Alien and Sedition Acts, 18-20

Ambrister, Robert, 153

American Mercury, 29

American System, 188, 212, 235

American Watchman (Delaware), 164

Ames, Fisher, 15, 56

Anderson, Patton, 80 n. 46

Anti-Masonic party, 224-225

Antrobus, Mr., 166

Arbuthnot, Alexander, 153

Armstrong, John, 122, 130

Armstrong, William, 106

Aurora (Philadelphia), 13, 27, 29, 85, 127-128, 165

Austin, Benjamin, 143 n. 87

Bache, Benjamin Franklin, 13

Bacon, Ezekiel, 114

Bagot, Charles, 148 n. 8, 151

Bank of the United States, first, 108-109; second, 142-143

Barbé-Marbois, François, 55

Barbour, James, 157, 211

Barden's Tavern, 26

Barlow, Joel, 111 n. 43, 113 n. 47

Bathhurst, Lord, 135 n. 58

Bayard, James, 35-38, 41, 93, 122

Bee (New London), 27

Benton, Thomas Hart, 133

Berkeley, Admiral, 77-78

Bernard, General, 145

Betts, Samuel R., 139-140

Beverly, Carter, 204 n. 70

Biddle, Nicholas, 163

Bidwell, Barnabas, 73, 77

Binns, John, 122, 223

Bishop, Abraham, 29

Blair, Francis P., 200 n. 49

Blue Light Federalists, see Federalist party

Bonaparte, Napoleon, 54-55, 73-74, 89, 106-107, 111 n. 43, 120

Bowdoin, James, 81 n. 51, 52

Breckenridge, John, 20, 45-46, 63, 70

Buchanan, James, 203-204

Burr, Aaron, 22-27, 30-36, 43, 66-68, 79-85

Burr, Theodosia, 25

Cabot, George, 92, 138

Cadore, Duc de, see Champagny

Calhoun, John C., 142, 147, 159, 190, 195-199, 209, 227

Campbell, George W., 148

Canning, George, 76, 87, 101, 171-174, 182-186

Canning, Stratford, 166, 172

Capodistrias, Count, 175

Carroll, Charles, 124, 232

Cass, Lewis, 194

Castlereagh, Lord, 90, 117, 125, 148, 153, 171

Champagny, Jean Baptiste, 100 n. 6, 106

de Chaumontfils, Leroy, 135 n. 56

the *Chesapeake* affair, 74-79

Christie, Gabriel, 35 n. 47

Claiborne, Governor, 107

Clarion (Nashville), 115

Clay, Henry, 80 n. 44, 115, 128, 133, 144, 147, 160-162, 190, 202-209, 215-216, 218-220

Clinton, DeWitt, 94, 118-119, 165, 187 n. 4

Clinton, George, 25, 43, 77, 93-94, 109

Coffee, John, 220 n. 29

Coleman, Littleton H., 212 n. 5